THERAPIES AND REHABILITATION IN
# Down Syndrome

# THERAPIES AND REHABILITATION IN
# Down Syndrome

*Edited by*
**JEAN-ADOLPHE RONDAL, PH.D., DR LING.**
*University of LIEGE*

and

**ALBERTO RASORE QUARTINO, MD**
*Ospedali Galliera, GENOA*

John Wiley & Sons, Ltd

Email (for orders and customer service enquiries): cs-books@wiley.co.uk
Visit our Home Page on www.wiley.com

***Other Wiley Editorial Offices***
John Wiley & Sons Inc., 111 River Street, Hoboken, NJ 07030, USA
Jossey-Bass, 989 Market Street, San Francisco, CA 94103-1741, USA
Wiley-VCH Verlag GmbH, Boschstr. 12, D-69469 Weinheim, Germany
John Wiley & Sons Australia Ltd, 42 McDougall Street, Milton, Queensland 4064, Australia
John Wiley & Sons (Asia) Pte Ltd, 2 Clementi Loop #02-01, Jin Xing Distripark, Singapore
129809
John Wiley & Sons Canada Ltd, 6045 Freemont Blvd, Mississauga, ONT, L5R 4J3.

Anniversary Logo Design: Richard J. Pacifico

***Library of Congress Cataloging-in-Publication Data***
Therapies and rehabilitation in Down syndrome / edited by Jean-Adolphe
Rondal, Alberto Rasore Quartino.
      p. ; cm.
   Includes bibliographical references and index.
   ISBN-13: 978-0-470-06006-3 (pbk. : alk. paper)
   ISBN-10: 0-470-06006-9 (pbk. : alk. paper)
   1.  Down syndrome–Patients–Rehabilitation.  2.  Children with mental
disabilities–Rehabilitation.  I.  Rondal, J. A.  II.  Rasore Quartino, Alberto.
   [DNLM: 1.  Down Syndrome–therapy.  2.  Down Syndrome–rehabilitation.
WS 107 T398 2007]
 RJ506.D68T454 2007
 616.85′884206–dc22
                                                                2006037887

***A catalogue record for this book is available from the British Library***
ISBN 978-0-470-06006-3

Typeset in 10/12 Times by SNP Best-set Typesetter Ltd, Hong Kong
Printed and bound in Great Britain by TJ International, Padstow, Cornwall

This book is printed on acid-free paper responsibly manufactured from sustainable forestry in
which at least two trees are planted for each one used for paper production.

# Contents

# Preface

This book stems from the presentations by a group of distinguished scientists gathered in the hills of a beautiful San Marino resort between 4 and 6 May 2006 for the Third International Symposium on Down Syndrome organized by the Republic of San Marino and the Down Syndrome Associations of Rimini in Italy and of San Marino.

We are grateful to the Secretariat of State for Health, Social Security, Social Affairs and National Insurance of the Republic of San Marino for their generous financial, logistic and administrative help and support.

The Down Syndrome Associations of Rimini and San Marino, The European Down Syndrome Association (EDSA), and the Fondazione Baccichetti per la Sindrome di Down also sponsored the event and should be warmly thanked for their support.

A number of the world's best specialists met in San Marino over those days to deliver addresses on various aspects of therapy and rehabilitation strategies for people with Down Syndrome. We are most grateful to those colleagues for agreeing to participate in the symposium and then to expand their presentations into full-scale chapters in this book.

We are indebted to the staff at Wiley Publishers, Chichester, particularly, Emma Hatfield, Project Editor, and Carole Millett, Assistant Editor, for their professionalism, their supportive stance, and the friendly personal relations they maintained with us throughout the publication process. Closer to us, we also acknowledge the precious collaboration of Anastasia Piat-Di Nicolantonio and Laurence Docquier in preparing the final manuscript and taking care of the many tasks involved in such a large-scale endeavour.

Jean-Adolphe Rondal, Alberto Rasore Quartino

# Authors' Affiliations

ARCHER, TAMSIN, The Down Syndrome Educational Trust, Portsmouth, United Kingdom

BACCICHETTI, CARLO, Università di Padova, Pediatria e Genetica Medica, Padua, Italy

BIRD, GILLIAN, The Down Syndrome Educational Trust, Portsmouth, United Kingdom

BUCKLEY, SUSAN, The Down Syndrome Educational Trust, Portsmouth, United Kingdom

COTTINI, LUCIO, Università di Udine, Facoltà di Scienze della Formazione, Udine, Friuli, Italy

DELABAR, JEAN-MAURICE, Université Paris Diderot-Paris7, EA3508, Modèles de régulatation géniques, Paris, France

FERRARI, LEA, Università di Padova, Facoltà di Psicologia, Padua, Italy

GUAZZO, GIOVANNI MARIA, Centro di Riabilitazione NeapoliSanit, Ottaviano, Campania, Italy

KOLA, ISMAIL, Merck Research Laboratories, Rahway, NJ, United States of America

MAHONEY, GERALD, Case Western Reserve University, Mandel School of Applied and Social Sciences, Cleveland, OH, United States of America

NOTA, LAURA, Università di Padova, Facoltà di Psicologia, Padua, Italy

PERERA, JUAN, Centro Principe de Asturias, Universidad de las Islas Baleares, Palma de Mallorca, Spain

PRITCHARD, MELANIE, Monash University, Institute of Medical Research, Clayton, Victoria, Australia

RASORE QUARTINO, ALBERTO, Ospedali Galliera, Pediatra e Genetica Medica, Genoa, Italy

ROMANO, CORRADO, Associazione OASI Maria Santissima, Pediatra e Genetica Medica, Troina, Sicily, Italy

RONDAL, JEAN-ADOLPHE, Université de Liège, Unité de Psycholinguistique, Liège, Belgium

SACKS, BENJAMIN, The Down Syndrome Educational Trust, Portsmouth, United Kingdom

SORESI, SALVATORE, Università di Padova, Facoltà di Psicologia, Padua, Italy

# Introduction

**JEAN-ADOLPHE RONDAL AND
ALBERTO RASORE QUARTINO**

The book is about therapy and rehabilitation, i.e., about changing for the better a pathological state of affairs: in this particular case the biological, medical, psychological, and social lifespan consequences of a condition known as Down Syndrome (DS) that is caused in most cases by a triplication of chromosome 21, called 'trisomy 21'. This pathological condition, documented for the first time in the nineteenth century by the observations of the Frenchman Seguin and later the Englishman Down, is the most prevalent cause (incidence roughly 1 case in 1300 live births) of moderate mental retardation (IQ around 50 in modal value). It affects males and females in equal proportions, determining important developmental delays and deficits. Life expectancy is approximately 60 years, though this has increased markedly in recent decades thanks to progress made in medicine and biology, a better social acceptance, and psychological care and stimulation (Rondal *et al.* 2004), and is still expected to continue to improve in the future. This has already prompted research on the disease in the adult years, and is now motivating interest in the scientific community in the disease's course during the advanced years in those affected, who can now be expected to remain a part of our societies for far longer than was earlier the case (life expectancy in the first half of the twentieth century was only a dozen years).

The chapters taken together supply a 'state of the art' accessible alike to the professional and to the educated lay person on the subject of the central issues concerning the syndrome and the major strategies and perspectives for genetic, pharmacological, and medical therapies and treatments, as well as cognitive, linguistic, educational and inclusive employment rehabilitation strategies and possibilities for people with DS from early infancy right through into the years of ageing and senility.

Owing to the consequences of a mostly random triplication of their chromosome 21 in all or a large number of their body cells, people with DS present from birth, and even before, a number of neurophysiological and physical anomalies that affect their development in various ways. When properly taken care of, as is the case for any human being, they do develop into lovely babies, motivated children and adolescents, and responsible adults, more often than not with exquisitely social personalities. It is the moral responsibility of developed societies to act in the best possible ways using the available resources, scientific and otherwise, to help more disadvantaged people to grow up, be educated, be cured of diseases and the like, and live and function in social settings to the best of their capacities.

Thanks to decades of research efforts, we know a great deal more about the various developmental difficulties met with by people with DS and the anomalies and pathological susceptibilities of various sorts with which they usually present. This knowledge is being translated into therapeutic and rehabilitation strategies intended to eliminate a number of these difficulties, reduce the others, and induce major improvements regarding health matters, physical, cognitive, and linguistic development, educability, and inclusive schooling and employment.

This book is original in at least three respects. Firstly, the authors do not simply focus on the identification of the problems or track the course of development for children with DS. Rather, they specify and discuss major therapeutic approaches. Secondly, the coverage is thoroughly comprehensive, extending from perspectives for future genetic therapy to questions of quality of life, passing on the way through immunology and hormonal and other therapies, addressing medical problems and the prevention and treatment of normal and pathological ageing, the more traditional fields of language, memory, learning, and psychomotoric rehabilitation, the parents' role, and an international perspective on inclusive schooling and employment.

The book will be of major interest not only to scientists in the various disciplines concerned with the many facets of Down Syndrome, but also to practitioners looking for guidelines for therapies and clinical application of research findings, as well as to educators, teachers, and educated parents.

To give some global indications regarding the particular content of individual chapters:

- Chapter 1 (Delabar) explains the current scientific point of view and perspectives on gene therapy in genetic syndromes of intellectual disability and overall Down Syndrome. DS is caused by the overexpression of a limited number of dosage-sensitive genes located on chromosome 21. It can be reasonably forecast that at least some of these genes will be replaced or neutralized in the future. However, the technical difficulties are formidable.
- Chapter 2 (Pritchard and Kola) discusses several pharmacological agents currently used with DS people and the biological bases of these. Some of the molecules proposed in recent years or earlier have not been demonstrated to be effective, or only shown to be partially so and with specific organic targets. Others are still under test for approval by the responsible administrative bodies. It is essential to inform professionals of the pros and cons of these pharmacological treatments.
- Chapter 3 (Romano) discusses carbon metabolism in DS, the hormonal imbalances characteristic of the condition, and the still debated question

of administering growth hormone supplement or replacement to DS children.

- Chapter 4 (Rasore Quartino) analyses the medical problems associated with DS (for example, congenital heart disease, gastrointestinal anomalies, growth retardation, sensory defects, immune function disorders, hypothyroidism, muscular hypotonia, dental anomalies, orthopaedic anomalies, sleep problems, coeliac disease, leukaemia, and atlanto-axial instability) and examines the therapeutic weaponry that should be used in these cases. The focus is on the whole of the lifespan, including the medical approach to the specific problems of ageing people with DS.
- Chapter 5 (Rondal) analyses the major language difficulties and deficits encountered in children, adolescents, and adults with DS. It reviews the various strategies that should be used to improve language development in this syndrome, starting with prelinguistic intervention from the first months of life. The question often raised by parents as to whether these children should be exposed to bilingual contexts, for example when these are needed for cultural reasons, is also addressed.
- Chapter 6 (Mahoney) exposes the cognitive difficulties and deficits present in DS people (the various memory registers, attentional lability and difficulties, difficult task avoidance, intellectual development, problem-solving difficulties, reasoning limitations, and so on) and specifies the rehabilitation strategies that can be used in these respects.
- Chapter 7 (Guazzo) analyses the perceptual and motor difficulties characteristic of DS people and unearths the procedures one needs to use to improve development and functioning in these domains.
- Chapter 8 (Soresi and Ferrari) analyses the role of parents not only as supports for development in their DS children and adolescents but also as co-rehabilitative agents in close collaboration with the trained professionals. Parents' role in this respect appears more and more essential to a favourable outcome in the general developmental and rehabilitation process.
- Chapter 9 (Cottini and Nota) discusses the realities, difficulties, and possibilities of the inclusion of DS children in normal schools (mainstreaming) and analyses the 25-year-old Italian experience of legal deinstitutionalization and compulsory mainstreaming.
- Chapter 10 (Buckley, Bird, Sacks and Archer) reports and analyses the results of two large-scale studies at several years' interval in the United Kingdom comparing the effects of mainstream or special schooling for teenagers with Down Syndrome.
- Chapter 11 (Perera) examines the realities, difficulties, and entrepreneurial realities of employment and inclusive working conditions for people with DS, considered in themselves and as a form of global therapy for these people.
- Chapter 12 (Baccichetti) exposes the prospects and recommendations regarding the quality of life of people with DS, and reports on the results

of an epidemiological study conducted with several hundred DS adults living in the community.

## REFERENCE

Rondal J.A., Rasore Quartino A. and Soresi S. (eds) (2004). *The adult with Down syndrome. A new challenge for society.* London: Whurr Publishers.

# 1 Perspectives on Gene-based Therapies

JEAN-MAURICE DELABAR

## SUMMARY

Aneuploidies, i.e. disorders in the number of copies of functional genomic elements, are common genomic disorders with a profound impact on the health of human populations. The phenotypic consequences of aneuploidies are numerous, and range from mental retardation and developmental abnormalities to susceptibility to common phenotypes and to various neoplasms. Trisomy 21 (Down syndrome, DS, T21) is the most frequent aneuploidy (1/700 births and 500 000 patients in Europe) and it is still, even after the improvements of prenatal diagnosis, far outside the range of rare diseases (<1/2000). This is one of the main genetic causes of mental retardation. This review focuses on new strategies that might allow us to counter some of the adverse effects of the phenotype.

## DOWN SYNDROME AND PHENOTYPES

T21 exerts a powerful downward effect on the intelligence quotient (IQ). In contrast to what occurs in normally developing children, there is a progressive IQ decline in DS, beginning in the first year of life. The ratio of mental age to chronological age is not constant. By adulthood, IQ is usually in the moderately to severely retarded level (IQ 25–55), with an upper limit on mental age of approximately 7–8 years, although a few individuals have an IQ in the lower normal range (70–80). The molecular basis and the genes involved in this early decline across development are not known. This low IQ corresponds to an overall mental retardation. The short-term memory development of individuals with DS has been the subject of considerable research. Recent observation of the development of encoding strategies during the ages of 5 to 8 years suggests that this is a complex process involving the maturation of attentional and inhibitory processes (Palmer 2000). Long-term memory is also impaired in DS patients, who learn visual-spatial sequences normally, but display impairment

*Therapies and Rehabilitation in Down Syndrome.* Edited by Rondal
© 2007 John Wiley & Sons Ltd

in the learning of visual-object patterns (Vicari *et al.* 2005). The alterations in the cognition processes have not yet been related to the neuropathological features of DS.

At a gross morphological level, DS brains are smaller than normal. A 15–20 per cent decrease is generally reported (Jernigan *et al.* 1998; Pinter *et al.* 2001). Three brain areas are mainly altered: the prefrontal cortex, hippocampus and cerebellum. Post-mortem studies and non-invasive brain imaging have revealed reduced sizes of the brain hemispheres, brain stem and cerebellum (Raz *et al.* 1995; Kesslak *et al.* 1994). *In vivo* magnetic resonance imaging (MRI) studies have also revealed the relative increase of specific brain regions such as the subcortical grey matter. Regional differences were also reported in a voxel-based MRI study (White *et al.* 2003). Neuronal number is reduced in distinct regions and abnormal neuronal morphology is observed, especially in the cerebral cortex. In fetuses, brain examination has revealed abnormal cortical lamination patterns (Golden and Hyman 1994), altered dendritic arborization and spine morphology, reduction of spine numbers (Schulz and Scholz 1992; Becker *et al.* 1991) and altered electrophysiological properties of cell membranes (Becker *et al.* 1991).

People with Down syndrome are also much more likely to develop dementia than the general public. The neuropathological changes seen in DS brains (beyond 35 years old) are identical to those seen in sporadic Alzheimer Disease (AD) in terms of pattern of distribution of lesions (plaques and tangles) and immunostaining properties of lesions, although the changes in DS seem more pronounced. These changes are associated with dementia in 30–50 per cent of the patients of over 50 years (Franceschi *et al.* 1990; Mann *et al.* 1990). The reasons why DS patients develop these lesions and that they are at increased risk for development of dementia are unknown. The current knowledge of the genes that predispose to or participate in the AD of DS does not yet provide a satisfactory explanation of their pathophysiology. AD is characterized by the deposition of senile plaques and neurofibrillary tangles in vulnerable brain regions. One hypothesis to explain the AD phenotype in DS is that triplication of the gene encoding the amyloid protein (APP) would lead to the overproduction of Aβ peptides; however, other HSA21 genes might also be involved in the process.

## MURINE MODELS

Mouse orthologs of HSA21 genes are located on chromosome 16 (MMU16), chromosome 10 (MMU10) and chromosome 17 (MMU17) (Fig. 1.1). Thus, the characterization of mouse models that have an extra copy of all or part of MMU16, MMU10 or MMU17 should be useful for the understanding of DS alterations. M. Davisson (Davisson *et al.* 1990) used radiation-induced translocations to produce Ts65Dn, a mouse trisomic for a long fragment of MMU 16

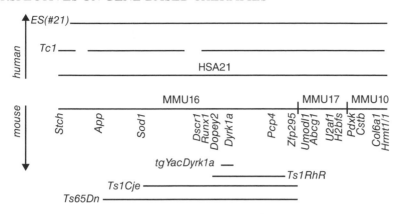

**Figure 1.1.** Existing Mouse models with partial trisomy.

(more than 20 Mb) syntenic to segment MRPL39-ZNF295 in humans (132 genes). A second partial trisomy 16 model has recently been developed, the Ts1Cje mouse (Sago *et al.* 1998). This mouse resulted from a reciprocal translocation between the end of chromosome 12 and the distal part of chromosome 16 at the level of the Sod1 gene: the partial trisomy 16 resulting from this event contains functional genes distal to Sod1 (one copy of Sod1 has been knocked out). The region present in three copies is syntenic to a smaller fragment than the syntenic region in Ts65Dn mice, corresponding to only 85 human genes (Fig. 1.1). The Ts65Dn mice present some features of DS: craniofacial abnormalities, developmental delay and impaired performance in various learning tests. In addition, alterations in long-term potentiation (LTP) and long-term depression (LTD) have been reported in young and old Ts65Dn mice (Siarey *et al.* 1997, 1999; Kleschevnikov *et al.* 2004) and stereological morphometric studies have demonstrated reduction in the volume of CA2 and in the mean neuron number in the dentate gyrus (Insausti *et al.* 1998). Electron microscopy showed that boutons and spines are enlarged and that abnormalities in the internal membranes are present in both models (Holtzman *et al.* 1996; Belichenko *et al.* 2005). Stereological measurements gave evidences of an age-related degeneration of septohippocampal cholinergic neurons and an astrocytic hypertrophy. Finally, high-resolution MRI and histological analysis revealed a reduction in cerebellar volume in Ts65Dn mice due to a reduction of both the internal granule layer and the molecular layer, with a parallel reduction in granule cell numbers (Baxter *et al.* 2000). In contrast, the brain, with the exception of the cerebellum, is not significantly smaller in segmentally trisomic mice and, indeed, tends to be larger than that of euploid mice if measurements of area at midline level are taken into account (a 9 per cent increase). Ts1Cje also show a cerebellum hypoplasia with a lower decrease in granule cell density (Olson *et al.* 2004). The Ts1Cje mice perform efficiently in the Morris water maze when the platform is visible, but show impairment in the hidden platform and probe tests, and in the reverse platform test (Sago *et al.* 1998), indicating that learning impairment is less severe than in Ts65Dn mice.

Recently two models of chimeric mice containing a large part of an extra human chromosome 21 with a varying degree of mosaicism have also been constructed (Shinohara *et al.* 2001; O'Doherty *et al.* 2005): the first one demonstrated a correlation between phenotype severity (learning impairment and heart defect with double outlet right ventricle and riding aorta) and the percentage of cells with an extra HSA21; the second model (Tc1) showed germ-line transmission resulting in living animals with various mosaicism and phenotypic alterations in behaviour, synaptic plasticity, cerebellar neuronal number and heart development (VSD and AVSD).

Smith and colleagues (1997) used smaller human chromosome fragments inserted into yeast artificial chromosomes to create an *in vivo* library spanning 1.8Mb of 21q22.2. Two YAC-transgenic mice presented brain abnormalities: tg230E8 (with 9 genes) had a high density of cortical neurons and tg152F7 (with 5 genes including DYRK1A, encoding a serine threonine kinase) had a 15 per cent heavier brain, with larger cortical (layer V) and hippocampal (dentate gyrus) neurons (15 per cent) than euploid mice. A smaller human fragment containing only the DYRK1A gene was used by Ahn *et al.* (2006) to generate a line of transgenic mice with heavier than normal brains (19 per cent heavier).

Other groups have also created models for single gene overexpression, and the observations of these models, together with other datasets, are intended to identify potential candidate genes.

## CANDIDATE GENES

### CRITERIA USED TO DEFINE CANDIDATE GENES

The basic rational assumptions guiding DS research are that: (i) individual chromosome 21 genes will show gene-dosage effects that increase expression by 50 per cent at the RNA and protein level; (ii) at least some of these increases will result in perturbations of the pathways and cellular processes in which these genes are involved; and (iii) these perturbations, possibly additively, will result in the neurodevelopmental and cognitive abnormalities that characterize the mental retardation of DS. These assumptions emphasize that, in comparison with mental retardation due to single-gene defects, DS presents unique complexities: there is no absent gene function, and there is a large number of candidate genes (more than 300) (Gardiner *et al.* 2004).

#### Chromosomic Localization

The gene must be localized on chromosome 21 – a condition that is now, as a result of the sequencing of human genome, easy to satisfy. Obviously genes other than those encoded by HSA21 are involved in DS phenotypes; but the primary cause of their dysregulation is thought to be a triplicated gene on HSA21. However, the question of the regional localization of the genes on the chromosome is also important: genotype–phenotype correlation studies in ten patients with partial trisomy 21 suggested that there is a region of about 2.5 Mb between the genes CBR and ERG that, if triplicated, is associated with a number of the features of DS. These include facial dismorphology (flat nasal bridge, protruding tongue, high arched palate, folded ears), hand and foot features, joint hyperlaxity, muscular hypotonia, short stature and mental retardation (Delabar *et al.* 1993). Pooling data from the literature permitted a comparison of 40 patients: 30 patients carrying this region in three copies presented a characteristic phenotype that included mental retardation, while among 9 individuals with a duplication of the proximal HSA21q region only 2 presented a weak form of mental retardation, indicating that a second locus (with lower penetrance) may be involved in mental retardation. A proposal has been made (6th chr21 workshop 1996) to rename the CBR–ERG region DCR-1 (Down syndrome chromosomal region 1). A gene localized outside this region would have a lower probability of becoming a strong player in mental retardation.

## Functions or Potential Functions

The protein characteristics must suggest a relevant function, and there is still a large number of genes of unknown function. Functional hypotheses might also come from the known target of the gene or from the interacting proteins. Analysis of pathways is also a source of relevant hypotheses (Gardiner *et al.* 2004; Pellegrini-Calace and Tramontano 2006).

## Territories of Expression

The gene must be found expressed in relevant body tissues; some expression studies have now been performed either on a large scale, to get a first glance at expression patterns (Gitton *et al.* 2002; Reymond *et al.* 2002), or more accurately at different developmental stages and in specific brain tissues, with results as follows: sim2 (single minded): *in situ* hybridization with human and rat fetuses showed that the corresponding gene is expressed during early fetal life in the central nervous system and in other tissues, including the facial, cranial, palatal, and primordial vertebral tissues (Dahmane *et al.* 1995); pcp4: this gene is expressed in the central nervous system, in the myenteric plexus, and in other ectoderm derivatives, for instance the lens, the hairy cells of the cochlea, the enamel organ and the hair follicles (Thomas *et al.* 2003); dopey2 (C21orf5): a wide but differential expression has been detected in the nervous system during embryogenesis, with a relatively lower level in the forebrain than in the midbrain and hindbrain, and the highest transcription intensity in the future cerebellum (Rachidi *et al.* 2006).

### Level of Expression in DS or in tg Mice

Transcriptome analyses of these mouse models have shown that most of the genes in 3 copies are 1.5-fold overexpressed. However some genes are more than 1.5-fold overexpressed and others are subjected to compensatory mechanisms with no change in expression or, more rarely, a decreased expression (Lyle *et al.* 2004; Dauphinot *et al.* 2005). Obviously a gene, expression of which is found to be compensated for, will not be a good candidate for a phenotype found in the studied tissue.

### Associated Phenotypic Changes in Murine Models

Finally, the best evidence remains the demonstration of a phenotype arising from overexpression in a mouse model.

## GENE-BASED CORRECTIVE STRATEGIES

With the identification of candidate genes is associated the possibility of designing corrective strategies directly targeting the gene products or targeting downward pathways. The main caveat to these strategies is that some genes are quite sensitive to a decreased gene dosage below the normal level; therefore attaining a level of 50 per cent of normal might induce dramatic consequences.

### RNA TARGETS

The first consequence of the presence of 3 copies of HSA21 genes is thought to be, for the largest part of the genes, an increase of the corresponding messenger RNA. The use of a new class of small RNAs, the 'small interfering RNAs', siRNAs, is one of the strategies permitting one to decrease, first, the amount of the targeted RNA and, second, the amount of encoded protein.

RNA interference is an ancient mechanism of gene regulation that plays a central role in controlling gene expression in all eukaryotes, including yeast. Using small interfering RNA molecules, essentially RNAi can selectively silence any gene in the genome. Once in a cell, a short double-stranded RNA (dsRNA) molecule is cleft by an RNAse called Dicer into 21–23 nucleotide guide RNA duplexes called siRNAs that become bound to the RNA-induced silencing complex (RISC). Within the RISC, one of the two strands of the siRNA is chosen as the antisense strand via cleavage of the passenger strand, so that they can target complementary sequences in messenger RNAs. After pairing with an siRNA strand, the targeted mRNA is cleft and undergoes degradation, thereby interrupting the synthesis of the disease-causing protein.

One example is an experiment targeting DSCR1, a gene that belongs to a family of conserved proteins, also termed calcipressins; the protein functions as a small cytoplasmic signalling molecule. Two groups (Hesser *et al.* 2004 and Arron *et al.* 2006) have established a regulatory role for DSCR1 that controls the level of NFAT, a transcription factor, in the nucleus. Using a siRNA targeting DSCR1, Hesser and colleagues have shown, in endothelial cells, that they can increase the NFAT activity that is reduced in DS.

A second example applied to a mouse model of amyotrophic lateral sclerosis targets the mutated form of superoxide dismutase 1 (SOD1), the first enzyme localized on HSA21. Ralph and colleagues, in 2005, generated a lentiviral vector to mediate expression of RNAi molecules. Injection of this vector into various muscle groups of mice, engineered to overexpress a mutated form of human SOD1, resulted in an efficient reduction of SOD1 expression, improved survival of vulnerable motor neurons and mediated an improved motor performance in these animals (Fig. 1.2).

## PROTEIN TARGETS

The second strategy directly targets the protein product of the candidate gene.

The following two examples illustrate the use of antibodies to decrease the amount of the amyloid beta (Abeta) peptide. In the 'amyloid cascade hypothesis' memory deficits in patients with Alzheimer disease are caused by increased brain levels of both soluble and insoluble amyloid beta peptide(s), which are derived from the larger amyloid precursor protein (APP) by sequential proteolytic processing (Hardy and Selkoe 2002). Bales *et al.* (2006) have found that Abeta can directly interact with the high-affinity choline transporter, which may impair acetylcholine release and related neurotransmission. Using an anti-Abeta antibody they treated mice that overexpress a mutation related to one of the mutations associated with familial AD by direct hippocampal perfusion, and restored hippocampal acetylcholine release and reduced impaired habituation learning.

In a similar study Lee and colleagues (2006) designed a monoclonal antibody targeting preferentially the higher-order Abeta structures and verified that this antibody is specific to fibrillar Abeta in brain sections of individuals with mild cognitive impairment, Down syndrome or AD. Intraperitoneal injections of this antibody to mice carrying the mutation 2576 found in familial AD induced significant improvements in spatial learning and memory relative to control mice (Fig. 1.3).

These results suggest that pathological Abeta conformers produced *in vivo* are capable of disrupting neuronal function, and substantiate the therapeutic potential of targeting Abeta oligomers for the treatment of AD in AD patients or DS patients.

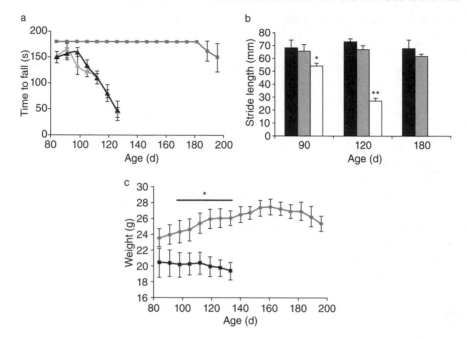

**Figure 1.2.** Silencing of SOD1 expression using shRNA mediates improved motor performance in SOD1G93A transgenic mice.
(a) Rotarod performance in transgenic mice injected with EIAV-SOD1HP1 (red, n = 6), EIAV-Emp (blue, n = 7) and uninjected controls (green, n = 5). (b) Hindlimb footprint analysis of stride length in EIAV-SOD1HP1–injected (grey), EIAV-Emp–injected (white) and wild-type (black) mice showing a significant improvement in stride length by shRNA expression compared with injected controls (* P < 0.01, ** P < 0.005, n = 4). (c) Weight measurements of EIAV-SOD1HP1–injected (red) and EIAV-Emp–injected (blue) animals. Mice receiving intramuscular injection of EIAV-SOD1HP1 were significantly heavier than injected controls (* P < 0.05, n = 6) (from Ralph *et al.* 2005).

## PROTEIN ACTIVITIES AS TARGETS

A third possibility is to use compounds acting to modify the activity of the targeted protein or the targeted pathway. Two examples are presented: the first one describes the targeting of the sonic hedgehog pathway in the Ts65Dn model and the second one illustrates the use of an inhibitor of Dyrk1a in a YAC transgenic model.

### Sonic Hedgehog Pathway

Roper and colleagues (2006) have demonstrated that, in cell culture, developing cerebellum granule cell precursors (GCPs) respond to the addition of Sonic

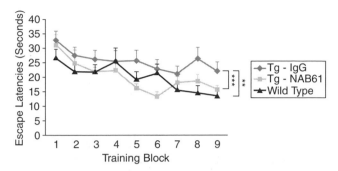

**Figure 1.3.** NAB61 improves spatial learning and memory. Performance in the hidden water maze. 17–19-month-old Tg2576 mice were administered an initial dose of 400 microg of NAB61 or nonspecific mouse IgG on day 3 with maintenance doses of 200 microg on days 0, 6, and 12. Performance on the visible water maze was tested on days 1–3 (four trials/block, two blocks/day) followed by the hidden water maze on days 4–13 (four trials/block, one block/day). Probe trials were interpolated throughout the hidden water maze on days 7, 10, and 13. *In the visible water maze*: NAB61-treated Tg2576, IgG-treated Tg2576, and non-transgenic mice all learned the visible water maze task. No significant differences were found between the three groups. Within-group analysis indicated that NAB61-treated Tg2576 and non-transgenic mice both showed significant improvements in escape latencies with time, whereas data from IgG-treated Tg2576 mice did not reach statistical significance (from Lee *et al.* 2006).

hedgehog protein by proliferating. This response is reduced in trisomic mice. These results indicate that failure to generate sufficient progeny from GCP is an important component of the granule cells deficit associated with reduced cerebellar size in adult Ts65Dn mice. On the day of birth, the number of progenitors is identical, but the number of mitotic GCP is significantly reduced in trisomic mice. By P6, the total number of precursor cells has been compromised to such an extent that normal levels of GCP production are not achieved in Ts65Dn mice. The authors show that an intrinsic deficit in the response of trisomic GCP to Shh underlies the reduced generation of GC in Ts65Dn mice. Introduction of a Shh pathway agonist early in development stimulated mitosis of GCP and corrected this deficit, to the extent that the number of GCP and the rate of mitosis were normal 1 week after treatment (Fig. 1.4).

## Dyrk1a Pathway

Minibrain kinase/dual-specificity tyrosine phosphorylation-regulated kinase (Mnb/Dyrk1A) is a proline-directed serine-threonine kinase (Kentrup *et al.* 1996; Himpel *et al.* 2001) encoded by a gene located within the Down syndrome chromosomal region 1 (DCR-1) involved in mental retardation in DS (Delabar *et al.* 1993; Korenberg *et al.* 1996). Its expression is elevated in DS brain fetuses (unpublished results) and in individuals with DS (Guimera *et al.*

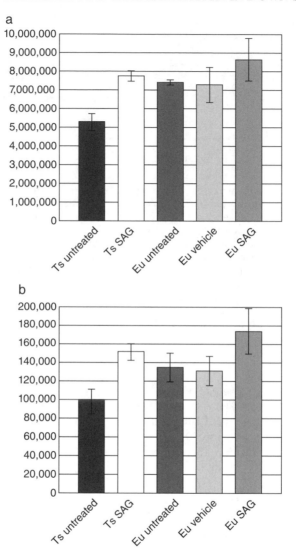

**Figure 1.4.** Mitotic and GCP deficits of trisomic mice are reversed by injection of a Shh pathway agonist. Progeny of Ts65Dn mothers received an s.c. injection of a Shh pathway agonist 20 g g SAG 1.1 Shh agonist (32) on the day of birth. The animals were killed, genotyped, and assessed by stereology at P6. ANOVA with multiple comparisons was used to analyse results. (a) For GCP, the trisomic agonist, euploid vehicle, and euploid-untreated groups were not different from each other, but were significantly increased relative to untreated trisomic mice (F = 5.6, P = 0.009, $\alpha$ = 0.05). (b) For mitotic cells, the trisomic agonist group was significantly different from trisomic untreated mice (F 3.06, P = 0.06, $\alpha$ = 0.05), but not different from euploid or euploid vehicle groups (from Roper *et al.* 2006).

1999). Several endogenous substrates for this kinase have been identified, such as transcription factor FKHR (Woods *et al.* 2001a), microtubule–associated protein tau (Woods *et al.* 2001b) and proteins engaged in endocytosis such as dynamin (Chen-Hwang *et al.* 2002) and synaptojanin (Adayev *et al.* 2006). It is thought to be involved in the control of neurogenesis and of neuronal plasticity. Yac transgenic mice carrying an extra copy of this gene present alterations of the brain morphology and of cognitive functions (Branchi *et al.* 2004; Chabert *et al.* 2004). This gene is also overexpressed in specific neurons of patients with Alzheimer disease (Ferrer *et al.* 2005). Magnetic resonance imaging was used to characterize brain morphology alterations during development (Fig. 1.5A): total brain volume of transgenic animals is found increased by 14–15 per cent in comparison with controls, and this difference is seen as early as 2 days postnatal.

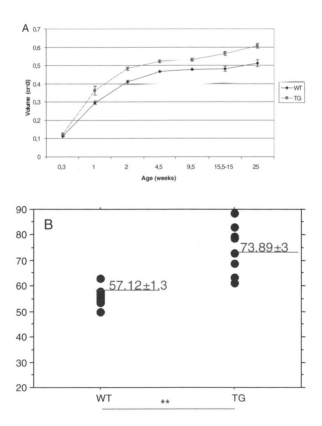

**Figure 1.5.** Dyrk1a overexpression modifies brain morphogenesis: MRI measurements were performed between day 7 and day 180 on isoflurane anaesthetized mice: controls and transgenic were from the same litters. **A:** total brain volumes in function of age and genotype; **B:** volume of the thalamus–hypothalamus area (**: $P < 0.001$).

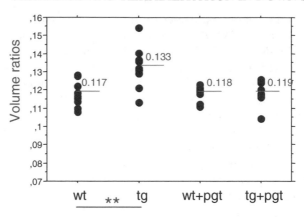

**Figure 1.6.** PGT-driven correction of the morphogenesis alterations. The relative volume of the thalamus–hypothalamus area was assessed for each group: wt: control + H2O; tg: transgenic + H2O; wt + PGT: control + polyphenols from green tea; tg + PGT: transgenic mice + polyphenols from green tea. ($F(1, 32) = 6.23$, $P < 0.02$.)

The regional assessment of the volumes permits the identification of a region, the thalamus–hypothalamus area, that is specifically increased in transgenic mice (30 per cent) (Fig. 1.5B; Sebrié *et al.*, submitted).

Kinases catalyse the addition of a phosphate group to various substrates. The main class of inhibitors of kinases are molecules taking the place of the donor molecule, ATP. Bain and colleagues (2003) have shown *in vitro* that dyrk1a is specifically inhibited by epigallocatechin gallate (EGCG), a natural molecule that is the main component of the polyphenols in green tea.

These observations were used to design a diet given to the gestating mothers and continued postnatally until the MRI analysis (2–4 months). It was found that polyphenols from green tea (PGT) correct the alterations in morphogenesis: the correction of the alterations seen on the total brain volumes is 35 per cent in males and 65 per cent in females. The PGT effect is more pronounced in the thalamus–hypothalamus region, producing a 91 per cent reduction of the relative increase (thalamus–hypothalamus volume/total brain volume) of this region. Polyphenols from green tea may exert their actions through a direct inhibition of dyrk1a (by EGCG) (Fig. 1.6).

These results suggest that it is possible to rescue a brain phenotype by a mild modulation that does not alter the wild type phenotype.

## FUTURE PROSPECTS

Targeting specific genes in animal models is now possible by using one of the strategies presented in this review. These corrective interventions may create side-effects, as has been the case with the antibody technology used in

Alzheimer disease. To avoid in human subjects the possible negative effects of the treatments and choose the best targets or the best combination of targets, meaning those that will allow corrections as nearly as possible back to a normal level, it will be necessary to develop numerous single-gene models in mice. These models together with models of partial trisomy will be assessed for the efficiency of the corrective strategies at morphological level and cognitive level. Nevertheless, even if many investigations have to be performed, it is remarkable that strategies targeting specific genes are already giving promising results. One may hope that similar strategies or the development of the strategies reported in this chapter will render it possible to reduce the burdens to which DS patients are subjected.

# REFERENCES

Adayev, T., Chen-Hwang, M.C., Murakami, N., Wang, R. and Hwang, Y.W. (2006). MNB/DYRK1A phosphorylation regulates the interactions of synaptojanin 1 with endocytic accessory proteins. *Biochem Biophys Res Commun.* 29;351(4):1060–5.

Ahn, K.J., Jeong, H.K., Choi, H.S., Ryoo, S.R., Kim, Y.J., Goo, J.S., Choi, S.Y., Han, J.S., Ha, I. and Song, W.J. (2006). DYRK1A BAC transgenic mice show altered synaptic plasticity with learning and memory defects. *Neurobiol Dis.* 22(3):463–72.

Arron, J.R., Winslow, M.M., Polleri, A., Chang, C.P., Wu, H., Gao, X., Neilson, J.R., Chen, L., Heit, J.J., Kim, S.K., Yamasaki, N., Miyakawa, T., Francke, U., Graef, I.A. and Crabtree, G.R. (2006). NFAT dysregulation by increased dosage of DSCR1 and DYRK1A on chromosome 21. *Nature.* 441(7093):595–600.

Bain, J., McLauchlan, H., Elliott, M. and Cohen, P. (2003). The specificities of protein kinase inhibitors: an update. *Biochem J.* 371(Pt 1):199–204.

Bales, K.R., Tzavara, E.T., Wu, S., Wade, M.R., Bymaster, F.P., Paul, S.M. and Nomikos, G.G. (2006). Cholinergic dysfunction in a mouse model of Alzheimer disease is reversed by an anti-A beta antibody. *J Clin Invest.* 116(3):825–32. (Epub 2006 Feb 23.)

Baxter, L.L., Moran, T.H., Richtsmeier, J.T., Troncoso, J. and Reeves, R.H. (2000). Discovery and genetic localization of Down syndrome cerebellar phenotypes using the Ts65Dn mouse. *Hum Mol Genet.* 9:195–202.

Becker, L.E., Mito, T., Takashima, S. and Onodera, K. (1991). Growth and development of the brain in Down syndrome. In C. Epstein (ed.), *The morphogenesis of Down syndrome*, pp. 133–52. New York: Wiley-Liss.

Belichenko, P.V., Masliah, E., Kleschevnikov, A.M., Villar, A.J., Epstein, C.J., Salehi, A. and Mobley, W.C. (2005). Synaptic structural abnormalities in the Ts65Dn mouse model of Down Syndrome. *J Comp Neurol.* 480(3):281–98.

Branchi, I., Bichler, Z., Minghetti, L., Delabar, J.M., Malchiodi-Albedi, F., Gonzalez, M.C., Chettouh, Z., Nicolini, A., Chabert, C., Smith, D.J., Rubin, E.M., Migliore-Samour, D. and Alleva, E. (2004). Transgenic mouse *in vivo* library of human Down syndrome critical region 1: association between DYRK1A overexpression, brain development abnormalities, and cell cycle protein alteration. *J Neuropathol Exp Neurol.* 63(5):429–40.

Chabert, C., Jamon, M., Cherfouh, A., Duquenne, V., Smith, D.J., Rubin, E. and Roubertoux, P.L. (2004). Functional analysis of genes implicated in Down syndrome: 1. Cognitive abilities in mice transpolygenic for Down Syndrome Chromosomal Region-1 (DCR-1). *Behav Genet.* 34(6):559–69.

Chen-Hwang, M.C., Chen, H.R., Elzinga, M. and Hwang, Y.W. (2002). Dynamin is a minibrain kinase/dual specificity Yak1-related kinase 1A substrate. *J Biol Chem.* 277(20):17597–604.

Dahmane, N., Charron, G., Lopes, C., Yaspo, M.L., Maunoury, C., Decorte, L., Sinet, P.M., Bloch, B. and Delabar, J.M. (1995). Down syndrome-critical region contains a gene homologous to Drosophila sim expressed during rat and human central nervous system development. *Proc Natl Acad Sci USA.* 92(20):9191–5.

Dauphinot, L., Lyle, R., Rivals, I., Dang, M.T., Moldrich, R.X., Golfier, G., Ettwiller, L., Toyama, K., Rossier, J., Personnaz, L., Antonarakis, S.E., Epstein, C.J., Sinet, P.M. and Potier, M.C. (2005). The cerebellar transcriptome during postnatal development of the Ts1Cje mouse, a segmental trisomy model for Down syndrome. *Hum Mol Genet.* 14(3):373–84.

Davisson, M.T., Schmidt, C. and Akeson, E.C. (1990). Segmental trisomy of murine chromosome 16: a new model system for studying Down syndrome. *Prog Clin Biol Res.* 360:263–80.

Delabar, J.M., Theophile, D., Rahmani, Z., Chettouh, Z., Blouin, J.L., Prieur, M., Noel, B. and Sinet, P.M. (1993). Molecular mapping of twenty-four features of Down syndrome on chromosome 21. *Eur J Hum Genet.* 1(2):114–24.

Ferrer, I., Barrachina, M., Puig, B., Martinez, de Lagran, M., Marti, E., Avila, J. and Dierssen, M. (2005). Constitutive Dyrk1A is abnormally expressed in Alzheimer disease, Down syndrome, Pick disease, and related transgenic models. *Neurobiol Dis.* 20(2):392–400.

Franceschi, M., Comola, M., Piattoni, F., Gualandri, W. and Canal, N. (1990). Prevalence of dementia in adult patients with trisomy 21. *Am J Med Genet.* Suppl 7:306–8.

Gardiner, K., Davisson, M.T. and Crnic, L.S. (2004). Building protein interaction maps for Down syndrome. *Brief Funct Genomic Proteomic.* Vol.3(2):142–56.

Gitton, Y., Dahmane, N., Baik, S., Ruiz i Altaba, A., Neidhardt, L., Scholze, M., Herrmann, B.G., Kahlem, P., Benkahla, A., Schrinner, S., Yildirimman, R., Herwig, R., Lehrach, H. and Yaspo, M.L. (2002). HSA21 expression map initiative. A gene expression map of human chromosome 21 orthologues in the mouse. *Nature.* 420(6915):586–90.

Golden, J.A. and Hyman, B.T. (1994). Development of the superior temporal neocortex is anomalous in trisomy 21. *J Neuropathol Exp Neurol.* 53:513–20.

Guimera, J., Casas, C., Estivill, X. and Pritchard, M. (1999). Human minibrain homologue (MNBH/DYRK1): characterization, alternative splicing, differential tissue expression, and overexpression in Down syndrome. *Genomics.* 1;57(3):407–18.

Hardy, J. and Selkoe, D.J. (2002). The amyloid hypothesis of Alzheimer's disease: progress and problems on the road to therapeutics. *Science.* 297:353–6.

Hesser, B.A., Liang, X.H., Camenisch, G., Yang, S., Lewin, D.A., Scheller, R., Ferrara, N. and Gerber, H.P. (2004). Down syndrome critical region protein 1 (DSCR1), a novel VEGF target gene that regulates expression of inflammatory markers on activated endothelial cells. *Blood.* 104(1):149–58.

Himpel, S., Panzer, P., Eirmbter, K., Czajkowska, H., Sayed, M., Packman, L.C., Blundell, T., Kentrup, H., Grotzinger, J., Joost, H.G. and Becker, W. (2001).

Identification of the autophosphorylation sites and characterization of their effects in the protein kinase DYRK1A. *Biochem J.* 359(3):497–505.

Holtzman, D.M., Santucci, D., Kilbridge, J., Chua-Couzens, J., Fontana, D.J., Daniels, S.E., Johnson, R.M., Chen, K., Sun, Y., Carlson, E., Alleva, E., Epstein, C.J. and Mobley, W.C. (1996). Developmental abnormalities and age-related neurodegeneration in a mouse model of Down syndrome. *Proc Natl Acad Sci USA.* 93:13333–8.

Insausti, A.M., Megias, M., Crespo, D., Cruz-Orive, L.M., Dierssen, M., Vallina, I.F., Insausti, R., Florez, J. and Vallina, T.F. (1998). Hippocampal volume and neuronal number in Ts65Dn mice: a murine model of Down syndrome. *Neurosci Lett.* 253:175–8.

Jernigan, T.L., Bellugi, U., Sowell, E., Doherty, S. and Hesselink, J.R. (1998). Cerebral morphologic distinctions between Williams and Down syndromes. *Arch Neurol.* 50:186–91.

Kentrup, H., Becker, W., Heukelbach, J., Wilmes, A., Schurmann, A., Huppertz, C., Kainulainen, H., Joost, H.G. (1996). Dyrk, a dual specificity protein kinase with unique structural features whose activity is dependent on tyrosine residues between subdomains VII and VIII. *J Biol Chem.* 271(7):3488–95.

Kesslak, J.P., Nagata, S.F., Lott, I. and Nalcioglu, O. (1994). Magnetic resonance imaging analysis of age-related changes in the brains of individuals with Down's syndrome. *Neurology.* 44:1039–45.

Kleschevnikov, A.M., Belichenko, P.V., Villar, A.J., Epstein, C.J., Malenka, R.C. and Mobley, W.C. (2004). Hippocampal long-term potentiation suppressed by increased inhibition in the Ts65Dn mouse, a genetic model of Down syndrome. *J Neurosci.* 24(37):8153–60.

Korenberg, J.R., Aaltonen, J., Brahe, C., Cabin, D., Creau, N., Delabar, J.M., Doering, J., Gardiner, K., Hubert, R.S., Ives, J., Kessling, A., Kudoh, J., Lafreniere, R., Murakami, Y., Ohira, M., Ohki, M., Patterson, D., Potier, M.C., Quackenbush, J., Reeves, R.H., Sakaki, Y., Shimizu, N., Soeda, E., Van Broeckhoven, C. and Yaspo, M.L. (1997). Report and abstracts of the Sixth International Workshop on Human Chromosome 21 Mapping 1996. Cold Spring Harbor, New York, USA. May 6–8, 1996. *Cytogenet Cell Genet.* 79(1–2):21–52.

Lee, E.B., Leng, L.Z., Zhang, B., Kwong, L., Trojanowski, J.Q., Abel, T. and Lee, V.M. (2006). Targeting amyloid-beta peptide (Abeta) oligomers by passive immunization with a conformation-selective monoclonal antibody improves learning and memory in Abeta precursor protein (APP) transgenic mice. *J Biol Chem.* 281(7):4292–9.

Lyle, R., Gehrig, C., Neergaard-Henrichsen, C., Deutsch, S. and Antonarakis, S.E. (2004). Gene expression from the aneuploid chromosome in a trisomy mouse model of down syndrome. *Genome Res.* 14(7):1268–74.

Mann, D.M., Royston, M.C. and Ravindra, C.R. (1990). Some morphometric observations on the brains of patients with Down's syndrome: their relationship to age and dementia. *J Neurol Sci.* 99:153–64.

O'Doherty, A., Ruf, S., Mulligan, C., Hildreth, V., Errington, M.L., Cooke, S., Sesay, A., Modino, S., Vanes, L., Hernandez, D., Linehan, J.M., Sharpe, P.T., Brandner, S., Bliss, T.V., Henderson, D.J., Nizetic, D., Tybulewicz, V.L. and Fisher, E.M. (2005). An aneuploid mouse strain carrying human chromosome 21 with Down syndrome phenotypes. *Science* 23;309(5743):2033–7.

Olson, L.E., Roper, R.J., Baxter, L.L., Carlson, E.J., Epstein, C.J. and Reeves, R.H. (2004). Down syndrome mouse models Ts65Dn, Ts1Cje, and Ms1Cje/Ts65Dn exhibit variable severity of cerebellar phenotypes. *Dev Dyn.* 230(3):581–9.

Palmer, S. (2000). Working memory: a developmental study of phonological recoding. *Memory.* (8):179–93.

Pellegrini-Calace, M. and Tramontano, A. (2006). Identification of a novel putative mitogen-activated kinase cascade on human chromosome 21 by computational approaches. *Bioinformatics.* 22(7):775–8.

Pinter, J.D., Eliez, S., Schmitt, J.E., Capone, G.T. and Reiss, A.L. (2001). Neuroanatomy of Down's syndrome: a high-resolution MRI study. *Am J Psychiatry.* 158:1659–65.

Rachidi, M., Lopes, C., Delezoide, A.L. and Delabar, J.M. (2006). C21orf5, a human candidate gene for brain abnormalities and mental retardation in Down syndrome. *Cytogenet Genome Res.* 112(1–2):16–22.

Ralph, G.S., Radcliffe, P.A., Day, D.M., Carthy, J.M., Leroux, M.A., Lee, D.C., Wong, L.F., Bilsland, L.G., Greensmith, L., Kingsman, S.M., Mitrophanous, K.A., Mazarakis, N.D. and Azzouz, M. (2005). Silencing mutant SOD1 using RNAi protects against neurodegeneration and extends survival in an ALS model. *Nat Med.* 11(4):429–33.

Raz, N., Torres, I.J., Briggs, S.D., Spencer, W.D., Thornton, A.E., Loken, W.J., Gunning, F.M., McQuain, J.D., Driesen, N.R. and Acker, J.D. (1995). Selective neuroanatomic abnormalities in Down's syndrome and their cognitive correlates: evidence from MRI morphometry. *Neurology.* 45:356–66.

Reymond, A., Marigo, V., Yaylaoglu, M.B., Leoni, A., Ucla, C., Scamuffa, N., Caccioppoli, C., Dermitzakis, E.T., Lyle, R., Banfi, S., Eichele, G., Antonarakis, S.E. and Ballabio, A. (2002). Human chromosome 21 gene expression atlas in the mouse. *Nature.* 420(6915):582–6.

Roper, R.J., Baxter, L.L., Saran, N.G., Klinedinst, D.K., Beachy, P.A. and Reeves, R.H. (2006). Defective cerebellar response to mitogenic Hedgehog signaling in Down syndrome mice. *Proc Natl Acad Sci USA.* 103(5):1452–6.

Sago, H., Carlson, E.J., Smith, D.J., Kilbridge, J., Rubin, E.M., Mobley, W.C., Epstein, C.J. and Huang, T.T. (1998). Ts1Cje, a partial trisomy 16 mouse model for Down syndrome, exhibits learning and behavioral abnormalities. *Proc Natl Acad Sci USA.* 95:6256–61.

Schulz, E. and Scholz, B. (1992). Neurohistological findings in the parietal cortex of children with chromosome aberrations. *J Hirnforsch.* 33(1):37–62. (In German.)

Sebrié, C., Chabert, C., Ledru, A., Guedj, F., Jean-Claude, Beloeil, J.C., Brigitte, Gillet, B. and Delabar, J.M. (submitted). *In vivo* MRI study of brain volumetric alterations in a transgenic YAC model of partial trisomy 21.

Shinohara, T., Tomizuka, K., Miyabara, S., Takehara, S., Kazuki, Y., Inoue, J., Katoh, M., Nakane, H., Iino, A., Ohguma, A., Ikegami, S., Inokuchi, K., Ishida, I., Reeves, R.H. and Oshimura, M. (2001). Mice containing a human chromosome 21 model behavioral impairment and cardiac anomalies of Down's syndrome. *Hum Mol Genet.* 10(11):1163–75.

Siarey, R.J., Stoll, J., Rapoport, S.I. and Galdzicki, Z. (1997). Altered long-term potentiation in the young and old Ts65Dn mouse, a model for Down Syndrome. *Neuropharmacology.* 36:1549–54.

Siarey, R.J., Carlson, E.J., Epstein, C.J., Balbo, A., Rapoport, S.I. and Galdzicki, Z. (1999). Increased synaptic depression in the Ts65Dn mouse, a model for mental retardation in Down syndrome. *Neuropharmacology.* 38(12):1917–20.

Smith, D.J., Stevens, M.E., Sudanagunta, S.P., Bronson, R.T., Makhinson, M., Watabe, A.M., O'Dell, T.J., Fung, J., Weier, H.U., Cheng, J.F. and Rubin, E.M. (1997). Functional screening of 2 Mb of human chromosome 21q22.2 in transgenic mice implicates minibrain in learning defects associated with Down syndrome. *Nat Genet.* 16(1):28–36.

Thomas, S., Thiery, E., Aflalo, R., Vayssettes, C., Verney, C., Berthuy, I. and Creau, N. (2003). PCP4 is highly expressed in ectoderm and particularly in neuroectoderm derivatives during mouse embryogenesis. *Gene Expr Patterns.* 3(1):93–7.

Vicari, S., Bellucci, S. and Carlesimo, G.A. (2005). Visual and spatial long-term memory: differential pattern of impairments in Williams and Down syndromes. *Dev Med Child Neurol.* 47(5):305–11.

White, N.S., Alkire, M.T. and Haier, R.J. (2003). A voxel-based morphometric study of nondemented adults with Down Syndrome. *Neuroimage.* 20:393–403.

Woods, Y.L., Rena, G., Morrice, N., Barthe,l A., Becker, W., Guo, S., Unterman, T.G. and Cohen, P. (2001a). The kinase DYRK1A phosphorylates the transcription factor FKHR at Ser329 in vitro, a novel in vivo phosphorylation site. *Biochem J.* 355(3):597–607.

Woods, Y.L., Cohen, P., Becker, W., Jakes, R., Goedert, M., Wang, X. and Proud, C.G. (2001b). The kinase DYRK phosphorylates protein-synthesis initiation factor eIF-2Bepsilon at Ser539 and the microtubule-associated protein tau at Thr212: potential role for DYRK as a glycogen synthase kinase 3-priming kinase. *Biochem J.* 355(3):609–15.

# 2 The Biological Bases of Pharmacological Therapies in Down Syndrome

MELANIE A. PRITCHARD AND ISMAIL KOLA

## SUMMARY

Individuals with Down syndrome exhibit a collection of characteristic disorders, some of which can be controlled by the administration of pharmacological agents. Although in some instances the biological action of the agent is understood, in many cases it is not, and this is especially true in the context of Down syndrome. In this chapter we will review some of the pharmacological therapies currently used to treat some of the disorders associated with Down syndrome. We will conclude with our view on how future pharmacotherapies will emerge and illustrate this by giving an example from our own research.

## INTRODUCTION

Down syndrome (DS), caused by an extra copy of all or part of chromosome 21, is the most common congenital birth defect in humans. Individuals with DS exhibit anomalies of every major organ system in the body, including defects of the skeleton and bone, craniofacial anomalies, immune deficits. endocrine defects, cognitive defects associated with abnormal brain development and function and, later in life, pathology akin to Alzheimer disease. Although the genetic aetiology of the disorder is well established, how this extra chromosomal material causes the characteristic traits associated with the syndrome is poorly understood, and this lack of understanding is reflected in the paucity of therapies specific for DS. There is no cure for DS. The best that medical science can currently offer is to treat some of the existing pathologies; but with very few exceptions, these treatments are not DS-specific – they are therapies used to treat members of the general population suffering from similar disorders. There is a valid reason for such an approach, as many of the

*Therapies and Rehabilitation in Down Syndrome.* Edited by Rondal
© 2007 John Wiley & Sons Ltd

disorders associated with DS appear to have the same clinical manifestation in non-DS individuals; however, in the non-DS population the symptoms usually occur in isolation, not in conjunction with a range of other confounding organ system anomalies.

## IMMUNE DEFICITS

DS individuals have an increased susceptibility to infection, presumably due to an inefficient immune system (Murphy *et al.* 1995). The DS thymus, one of the major organs involved in the immune response, is structurally abnormal. There is poor demarcation of the cortex and medulla, and marked cortical thymocyte depletion (Murphy *et al.* 1995). The relative proportions of the major circulating immune cell subsets, namely, T cells, B cells and natural killer (NK) cells, are also abnormal (Cossarizza *et al.* 1990). It has been proposed that T cells fail to mature correctly in the DS thymus (Burgio *et al.* 1983), which may result in the higher than normal frequency of autoimmune disorders such as vitiligo and alopecia observed in DS (Scherbenske *et al.* 1990). The cause(s) of diminished immune cell function is/are unknown, but a number of genes encoded on chromosome 21 and over-expressed in DS have been implicated. Examples include: *ETS2*; the interferon alpha and gamma receptor genes, *IFNAR1/2* and *IFNGR*; *CD18*; the leukocyte function associated beta chain (LFA-1β); and *AF-1*, the accessory factor for IFN-γ responsiveness.

It has been known since the 1970s that a variety of DS cells, including thymocytes, are hypersensitive to the anti-proliferative actions of IFNγ, most probably owing to an increase in the number of IFNGR molecules on DS cells and elevated levels of AF-1 (Murphy *et al.* 1995). As well as inhibiting cellular proliferation, interferons induce cell death pathways (Boehm *et al.* 1997); thus it is possible that, during development, populations of cells that are exquisitely sensitive to the anti-cellular effects of endogenous interferons are killed. Evidence for this comes from a study in which anti-interferon antibodies, designed to block interferon functions, were administered *in utero* to pregnant female mice carrying trisomy-16 fetuses. Mice trisomic for chromosome 16 are a well-recognized model for human chromosome 21 trisomy, with late-stage trisomy-6 fetuses exhibiting some of the features of DS. Administration of anti-interferon antibodies resulted in marked improvement in a number of morphological features in the trisomy-16 animals (Maroun 1995). Also, a study by the same researchers showed that anti-gamma interferon antibodies could prevent the premature death of trisomy-16 mouse cortical neurons (Hallam and Maroun 1998). Thus it is possible that anti-interferon therapy may improve some of the defects associated with DS, such as reduced thymic cell populations and reduced neuronal numbers. Although the use of interferon antagonists as therapies for DS is in the early experimental phase and most of the studies have been performed by one research group in animal models, this area of endeavour seems to hold some promise. Indeed, the same group has formed a company to develop anti-interferon drugs for clinical testing.

Currently, two approaches exist for the treatment of DS immune system disorders. In the first, the symptoms (infections) are treated using standard antibiotic/antiviral regimes. A second, more controversial, approach involves the supplementation of zinc. Zinc plays a central role in the immune system (reviewed in Shankar and Prasad 1998) and its levels have been found to be reduced in some individuals with DS (Romano *et al.* 2002). Zinc supplements have been shown to boost the DS immune system by causing an increase in the number of circulating T cells (Franceschi *et al.* 1988) and by normalizing some humoral and cellular immune parameters (Licastro *et al.* 1994), thus reducing the incidence of recurrent infections (Licastro *et al.* 1994). The positive effect of zinc is thought to occur because thymic hormones such as thymulin and many enzymes require zinc for their activity (reviewed in Shankar and Prasad 1998). Although zinc supplements have been advocated by some, other studies (for instance, Lockitch *et al.* 1989) showed no demonstrable benefit of zinc supplementation. Crucially, no information is available on the possible detrimental effects of chronic zinc administration.

## ENDOCRINE DYSFUNCTION – THE DOWN SYNDROME THYROID

Normal levels of thyroid hormones are required for growth and cognitive function. Depending on the report, between 0.7 per cent and 2.9 per cent of infants with DS have congenital hypothyroidism (Gruneiro de Papendieck *et al.* 2002). The prevalence of thyroid dysfunction in adults with DS has varied between 3 per cent and 54 per cent (Karlsson *et al.* 1998 and references therein) and is due to autoimmunity or thyroiditis. These abnormalities result in decreased levels of thyroxine and increased levels of thyroid-stimulating hormone (TSH). Treatment involves a blood test to determine thyroid hormone levels and, if indicated, the administration of synthetic thyroxine. Zinc supplements have also been reported to restore hormone levels (Bucci *et al.* 1999; Licastro *et al.* 1992; Napolitano *et al.* 1990), but this is still controversial.

## NEUROLOGICAL DEFECTS

There are a number of neurological anomalies associated with DS. Those occurring in early life include intellectual impairment, hypotonia and seizures, which are sometimes called infantile spasms. Later in life DS individuals develop Alzheimer-like pathology in the brain, and experience seizures of a type strongly connected with Alzheimer disease.

The prevalence of epilepsy in DS ranges between 8 per cent and 13 per cent, depending on the report. For infantile spasms, the mean age of onset in one study was 7.6 months (Nabbout *et al.* 2001). In adults, the mean age of onset is around 37 years of age (Puri *et al.* 2001). The cause of seizures is unknown, but can probably be attributed to the inherent structural abnormalities of the DS brain (Goldberg-Stern *et al.* 2001 and references therein).

Antiepilepic drugs such as vigabatrin, adenocorticotropin and valproic acid are used to treat seizures effectively in both young and older DS individuals; however, the modes of action of these drugs are generally unknown. For instance, valproic acid (VPA) has been used for decades as an anticonvulsant. It was thought to interact with voltage-sensitive sodium channels to inhibit the repetitive firing of neurons and to increase the levels of the inhibitory neurotransmitter GABA (Johannessen 2000); but the mechanism by which it induced these effects was unknown. Recently, VPA was found to act as a histone deacetylase (HDAC) inhibitor, causing the transcriptional activation of a variety of genes (Kernochan *et al.* 2005; Phiel *et al.* 2001). Interestingly, a recent report demonstrated that VPA exerts different effects on gene expression in different cell types, adding further complication. Qiao and colleagues (2006) reported that, in fibroblasts, VPA increased the expression of the adiponectin promoter, but had a repressive effect on the same promoter in adipocytes. What is highly likely is that these generalized transcriptional effects of VPA contribute to the adverse reactions associated with its administration, which include hyperammonaemia, hepatotoxicity and pancreatitis.

Almost without exception, individuals with DS develop the neuropathology of Alzheimer disease by their fourth decade (Cork 1990; Mann 1988; Wisniewski *et al.* 1985), which is characterized by the appearance of β-amyloid plaques, neurofibrillary tangles, degeneration of certain neuronal populations and, in some cases, dementia (Stanton and Coetzee 2004). Loss of basal forebrain cholinergic neurons (BFCNs) is a prominent feature of Alzheimer disease and DS (Cooper *et al.* 2001). BFCNs supply the major cholinergic input to the hippocampus and the neocortex. These neurons have an important role in attention, learning and memory. The neurotransmitter acetylcholine is synthesized by BFCNs and released at the synapse, where it is hydrolysed to choline and acetate by the enzyme acetylcholinesterase (AChE) (Small 2005). The degeneration of BFCNs was linked to a cholinergic deficit in the Alzheimer disease brain and prompted pharmacological intervention in the form of a drug called donepezil (or Aricept). Donepezil inhibits the actions of AChE, thereby boosting cholinergic neurotransmission in the brain (Small 2005).

In Alzheimer disease, donepezil has been widely tested. A META analysis combining data on 2228 Alzheimer disease patients concluded that donepezil was efficacious and safe for the treatment of mild to moderate Alzheimer disease (Birks 2006). However, one study testing donepezil in 565 patients with Alzheimer disease in a randomized, double-blinded trial concluded that no significant benefits were observed with donepezil compared to placebo in progression of disability, rate of institutionalization or behavioural or psychological symptoms (Courtney *et al.* 2004).

Donepezil is one of the few drugs that have been specifically tested in DS. However, only a small number of studies have been conducted and the number of individuals involved in these studies is small. Kishnani and colleagues (1999) treated four people with DS aged between 24 and 64 years of age for an average of nine months. They recorded improvements in communication, expressive language, attention and mood stability as reported by their carers in all four individuals. Another study treated three individuals with DS, a 59-year-old woman, a 65-year-old woman and a 57-year-old man. All three suffered adverse reactions that subsided when donepezil was withdrawn (Hemingway-Eltomey and Lerner 1999). The first randomized, double-blinded placebo-controlled study on the efficacy and safety of donepezil as a treatment for dementia in DS was reported in 2002. The study found that donepezil was well tolerated and safe and, importantly, dementia scores for the treated group improved over the treatment period (Prasher *et al.* 2002). However, the number of individuals enrolled in the trial was again small, with only fourteen DS people receiving the drug and thirteen the placebo. Donepezil has also been found to improve cognitive function in younger individuals with DS (Heller *et al.* 2003; Johnson *et al.* 2003; Kondoh *et al.* 2005).

The pharmacological action of donepezil as an AChE inhibitor is known; but recently it was discovered that the actions of donepezil may not be restricted to the cholinergic system in the brain. Donepezil also modulates the activity of the glutamate receptor, NMDA, in rat cortical neurons, suggesting that it has effects on the glutamatergic system, which is also down-regulated in the brains of patients with Alzheimer disease. Thus, at therapeutic doses, donepezil, in addition to stimulating the cholinergic system via the inhibition of cholinesterases, augments the activity of the NMDA system, bringing these two transmitter systems back to normal levels to improve the learning, memory, and cognition of the patients (Moriguchi *et al.* 2005). In another study, Takatori (2006) found that AchE inhibitors such as donepezil protected cortical neurons from glutamate-induced toxicity mediated by nicotinic acetylcholine receptors via the phosphatidylinositol-3-kinase-Akt pathway, culminating in an up-regulation of the anti-apoptotic protein, Bcl-2.

Another drug, piracetam, has been tested in DS individuals in an effort to improve cognition. Piracetam, a cyclic derivative of γ-amino butyric acid (GABA), is classified as a nootropic, a class of drug thought to enhance cognitive function. The physiological or pharmacological basis by which piracetam exerts its actions is unknown; however, it has been variously reported to act on both glutamatergic and cholinergic neurotransmission, to enhance membrane fluidity, to increase blood flow, to augment corticosteroid function and to modulate calcium channel function (Lobaugh *et al.* 2001; Moran *et al.* 2002). Benefits of piracetam treatment have been reported anecdotally and in testimonials by parents administering piracetam to their DS children; but only two scientific studies have been conducted. One was a double-blinded, placebo-controlled study in which eighteen children with DS completed the trial. These children were aged between 6.5 and 13 years and had mild to moderate intellectual disability. The study concluded that piracetam therapy did not enhance cognition or behaviour; indeed, it was associated with adverse side- effects in seven of eleven children treated (Lobaugh *et al.* 2001). The second study tested piracetam in the Ts65Dn mouse model of DS. Interestingly, this study reported a beneficial effect of the drug on learning and memory in normal control mice, but in one of the more demanding cognitive tests, piracetam, at all doses tested, impaired the performance of Ts65Dn trisomic mice (Moran *et al.* 2002).

## PERSPECTIVE

When considering the examples we have given here, it is apparent that although there are some therapies with reasonable efficacy for some of the characteristic pathologies associated with DS, major deficiencies remain for most treatments. One of the major problems is that no large-scale controlled studies have been conducted in DS individuals. Although donepezil has been tested in DS and seems to hold promise for either improving cognition generally or for the treatment of dementia, the results are far from conclusive, owing to the limited number of trials conducted and the low number of subjects tested. Heller and colleagues (2006) have provided an extremely useful treatise on the issues to consider when designing clinical trials for the DS population, with a particular emphasis on children. They address topics such as study design, recruitment and retention of subjects, choice of medication and the measurement of efficacy and safety. In particular, efficacy and safety are of critical importance, since it is apparent that for many of the treatments used there is scant information on the correct dosage or possible side-effects for people with DS. Of concern is that it may not be possible to extrapolate data about any drug tested on the general population and apply it to the situation in DS, since cellular function and hence pharmacokinetic parameters may be very different in DS. Graphic indicators of this come from the studies that revealed that DS cells are acutely more sensitive to $\gamma$-interferon (see earlier) and to some of the chemotherapeutic agents used to combat the childhood leukaemia characteristic of DS, such as methotrexate (Drabkin and Erickson 1995), dexamethasone and etoposide (Gamis 2005). Also, when piracetam was administered to trisomic mice the effect was detrimental and opposite to the beneficial effect observed in normal, euploid animals (Moran *et al.* 2002). Finally, for the most part, we treat the symptoms while the biological bases of the therapies remain elusive. Thus, it is our opinion, shared by others, that it is crucial to elucidate the normal functions of chromosome 21 genes and understand how and why over-expression causes particular traits in DS. Only then will we be in a position to develop effective pharmacological therapies based on an understanding of the biological/molecular mechanisms involved.

There are many groups in the world attempting to elucidate the functions of the genes located on human chromosome 21. Our group has worked on *ETS2, GABPα, ADAMTS-1, DSCR1* and *ITSN1*. The following is an example, using *ETS2*, of how basic research into the mechanisms of action of chromosome 21 genes may allow the development of future pharmacotherapies.

## *ETS2* IN DOWN SYNDROME

*Ets2* is a transcription factor known to regulate the expression of numerous genes involved in cell cycle regulation, cell survival and tissue remodelling (reviewed in Sementchenko and Watson 2000). Our group revealed that over-expression of *Ets2* in the mouse produced some of the skeletal abnormalities characteristic of DS (Sumarsono *et al.* 1996). We further showed that *Ets2* transgenic mice had a smaller thymus, similar to that seen in DS (Wolvetang *et al.* 2003a) and increased neuronal apoptosis (Wolvetang *et al.* 2003b), and that this was due to the pro-apoptotic actions of *Ets2*. We also demonstrated that some of the genes involved in the apoptotic pathway were dysregulated in mice harbouring an extra dose of *Ets2*, as they were in DS tissues. These included up-regulation of the pro-apoptotic genes *p53* and *Bax* and down-regulation of the anti-apoptotic gene, *Bcl-2* (Wolvetang *et al.* 2003a). When *Ets2* transgenic mice were crossed onto a *p53* null background, the thymic apoptosis phenotype was rescued, indicating that the induction of apoptosis by *Ets2* was dependent on *p53* (Wolvetang *et al.* 2003a).

In addition to its role in promoting apoptosis, *Ets2* possesses other functions. The gene that codes for β-amyloid precursor protein (β-*APP*), a protein centrally involved in plaque formation in DS and Alzheimer disease, is located on chromosome 21. In DS β-APP expression is three- to fourfold higher than that expected from the 1.5-fold increased gene dosage, suggesting that other genes on chromosome 21 directly or indirectly further up-regulate β-APP gene expression. We have shown that *Ets2* transactivates the β-*APP* gene via specific *ets* binding sites in the β-*APP* promoter and that brains and primary neuronal cultures from *Ets2* transgenic mice display molecular abnormalities also seen in DS, such as elevated expression of β-APP protein (Wolvetang *et al.* 2003c).

Thus, we are beginning to build a picture of the cellular functions of *Ets2*. Dissecting the biological pathways in which each chromosome 21 gene is involved will enable us to identify targets for new drug therapies that will act specifically in the pathways disrupted in DS. Until we understand the aberrant cellular mechanisms triggered by an extra copy of the genes on chromosome 21, rational, truly effective therapies will remain elusive.

# REFERENCES

Birks, J. (2006). Cholinesterase inhibitors for Alzheimer's disease. *Cochrane Database Syst Rev.* Jan 25;(1):CD005593.

Boehm, U., Klamp, T., Groot, M. and Howard, J.C. (1997). Cellular responses to interferon-gamma. *Annu Rev Immunol.* 15:749–95.

Bucci, I., Napolitano, G., Giuliani, C., Lio, S., Minnucci, A., Di Giacomo, F., Calabrese, G., Sabatino, G., Palka, G. and Monaco, F. (1999). Zinc sulfate supplementation improves thyroid function in hypozincemic Down children. *Biol Trace Elem Res.* 67(3):257–68.

Burgio, G.R., Ugazio, A., Nespoli, L. and Maccario, R. (1983). Down syndrome: a model of immunodeficiency. *Birth Defects Orig Artic Ser.* 19(3):325–7.

Cooper, J.D., Salehi, A., Delcroix, J.D., Howe, C.L., Belichenko, P.V., Chua-Couzens, J., Kilbridge, J.F., Carlson, E.J., Epstein, C.J. and Mobley, W.C. (2001). Failed retrograde transport of NGF in a mouse model of Down's syndrome: reversal of cholinergic neurodegenerative phenotypes following NGF infusion. *Proc Natl Acad Sci USA.* 98(18):10439–44.

Cork, L.C. (1990). Neuropathology of Down syndrome and Alzheimer disease. *Am J Med Genet Suppl.* 7:282—6.

Cossarizza, A., Monti, D., Montagnani, G., Ortolani, C., Masi, M., Zannotti, M. and Franceschi, C. (1990). Precocious aging of the immune system in Down syndrome: alteration of B lymphocytes, T-lymphocyte subsets, and cells with natural killer markers. *Am J Med Genet Suppl.* 7:213–18.

Courtney, C., Farrell, D., Gray, R., Hills, R., Lynch, L., Sellwood, E., Edwards, S., Hardyman, W., Raftery, J., Crome, P., Lendon, C., Shaw, H., Bentham, P. and AD2000 Collaborative Group. (2004). Long-term donepezil treatment in 565 patients with Alzheimer's disease (AD2000): randomised double-blind trial. *Lancet.* 363(9427):2105–15.

Drabkin, H.A. and Erickson, P. (1995). Down syndrome and leukemia, an update. *Prog Clin Biol Res.* 393:169–76.

Franceschi, C., Chiricolo, M., Licastro, F., Zannotti, M., Masi, M., Mocchegiani, E. and Fabris, N. (1988). Oral zinc supplementation in Down's syndrome: restoration of thymic endocrine activity and of some immune defects. *J Ment Defic Res.* 32(Pt 3):169–81.

Gamis, A.S. (2005). Acute myeloid leukemia and Down syndrome evolution of modern therapy – state of the art review. *Pediatr Blood Cancer.* 44(1):13–20.

Goldberg-Stern, H., Strawsburg, R.H., Patterson, B., Hickey, F., Bare, M., Gadoth, N. and Degrauw, T.J. (2001). Seizure frequency and characteristics in children with Down syndrome. *Brain Dev.* 23(6):375–8.

Gruneiro de Papendieck, L., Chiesa, A., Bastida, M.G., Alonso, G., Finkielstain, G. and Heinrich, J.J. (2002). Thyroid dysfunction and high thyroid stimulating hormone levels in children with Down's syndrome. *J Pediatr Endocrinol Metab.* 15(9):1543–8.

Hallam, D.M. and Maroun, L.E. (1998). Anti-gamma interferon can prevent the premature death of trisomy 16 mouse cortical neurons in culture. *Neurosci Lett.* 252(1):17–20.

Heller, J.H., Spiridigliozzi, G.A., Sullivan, J.A., Doraiswamy, P.M., Krishnan, R.R. and Kishnani, P.S. (2003). Donepezil for the treatment of language deficits in adults with Down syndrome: a preliminary 24-week open trial. *Am J Med Genet A.* 116(2):111–16.

Heller, J.H., Spiridigliozzi, G.A., Crissman, B.G., Sullivan-Saarela, J.A., Li, J.S. and Kishnani, P.S. (2006). Clinical trials in children with Down syndrome: issues from a cognitive research perspective. *Am J Med Genet C Semin Med Genet.* 142C:187–95.

Hemingway-Eltomey, J.M. and Lerner, A.J. (1999). Adverse effects of donepezil in treating Alzheimer's disease associated with Down's syndrome. *Am J Psychiatry.* 156(9):1470.

Johannessen, C.U. (2000). Mechanisms of action of valproate: a commentatory. *Neurochem Int.* 37(2–3):103–10.

Johnson, N., Fahey, C., Chicoine, B., Chong, G. and Gitelman, D. (2003). Effects of donepezil on cognitive functioning in Down syndrome. *Am J Ment Retard.* 108(6):367–72.

Karlsson, B., Gustafsson, J., Hedov, G., Ivarsson, S.-A. and Annerén, G. (1998). Thyroid dysfunction in Down's syndrome: relation to age and thyroid autoimmunity. *Arch Dis Child.* 79:242–5.

Kernochan, L.E., Russo, M.L., Woodling, N.S., Huynh, T.N., Avila, A.M., Fischbeck, K.H. and Sumner, C.J. (2005). The role of histone acetylation in SMN gene expression. *Hum Mol Genet.* 14(9):1171–82.

Kishnani, P.S., Sullivan, J.A., Walter, B.K., Spiridigliozzi, G.A., Doraiswamy, P.M. and Krishnan, K.R. (1999). Cholinergic therapy for Down's syndrome. *Lancet.* 353(9158):1064–5.

Kondoh, T., Amamoto, N., Doi, T., Hamada, H., Ogawa, Y., Nakashima, M., Sasaki, H., Aikawa, K., Tanaka, T., Aoki, M., Harada, J. and Moriuchi, H. (2005). Dramatic improvement in Down syndrome-associated cognitive impairment with donepezil. *Ann Pharmacother.* 39(3):563–6.

Licastro, F., Mocchegiani, E., Zannotti, M., Arena, G., Masi, M. and Fabris, N. (1992). Zinc affects the metabolism of thyroid hormones in children with Down's syndrome: normalization of thyroid stimulating hormone and of reversal triiodothyronine plasmic levels by dietary zinc supplementation. *Int J Neurosci.* 65(1–4):259–68.

Licastro, F., Chiricolo, M., Mocchegiani, E., Fabris, N., Zannotti, M., Beltrandi, E., Mancini, R., Parente, R., Arena, G. and Masi, M. (1994). Oral zinc supplementation in Down's syndrome subjects decreased infections and normalized some humoral and cellular immune parameters. *J Intellect Disabil Res.* 38(Pt 2):149–62.

Lobaugh, N.J., Karaskov, V., Rombough, V., Rovet, J., Bryson, S., Greenbaum, R., Haslam, R.H. and Koren, G. (2001). Piracetam therapy does not enhance cognitive functioning in children with down syndrome. *Arch Pediatr Adolesc Med.* 155(4):442–8.

Lockitch, G., Puterman, M., Godolphin, W., Sheps, S., Tingle, A.J. and Quigley, G. (1989). Infection and immunity in Down syndrome: a trial of long-term low oral doses of zinc. *J Pediatr.* 114(5):781–7.

Mann, D.M. (1988). Alzheimer's disease and Down's syndrome. *Histopathology.* 13(2):125–37.

Maroun, L.E. (1995). Anti-interferon immunoglobulins can improve the trisomy 16 mouse phenotype. *Teratology.* 51(5):329–35.

Moran, T.H., Capone, G.T., Knipp, S., Davisson, M.T., Reeves, R.H. and Gearhart, J.D. (2002). The effects of piracetam on cognitive performance in a mouse model of Down's syndrome. *Physiol Behav.* 77(2–3):403–9.

Moriguchi, S., Zhao, X., Marszalec, W., Yeh, J.Z. and Narahashi, T. (2005). Modulation of N-methyl-D-aspartate receptors by donepezil in rat cortical neurons. *J Pharmacol Exp Ther.* 315(1):125–35.

Murphy, M., Insoft, R.M., Pike-Nobile, L. and Epstein, L.B. (1995). A hypothesis to explain the immune defects in Down syndrome. *Prog Clin Biol Res.* 393:147–67.

Nabbout, R., Melki, I., Gerbaka, B., Dulac, O. and Akatcherian, C. (2001). Infantile spasms in Down syndrome: good response to a short course of vigabatrin. *Epilepsia.* 42(12):1580–3.

Napolitano, G., Palka, G., Lio, S., Bucci, I., De Remigis, P., Stuppia, L. and Monaco, F. (1990). Is zinc deficiency a cause of subclinical hypothyroidism in Down syndrome? *Ann Genet.* 33(1):9–15.

Phiel, C.J., Zhang, F., Huang, E.Y., Guenther, M.G., Lazar, M.A. and Klein, P.S. (2001). Histone deacetylase is a direct target of valproic acid, a potent anticonvulsant, mood stabilizer, and teratogen. *J Biol Chem.* 276(39):6734–41.

Prasher, V.P., Huxley, A., Haque, M.S. and Down Syndrome Ageing Study Group. (2002). A 24-week, double-blind, placebo-controlled trial of donepezil in patients with Down syndrome and Alzheimer's disease – pilot study. *Int J Geriatr Psychiatry.* 17(3):270–8.

Puri, B.K., Ho, K.W. and Singh, I. (2001). Age of seizure onset in adults with Down's syndrome. *Int J Clin Pract.* 55(7):442–4.

Qiao, L., Schaack, J. and Shao, J. (2006). Suppression of adiponectin gene expression by histone deacetylase inhibitor valproic acid. *Endocrinology.* 147(2):865–74.

Romano, C., Pettinato, R., Ragusa, L., Barone, C., Alberti, A. and Failla, P. (2002). Is there a relationship between zinc and the peculiar comorbidities of Down syndrome? *Down's Syndr Res Pract.* 8(1):25–8.

Scherbenske, J.M., Benson, P.M., Rotchford, J.P. and James, W.D. (1990). Cutaneous and ocular manifestations of Down syndrome. *J Am Acad Dermatol.* 22(5 Pt 2):933–8.

Sementchenko, V.I. and Watson, D.K. (2000). Ets target genes: past, present and future. *Oncogene.* 19(55):6533–48.

Shankar, A.H. and Prasad, A.S. (1998). Zinc and immune function: the biological basis of altered resistance to infection. *Am J Clin Nutr.* 68(2 Suppl):447S–463S.

Small, D.H. (2005). Acetylcholinesterase inhibitors for the treatment of dementia in Alzheimer's disease: do we need new inhibitors? *Expert Opin Emerg Drugs.* 10(4):817–25.

Stanton, L.R. and Coetzee, R.H. (2004). Down's syndrome and dementia. *Adv Psych Treat.* 10:50–8.

Sumarsono, S.H., Wilson, T.J., Tymms, M.J., Venter, D.J., Corrick, C.M., Kola, R., Lahoud, M.H., Papas, T.S., Seth, A. and Kola, I. (1996). Down's syndrome-like skeletal abnormalities in Ets2 transgenic mice. *Nature.* 8;379(6565):534–7.

Takatori, Y. (2006). Mechanisms of neuroprotective effects of therapeutic acetylcholinesterase inhibitors used in treatment of Alzheimer's disease. *Yakugaku Zasshi.* (The Pharmaceutical Society of Japan) 126(8):607–16.

Wisniewski, K.E., Wisniewski, H.M. and Wen, G.Y. (1985). Occurrence of neuropathological changes and dementia of Alzheimer's disease in Down's syndrome. *Ann Neurol.* 17:278–82.

Wolvetang, E.J., Wilson, T.J., Sanij, E., Busciglio, J., Hatzistavrou, T., Seth, A., Hertzog, P.J. and Kola, I. (2003a). ETS2 overexpression in transgenic models and in Down syndrome predisposes to apoptosis via the p53 pathway. *Hum Mol Genet.* 12(3):247–55.

Wolvetang, E.J., Bradfield, O.M., Hatzistavrou, T., Crack, P.J., Busciglio, J., Kola, I. and Hertzog, P.J. (2003b). Overexpression of the chromosome 21 transcription factor Ets2 induces neuronal apoptosis. *Neurobiol Dis.* 14(3):349–56.

Wolvetang, E.W., Bradfield, O.M., Tymms, M., Zavarsek, S., Hatzistavrou, T., Kola, I. and Hertzog, P.J. (2003c). The chromosome 21 transcription factor ETS2 transactivates the beta-APP promoter: implications for Down syndrome. *Biochim Biophys Acta.* 1628(2):105–10.

# 3 Carbon Metabolism, Immunology and Growth Hormone

## CORRADO ROMANO

## SUMMARY

This chapter is devoted to giving a brief update on carbon metabolism, immunology, and growth hormone in Down syndrome (DS). For the sake of clarity, the three topics will be addressed separately. Carbon metabolism has been considered in DS since the pivotal studies of Lejeune (1979). Recent evidence suggests that an impairment of carbon metabolism may be a risk factor for DS in the mothers, and may modulate the phenotype of people with DS. The immunological derangement in DS consists in a mild immune deficiency, which can be easily counteracted with the use of the available vaccines and antibiotics as well as an active lifestyle, coupled with a susceptibility to immune disorders, such as thyroid disorders and coeliac disease. An implication of growth hormone in growth retardation and ovarian function in people with DS has also been suggested, and is discussed in the final part of the chapter.

## CARBON METABOLISM

Interest in carbon metabolism in Down syndrome (DS) started from the pivotal study of Jerome Lejeune (1979). The point of departure of his reasoning was the existence of several metabolic diseases that caused intellectual disability. This fact suggested to him that a perturbation of the carbon cycle might be important. He reviewed the diseases having some symptoms in common with DS, and deduced the existence of a collagen disturbance from the similarities to hypothyroidism and iminodipeptiduria, of an oxygen disturbance from the similarities to hypothyroidism and haemoglobinopathies, a cholinergic disturbance from the similarities to Alzheimer disease, and a carbon-cycle disturbance from the similarities to Lesch–Nyhan's disease. He stated that the pathology of trisomy 21 allowed one to detect a disturbance close to the 10 formyl-tetrahydrofolate entry of the folate cycle. He concluded his analysis by voicing a suspicion that a possible effect of the excess of super-

*Therapies and Rehabilitation in Down Syndrome.* Edited by Rondal
© 2007 John Wiley & Sons Ltd

oxide dysmutase A and of the increase of glutathion peroxidase leads to a difficulty in dioxygenations and in non-aromatic hydroxylations, with a relative retardation of some reactions requiring FAD. He drew a famous 'simplified' schema showing that these metabolic deviations could provoke a disturbance of the collagen and of the synthesis of chemical mediators, in accordance with the indications furnished by the comparative pathogenesis of the various disease conditions studied. The conclusion of his article was the suggestion that these heuristic reflections opened the way to further investigations.

Unfortunately, nothing more came out in the medical literature up to 2002, when Chango *et al.* (2002) published an interesting article on the impact of genetic polymorphisms involved in the carbon metabolism on trisomy 21. They observed that the phenotypic expression of DS is variable, and noted that homocysteine levels have been found to be decreased in children with DS. Such a finding could reasonably be hypothetized to be due to the location of the cystathionine β-synthase (CBS) gene on chromosome 21, and its involvement in carbon metabolism. Moreover, they suggested that the study of the regulation of carbon metabolism in DS becomes important in the light of a possible normalization of the metabolic imbalance and the detection of increased sensitivity to therapeutic interventions. The consequence of such an assumption is that the evaluation of single nucleotide polymorphisms in genes involved in carbon metabolism needs to be addressed in individuals with trisomy 21. Chango *et al.* (2002) maintained that an imbalance of methylation and folate metabolism in trisomy 21 may foster an effect on both the person with DS and his/her mother. The pathway involved in the person with DS seems to be the triplication of the CBS gene, causing a decrease of homocysteine, S-adenosylmethionine, and S-adenosylhomocysteine, whereas in the mothers of persons with DS a decrease in folates, attributable to the action of inappropriate diet, smoking and oral contraceptives, and genetic polymorphisms may be the causative agents.

On the basis of such knowledge, we started to study some genes involved in carbon metabolism and homocysteine, Vitamin $B_{12}$ and folate blood levels in persons with DS, their mothers and age-matched related controls. We found (Bosco *et al.* 2003) that methionine synthase (MTR) 2756 (A → G) polymorphism, double heterozygosity methionine synthase 2756 AG/methionine synthase reductase (MTRR) 66 AG, and elevated homocysteinaemia are three risk factors for having a child with DS, at least in the Sicilian population.

We envisaged (Guéant *et al.* 2003) that genetic determinants of folate and Vitamin $B_{12}$ metabolism may build up a common pathway leading to neural tube defects (NTDs) and DS. The genetic determinant methionine synthase (MTR) 2756 A → G polymorphism is associated in Sicily (Guéant-Rodriguez *et al.* 2003) with an odds ratio of 2.62 for the NTD case (*p*-value 0.046, 95 per cent CI 1.05–6.75), of 3.8 for DS case (*p*-value 0.009, 95 per cent CI 1.4–10.5), and of 3.5 for DS mother (*p*-value 0.028, 95 per cent CI 1.2–10.9). Reviewing the data on the respective influence of genetic determinants of carbon metabolism on the occurrence of NTDs and DS throughout North America and Europe, we can see clearly that the same determinant has a different effect according to the population involved. The genetic determinant methylenetetrahydrofolate reductase (MTHFR) 677 C → T has in North America a risk effect for NTDs and a risk/neutral effect for DS, whereas in North-Western Europe it has a risk effect for both conditions, and in Central and South-Western Europe it is neutral for both conditions (Bosco *et al.* 2003; Chadeaufaux-Vekemans *et al.* 2002; De Franchis *et al.* 1995; Guéant-Rodriguez *et al.* 2003; Hassold *et al.* 2001; Hobbs *et al.* 2000; James *et al.*1999; Papatreu *et al.*1996; van der Put *et al.* 1995). The genetic determinant MTHFR 677 C → T / 1298 A → C has in North-Western Europe a risk effect for NTDs and is neutral in Central and South-Western Europe for NTDs and DS (Guéant-Rodriguez *et al.* 2003; Stegmann *et al.* 1999; van der Put *et al.* 1998). The genetic determinant MTR 2756 A → G is protective for NTDs in North America, is neutral for NTDs in North-Western Europe, and has a risk effect for both NTDs and DS in Central and South-Western Europe (Bosco *et al.* 2003; Christensen *et al.* 1999; Guéant-Rodriguez *et al.* 2003; Ueland *et al.* 2001; van der Put *et al.* 1997). The genetic determinant MTRR 66 A → G has a risk effect for NTDs and DS in North America, is neutral for NTDs and has a risk effect for DS in North-Western Europe, and has a risk effect for NTDs and is neutral for DS in Central and South-Western Europe (Hobbs *et al.* 2000; James *et al.*1999; O'Leary *et al.* 2002).

A recent article from Martinez-Frias *et al.* (2006) has addressed the maternal polymorphisms 677C-T and 1298A-C of MTHFR and 66A-G MTRR genes, comparing 91 mothers of persons with DS and 90 control mothers. They evaluated mean total plasma homocysteine concentration and found that mothers of DS cases ($16.59 \pm 7.89\,\mu mol/L$) had a statistically significant ($t = 2.54; p < 0.02$) increase compared to the control mothers ($14.03 \pm 5.45\,\mu mol/L$), confirming our data (Bosco *et al.* 2003). Furthermore, they observed that the same genotype combinations could have different effects on maternal homocysteine levels of mothers of persons with DS and of control mothers. Different polymorphisms may act jointly, totally modifying their individual effects, and some of those effects are different in mothers of live-born DS children, and in mothers of live-born control children. The final question raised by such authors can be shared by all of us: 'What is the mechanism by which carbon metabolism alterations could be related to an increased risk for DS?'. They have suggested three possible answers: fetal viability, alterations in DNA methylation, and altered segregation of chromosome 21. Isotalo *et al.* (2000) observed all the nine possible genotype combinations of the polymorphisms 677C-T and 1298A-C in the MTHFR gene in fetuses, while this was not true in newborn infants, where CTCC and TTCC genotypes were never recognized, and the TTAC combination was very infrequent (0.62 per cent). These results suggest that some genotype combinations affect fetal viability, and so thereafter all the studies on mothers of live-born DS children compared with control mothers will present with the same resultant bias. The second answer has been recently strengthened by Wang *et al.* (2004), who proved that folate deficiency in human lymphocyte culture is an important risk factor for human chromosome 17 and 21 aneuploidies. The third answer is the most difficult to prove, and has its basis in the fact that there is evidence for some specific recombination peculiarities affecting chromosome 21 (Lamb *et al.* 1997; Laurent *et al.* 2003).

As was suggested by Chango *et al.* (2002), the impact of carbon metabolism imbalance is not only on the mother of a child with DS, but also on the person with DS. We observed in a recent study (Guéant *et al.* 2005) that there is evidence of an association between total plasma homocysteine, MTHFR 677 T and transcobalamin 776 G alleles and the intelligence quotient (IQ) of patients with DS. We suggested that this association may be related to a defective remethylation of homocysteine. Our results showed that IQ was significantly lower in patients with DS having total plasma homocysteine >7.5 µmol/L, being carriers of MTHFR 677 T and transcobalamin 776 G. Furthermore, total plasma homocysteine >9.6 µmol/L is significantly associated with an IQ below 40.

What therapeutic perspectives may be envisaged from the above-mentioned results? First of all, mouse models may be useful in order to give support to the several hypotheses involved. Secondly, the decrease of homocysteine can be a target to be achieved, notwithstanding the need for longitudinal studies. Finally, experimental supplementation designs are needed in order to determine the best possible treatments, acquire longitudinal data and achieve a cost–benefit balance.

## IMMUNOLOGY

The increased morbidity and mortality of people with DS has often been linked to an immune-system disorder (Burgio *et al.* 1975). The truth is that in the 1970s people with DS showed an early mortality and much more morbidity than the general population. Respiratory diseases were 60 times more frequent and infectious diseases were 12 times more frequent in the population with DS. These differences from the general population have progressively decreased, mainly as a result of improvements in environmental hygiene and the use of vaccines and antibiotics. This fact is not without meaning: DS brings to the affected people a mild immune deficiency, which can be easily addressed with the use of the available vaccines, the practice of an active life, which helps to eliminate the stagnation of bronchial secretions, and quick treatment with antibiotics in case of infection. The remaining aspect of immunological disorder in DS is made up of those autoimmune disorders that are more frequent in DS, i.e. principally thyroid disorders and coeliac disease.

Thyroid disorders in DS can for the most part be divided into congenital hypothyroidism, acquired hypothyroidism, and hyperthyroidism. Since 1984 (Fort *et al*. 1984) it has been known that persistent primary congenital hypothyroidism can be found in 1:141 infants with DS, an incidence 28 times greater than that in the general population. Only recently, van Trotsenburg *et al*. (2006) have suggested that DS infants have a novel type of persistent mild congenital hypothyroidism, presumably of thyroidal origin, with a direct relation to the trisomic state of chromosome 21, hypothetically through genomic dosage imbalance of dosage-sensitive genes interfering with thyroid hormone production, and not linked to any immunological disorder. Conversely, acquired or postnatal hypothyroidism is usually linked to an autoimmune disorder, and thyroid autoantibodies are found in 13–34 per cent of patients with DS (Fialkow *et al*. 1971; Fort *et al*. 1984; Ivarsson *et al*. 1997; Kinnell *et al*. 1987; Korsager *et al*. 1978; Loudon *et al*. 1985; Murdoch *et al*. 1977; Sare *et al*. 1978; Sharav *et al*. 1988). This autoimmune disorder is at the root of the increased prevalence of both acquired hypothyroidism and hyperthyroidism in DS (Pueschel and Pezzullo 1985). The prevalence of acquired hypothyroidism in adults with DS has been assessed as in the range 3–54 per cent (Cutler *et al*. 1986; Ivarsson *et al*. 1997; Kinnell *et al*. 1987; Korsager *et al*. 1978; Murdoch *et al*. 1977; Rubello *et al*. 1995; Sare *et al*. 1978; Sharav *et al*. 1988), and is also increased in children with DS (Cutler *et al*. 1986; Fort *et al*. 1984; Ivarsson *et al*. 1997; Loudon *et al*. 1985; Pueschel and Pezzullo 1985; Sare *et al*. 1978). A longitudinal study from Karlsson *et al*. (1998) on 85 children with DS followed up annually for up to 15 years has shed new light on the relation to age and autoimmunity in thyroid dysfunction of DS. The authors found hypothyroidism in 30 subjects (35.2 per cent), and hyperthyroidism in two subjects (2.3 per cent). Half the patients with hypothyroidism acquired the condition before the age of eight years, but only one showed thyroid antibodies at diagnosis. Conversely, most patients who developed hypothyroidism after this age displayed thyroid antibodies. Thyroxine treatment had a positive impact, which was demonstrated by the fact that growth velocity increased in the year after the onset of treatment compared to the year before. The important lesson to be gathered from this study is that thyroid dysfunction is common in children with DS and warrants annual screening, but the finding of thyroid antibodies in these children is uncommon up to the age of eight years, when they eventually become common. The practical consequences of these results, those useful for the physician who cares for a person with DS, are (1) that hypothyroidism may appear in a person with DS at any age; (2) thyroid antibodies are not diagnostic, because they can be positive in euthyroidism and negative in hypothyroidism; and, finally, (3) the best clinical feature diagnostic of hypothyroidism is the decreased growth velocity throughout the year before the diagnosis. A yearly check-up of thyroid-stimulating hormone (TSH) dosage is warranted in all people with DS: increased values suggest the need to assess $T_4$; if this is normal, a re-evaluation is needed after three months. If the trend of progressive TSH increase and $T_4$ decrease is confirmed, the initiation of treatment with L-thyroxin is justified.

Coeliac disease (CD) is the second most important autoimmune disorder of DS. Since the first report (Bentley 1975) of a boy with DS and CD in 1975, the prevalence of this condition in people with DS has been assessed as follows in the countries listed: 0.8 per cent in Finland (Simila and Kokkonen 1990), 3 per cent in Estonia (Uibo et al. 2006), 3.2–7.1 per cent in the USA (Mackey et al. 2001; Pueschel et al. 1999; Zachor et al. 2000), 3.6 per cent in Argentina (Rumbo et al. 2002), 3.7 per cent in Tunisia (Zitouni et al. 2003), 4.6 per cent in Italy (Bonamico et al. 2001), 5.6 per cent in Brazil (Nisihara et al. 2005), 6.3 per cent in Turkey (Cogulu et al. 2003) and in Spain (Carnicer et al. 2001), 7 per cent in the Netherlands (George et al. 1996), 8 per cent in Malta (Sciberras et al. 2004), 12 per cent in North Moravia (Kolek et al. 2003), and 16.9–18.6 per cent in Sweden (Jansson and Johansson 1995; Carlsson et al. 1998). The significance of the above-quoted results is that they show a higher prevalence of CD in people with DS, contrasting with 0.33 per cent–1.2 per cent in the general population (Van Heel and West 2006), which correlates with the proneness to autoimmune disorders found in trisomy 21. CD is an autoimmune disorder, because it is characterized by intestinal villous atrophy with crypt hyperplasia and increased intraepithelial lymphocyte infiltration, triggered by the ingestion of gluten in genetically predisposed individuals (Hill et al. 2005). DS sufferers are considered to be a high-risk group for CD, and screening them for it is recommended by the North American Society for Pediatric Gastroenterology (Hill et al. 2005). The way this screening can be set up in the clinical setting has been clearly suggested by Cataldo et al. (2005): the first step should be the assay of IgA levels in order to exclude IgA deficiency; the second step should be the assay of IgA and IgG antigliadin antibodies (IgA AGA and IgG AGA), IgA antitransglutaminase antibodies (IgA tTG), and IgA antiendomysium antibodies (EMA). This screening should be repeated each year after the introduction of gluten to the diet. Those who are AGA-, EMA- and tTG-positive are offered a confirmatory intestinal biopsy. Subsequently to the diagnosis, a gluten-free diet should be started, and the best achievable quality of life can be arrived at in this way. Catassi et al. (2002) published the evidence that CD is associated with a moderately increased risk for non-Hodgkin lymphoma, but the association does not represent a great enough risk to justify early mass screening for CD in the general population. Whereas there is evidence that children with DS have an increased risk of malignancies (Hermon et al. 2001), this is not true for adults with DS, if the standardized incidence ratios (Hermon et al. 2001) and the standardized mortality ratios (Hill et al. 2003) for lymphoma, non-Hodgkin lymphoma and stomach, small intestine, or colon cancers do not show any significant difference from those of the general population. A third study (Yang et al. 2002) shows that adults with DS are at decreased risk for malignancies. I do not know about studies on the risk of lymphoma in people with both DS and CD. A recent article (Swigonski *et al.* 2006) addresses the cost-effectiveness of screening for CD in asymptomatic children with DS, aiming at preventing lymphoma. The results are that a screening strategy costs more than 500 000 $US per life-year gained, and screening all asymptomatic children with DS for CD costs almost 5 million $US. The authors (Swigonski *et al.* 2006) maintain that such results do not support the cost-effectiveness of screening. In the same issue of the *Journal*, Kawatu and LeLeiko (2006) comment on that article, pointing out that 'absence of evidence of effect is not synonymous with lack of effect', and highlighting the effect of CD on the linear growth of children with DS, which had not been addressed by Swigonski *et al.* (2006). The only fair current conclusion to this debate would be that more data are needed from high-quality randomized clinical trials of screening versus no-screening strategies.

## GROWTH HORMONE

Short stature is a peculiar feature of DS (Cronk *et al.* 1988). The growth retardation of children with DS starts prenatally (Kurjak and Kirkinen 1982), and after birth growth velocity is most reduced between 6 months and 3 years (Cronk *et al.* 1988; Sara *et al.* 1983), with a subsequent normality up to puberty, which occurs early and is associated with an impaired growth spurt (Cronk *et al.* 1988; Arnell *et al.* 1996). Children with DS must be followed up on specific growth charts, now available for the USA (Cronk *et al.* 1988), Sicily (Piro *et al.* 1990), the Netherlands (Cremers *et al.* 1996), France (Toledo *et al.* 1999), Sweden (Myrelid *et al.* 2002), the UK and Ireland (Styles *et al.* 2002), and Japan (Kimura *et al.* 2003), in order to diagnose early the associated diseases, such as CD and thyroid disorders, which further decrease the growth, if not treated. Growth hormone (GH) has a major influence on growth in normal children from the age of 6–9 months (Sara *et al.* 1983). The consequence is that children with DS start to reduce their growth when GH starts to have a heavy influence on it. A link between GH and growth retardation in DS can be suggested by these facts, but has not yet been proved. Annerén *et al.* (1986, 1990) maintain that growth retardation is due in DS to a delayed maturation with incomplete switching from the fetal form of insulin-like growth factor (IGF) to the production of IGF-1 regulated by GH. This assumption is based on a number of their results and findings: (1) growth retardation in DS is striking after 6 months of age, when GH starts to act; (2) GH modulates the action of IGF; and (3) low levels of IGFs, assayed by the RIA method throughout the lifespan of people with DS, are found. These results have not been confirmed by subsequent studies by other research groups (Barreca *et al.* 1994; Hestnes *et al.* 1991; Ragusa *et al.* 1998). Hestnes *et al.* (1991) found in 29 adults with DS normal IGF-1 serum levels and no correlation between IGF-1 and GH. Barreca *et al.* (1994) found IGF-1 deficiency only in 36 per cent of 39 subjects with DS, and denied that the cause could be an impairment in the GH–IGF-1 axis, because GH peaks after arginine stimulus did not show any statistically significant difference between IGF-1 low-level and normal-level groups. Ragusa *et al.* (1998) assayed the blood IGF-1 with an RIA method in 113 children and adolescents with DS: they found significantly lower mean values, but 85 per cent of cases were in the normal range and showed variations correlated to the pubertal stage, reaching their peak in the fourth of Tanner's stages. Pueschel (1993) showed that GH peaks were significantly lower in eight children with DS and growth retardation only after clonidine stimulus and not after L-dopa or growth-hormone releasing hormone (GHRH) stimuli. These results suggest the hypothalamic dysfunction that can lead to low GH secretion and growth retardation. Castells *et al.* (1996) confirmed such a hypothesis in 14 children with DS. Arvat *et al.* (1996) showed that GH response to GHRH stimulus is significantly lower ($p < 0.001$) in adults with DS versus children with DS, and versus control adults and control children ($p < 0.01$): this proves that GH secretion after stimulus in DS follows an accelerated age-related decrease, and suggests the existence of a precocious impairment of central cholinergic activity in DS, which, in turn, could cause somatostatinergic hyperactivity and reduced GH secretion. Beccaria *et al.* (1998) confirmed that the potentiating effect of pyridostigmine but not that of arginine is impaired in adults with DS, in whom a reduced somatotrope responsiveness to GHRH is also present. These findings indicate that in DS the pituitary GH releasable pool is fully preserved, while an impairment of the tuberoinfundibular cholinergic pathways could lead to somatostatinergic hyperactivity and low somatotrope responsiveness to GHRH.

Treatment with GH has been carried out in children with DS, but no long-term studies on large samples have been published, and the results are provisional. A report on 15 children with DS treated for three years (Annerén *et al.* 1999) maintains that 'GH treatment results in normal growth velocity in Down's syndrome but does not affect head circumference or mental or gross motor development. Growth velocity declines after treatment stops.' The same study concludes by saying 'we and others do not recommend GH treatment of children with DS without proven GH deficiency'.

Cento *et al.* (1997) have shown that ovarian sensitivity to follicle-stimulating hormone (FSH) administration, expressed in terms of oestradiol production, was significantly blunted in normo-ovulating women with DS versus the controls. Plasma levels of GH were decreased in the group with DS. Continuing their research path, Cento *et al.* (1998) proved that GH administration normalizes ovarian response to FSH in the early stages of follicle maturation of women with DS. From these studies attention focuses on GH's role in the ovarian function of women with DS. On the other hand, other studies (Frendo *et al.* 2000; Massin *et al.* 2001) have also demonstrated a prenatal origin of GH impairment in DS. These authors have first shown that the formation of syncytiotrophoblast is abnormal in DS, since cytotrophoblasts aggregate in culture, but do not fuse or fuse poorly. This fact is coupled with a decreased production of human chorionic gonadotropin (HCG) from the placenta and of pregnancy-specific hormones synthesized by syncytiotrophoblast, such as human placental lactogen (HPL), placental growth hormone (PGH) and leptin. Recently, the assay of PGH has been proposed (Baviera *et al.* 2004) in the prenatal screening of trisomy 21, because of its significantly elevated serum levels in pregnancies affected by chromosomal aneuploidies.

## REFERENCES

Annerén, G., Sara, V.R., Hall, K. and Tuvemo, T. (1986). Growth and somatomedins responses to growth hormone in Down's syndrome. *Arch Dis Child.* 61:48–52.

Annerén, G., Gustavson, K.H., Sara, V.R. and Tuvemo, T. (1990). Growth retardation in Down syndrome in relation to insulin-like growth factors and growth hormone. *Am J Med Genet Suppl.* 7:59–62.

Annerén, G., Tuvemo, T., Carlsson-Skwirut, C., Lonnerholm, T., Bang, P., Sara, V.R. and Gustafsson, J. (1999). Growth hormone treatment in young children with Down's syndrome: effects on growth and psychomotor development. *Arch Dis Child.* 80:334–8.

Arnell, H., Gustafsson, J., Ivarsson, S.A. and Annerén, G. (1996). Growth and pubertal development in Down syndrome. *Acta Paediatr.* 85:1102–6.

Arvat, E., Gianotti, L., Ragusa, L., Valetto, M.R., Cappa, M., Aimaretti, G., Ramunni, J., Grottoli, S., Camanni, F. and Ghigo, E. (1996). The enhancing effect of pyridostigmine on the GH response to GHRH undergoes an accelerated age-related reduction in Down syndrome. *Dementia.* 7:288–92.

Barreca, A., Rasore, Quartino, A., Acutis, M.S., Ponzani, P., Damonte, G., Miani, E., Balestra, V., Giordano, G. and Minuto, F. (1994). Assessment of growth hormone insulin like growth factor-I axis in Down's syndrome. *J Endocrinol Invest.* 17:431–6.

Baviera, G., Carbone, C., Corrado, F. and Mastrantonio, P. (2004). Placental growth hormone in Down's syndrome screening. *J Matern Fetal Neonatal Med.* 16:241–3.

Beccaria, L., Marziani, E., Manzoni, P., Arvat, E., Valetto, M.R., Gianotti, L., Ghigo, E. and Chiumello, G. (1998). Further evidence of cholinergic impairment of the neuroendocrine control of the GH secretion in Down's syndrome. *Dement Geriatr Cogn Disord.* 9:78–81.

Bentley, D. (1975). A case of Down's syndrome complicated by retinoblastoma and celiac disease. *Pediatrics.* 56:131–3.

Bonamico, M., Mariani, P., Danesi, H.M., Crisogianni, M., Failla, P., Gemme, G., Rasore Quartino, A., Giannotti, A., Castro, M., Balli, F., Lecora, M., Andria, G., Guariso, G., Gabrielli, O., Catassi, C., Lazzari, R., Balocco, N.A., De Virgiliis, S., Culasso, F., Romano, C. and SIGEP (Italian Society of Pediatric Gastroenterology and Hepatology), Medical Genetic Group. (2001). Prevalence and clinical picture of celiac disease in Italian Down syndrome patients: a multicenter study. *J Pediatr Gastroenterol Nutr.* 33:139–43.

Bosco, P., Guéant-Rodriguez, R.-M., Anello, G., Barone, C., Namour, F., Caraci, F., Romano, A., Romano, C. and Guéant, J.-L. (2003). Methionine synthase (MTR) 2756 (A → G) polymorphism, double heterozygosity methionine synthase 2756 AG/methionine synthase reductase (MTRR) 66 AG, and elevated homocysteinemia are three risk factors for having a child with Down Syndrome. *Am J Med Genet.* 121A:219–24.

Burgio, G.R., Ugazio, A.G., Nespoli, L., Marcioni, A.F., Bottelli, A.M. and Pasquali, F. (1975). Derangements of immunoglobulin levels, phytohemagglutinin responsiveness and T and B cell markers in Down's syndrome at different ages. *Eur J Immunol.* 5:600–3.

Carlsson, A., Axelsson, I., Borulf, S., Bredberg, A., Forslund, M., Lindberg, B., Sjoberg, K. and Ivarsson, S.A. (1998). Prevalence of IgA-antigliadin antibodies and IgA-antiendomysium antibodies related to celiac disease in children with Down syndrome. *Pediatrics.* 101:272–5.

Carnicer, J., Farre, C., Varea, V., Vilar, P., Moreno, J. and Artigas, J. (2001). Prevalence of coeliac disease in Down's syndrome. *Eur J Gastroenterol Hepatol.* 13:263–7.

Castells, S., Beaulieu, I., Torrado, C., Wisniewski, K.E., Zarny, S. and Gelato, M.C. (1996). Hypothalamic versus pituitary dysfunction in Down's syndrome as cause of growth retardation. *J Intellect Disabil Res.* 40:509–17.

Cataldo, F., Scola, L., Piccione, M., Giuffre, M., Crivello, A., Forte, G.I., Lio, D. and Corsello, G. (2005). Evaluation of cytokine polymorphisms (TNFalpha, IFNgamma and IL-10) in Down patients with coeliac disease. *Dig Liver Dis.* 37:923–7.

Catassi, C., Fabiani, E., Corrao, G., Barbato, M., De Renzo, A., Carella, A.M., Gabrielli, A., Leoni, P., Carroccio, A., Baldassarre, M., Bertolani, P., Caramaschi, P., Sozzi, M., Guariso, G., Volta, U., Corazza, G.R. and Italian Working Group on Coeliac Disease and Non-Hodgkin's-Lymphoma. (2002). Risk of non-Hodgkin lymphoma in celiac disease. *JAMA.* 287:1413–19.

Cento, R.M., Ragusa, L., Proto, C., Alberti, A., Fiore, G., Colabucci, F. and Lanzone, A. (1997). Ovarian sensitivity to follicle stimulating hormone is blunted in normoovulatory women with Down's syndrome. *Hum Reprod.* 12:1709–13.

Cento, R.M., Ragusa, L., Proto, C., Alberti, A., Fiore, G., Soranna, L., Colabucci, F. and Lanzone, A. (1998). Growth hormone administration normalizes the ovarian responsiveness to follicle-stimulating-hormone in the early stages of the follicular maturation in women with Down Syndrome. *J Endocrinol Invest.* 21:342–7.

Chadeaufaux-Vekemans, B., Coude, M., Muller, F., Oury, J., Cali, A. and Kamoun, P. (2002). Methylenetetrahydrofolate reductase polymorphisms in the etiology of Down syndrome. *Pediat Res.* 51:766–7.

Chango, A., Mircher, C., James, S.J., Réthoré, M.O. and Nicolas, J-P. (2002). Métabolisme des substrats monocarbonés et trisomie 21: analyse de l'impact des polymorphisms génétiques. *Ann Biol Clin (Paris).* 60:647–53.

Christensen, B., Arbour, L., Tran, P., Leclerc, D., Sabbaghian, N., Platt, R., Gilfix, B.M., Rosenblatt, D.S., Gravel, R.A., Forbes, P. and Rozen, R. (1999). Genetic polymorphisms in methylenetetrahydrofolate reductase and methionine synthase, folate levels in red blood cells, and risk of neural tube defects. *Am J Med Genet.* 84:151–7.

Cogulu, O., Ozkinay, F., Gunduz, C., Cankaya, T., Aydogdu, S., Ozgenc, F., Kutukculer, N. and Ozkinay, C. (2003). Celiac disease in children with Down syndrome: importance of follow-up and serologic screening. *Pediatr Int.* 45:395–9.

Cremers, M.J., van der Tweel, I., Boersma, B., Wit, J.M. and Zonderland, M. (1996). Growth curves of Dutch children with Down's syndrome. *J Intellect Disabil Res.* 40:412–20.

Cronk, C., Crocker, A.C., Pueschel, S.M., Shea, A.M., Zackai, E., Pickens, G. and Reed, R.B. (1988). Growth charts for children with Down syndrome: 1 month to 18 years of age. *Pediatrics*. 81:102–10.

Cutler, A.T., Benezra-Obeiter, R. and Brink, S.J. (1986). Thyroid function in young children with Down syndrome. *Am J Dis Child*. 140:479–83.

De Franchis, R., Sebastio, G., Andria, G. and Mastroiacovo, P. (1995). Spina bifida, 677T → C mutation, and role of folate. *Lancet*. 346:1073.

Fialkow, P.J., Blumberg, B.S., London, W.T., Sutnick, A.J. and Thuline, H.C. (1971). Thyroid antibodies and Australia antigen in Down's syndrome. *Journal of Mental Deficiency Research*. 15:177–80.

Fort, P., Lifshitz, F., Bellisario, R., Davis, J., Lanes, R., Pugliese, M., Richman, R., Post, E.M. and David, R. (1984). Abnormalities of thyroid function in infants with Down syndrome. *J Pediatr*. 104:545–9.

Frendo, J.L., Vidaud, M., Guibourdenche, J., Luton, D., Muller, F., Bellet, D., Giovagrandi, Y., Tarrade, A., Porquet, D., Blot, P. and Evain-Brion, D. (2000). Defect of villous cytotrophoblast differentiation into syncytiotrophoblast in Down's syndrome. *J Clin Endocrinol Metab*. 85:3700–7.

George, E.K., Mearin, M.L., Bouquet, J., von Blomberg, B.M., Stapel, S.O., van Elburg, R.M. and de Graaf, E.A. (1996). High frequency of celiac disease in Down syndrome. *J Pediatr*. 128:555–7.

Guéant, J.-L., Guéant Rodriguez, R.-M., Anello, G., Bosco, P., Brunaud, L., Romano, C., Ferri, R., Romano, A., Candito, M. and Namour, B. (2003). Genetic determinants of folate and Vitamin $B_{12}$ metabolism: a common pathway in neural tube defect and Down syndrome? *Clin Chem Lab Med*. 41:1473–7.

Guéant, J.-L., Anello, G., Bosco, P., Guéant-Rodriguez, R.-M., Romano, A., Barone, C., Gérard, P. and Romano, C. (2005). Homocysteine and related genetic polymorphisms in Down's syndrome IQ. *J Neurol Neurosurg Psychiatry*. 76:706–9.

Guéant-Rodriguez, R.M., Rendeli, C., Namour, B., Venuti, L., Romano, A., Anello, G., Bosco, P., Debard, R., Gérard, P., Viola, M., Salvaggio, E. and Guéant, J.L. (2003). Transcobalamin and methionine synthase reductase mutated polymorphisms aggravate the risk of neural tube defects in humans. *Neurosci Lett*. 344:189–92.

Hassold, T.J., Burrage, L.C., Chan, E.R., Judis, L.M., Schwartz, S., James, S.J., Jacobs, P.A. and Thomas, N.S. (2001). Maternal folate polymorphisms and the etiology of human nondisjunction. *Am J Hum Genet*. 69:434–9.

Hermon, C., Alberman, E., Beral, V. and Swerdlow, A.J. (2001). Mortality and cancer incidence in persons with Down's syndrome, their parents and siblings. *Ann Hum Genet*. 65:167–76.

Hestnes, A., Stovner, L.J., Husoy, O., Folling, I. and Sjaastad, O. (1991). Somatomedin C (insulin-like growth factor 1) in adults with Down's syndrome. *J Ment Defic Res*. 35:204–8.

Hill, D.A., Gridley, G., Cnattingius, S., Mellemkjaer, L., Linet, M., Adami, H.O., Olsen, J.H., Nyren, O. and Fraumeni, J.F. Jr. (2003). Mortality and cancer incidence among individuals with Down syndrome. *Arch Intern Med*. 163:705–11.

Hill, I.D., Dirks, M.H., Liptak, G.S., Colletti, R.B., Fasano, A., Guandalini, S., Hoffenberg, E.J., Horvath, K., Murray, J.A., Pivor, M. Seidman, E.G. and North American Society for Pediatric Gastroenterology, Hepatology and Nutrition. (2005). Guideline for the diagnosis and treatment of celiac disease in children: recommendations of the North American Society for Pediatric Gastroenterology, Hepatology and Nutrition. *J Pediatr Gastroenterol Nutr*. 40:1–19.

Hobbs, C.A., Sherman, S.L., Yi, P., Hopkins, S.E., Torfs, C.P., Hine, R.J., Progribna, M., Rozen, R. and James, S.J. (2000). Polymorphisms in genes involved in folate metabolism as maternal risk factors for Down syndrome. *Am J Hum Genet.* 67:623–30.

Isotalo, P.A., Wells, G.A. and Donnelly, J.G. (2000). Neonatal and fetal methylenetetrahydrofolate reductase genetic polymorphisms: an examination of C677T and A1298C mutations. *Am J Hum Genet.* 67:986–90.

Ivarsson, S.A., Ericsson, U.B., Gustafsson, J., Forslund, M., Vegfors, P. and Annerén, G. (1997). The impact of thyroid autoimmunity in children and adolescents with Down syndrome. *Acta Paediatr.* 86:1065–7.

James, S.J., Pogribna, M., Pogribny, I.P., Melnyk, S., Hine, R.J., Gibson, J.B., Yi, P., Tafoya, D.L., Swenson, D.H., Wilson, V.L. and Gaylor, D.W. (1999). Abnormal folate metabolism and methylenetetrahydrofolate reductase (MTHFR) gene may be maternal risk factors for Down syndrome. *Am J Clin Nutr.* 70:495–501.

Jansson, U. and Johansson, C. (1995). Down syndrome and celiac disease. *J Pediatr Gastroenterol Nutr.* 21:443–5.

Karlsson, B., Gustafsson, J., Hedov, G., Ivarsson, S.-A. and Annerén, G. (1998). Thyroid dysfunction in Down's syndrome: relation to age and thyroid autoimmunity. *Arch Dis Child.* 79:242–5.

Kawatu, D. and LeLeiko, N.S. (2006). Screening for celiac disease in asymptomatic children with Down syndrome: cost-effectiveness of preventing lymphoma. *Pediatrics.* 118:816–17.

Kimura, J., Tachibana, K., Imaizumi, K., Kurosawa, K. and Kuroki, Y. (2003). Longitudinal growth and height velocity of Japanese children with Down's syndrome. *Acta Paediatr.* 92:1039–42.

Kinnell, H.G., Gibbs, N., Teale, J.D. and Smith, J. (1987). Thyroid dysfunction in institutionalised Down's syndrome adults. *Psychol Med.* 17:387–92.

Kolek, A., Vospelova, J., Hermanova, Z., Santava, A. and Tichy, M. (2003). Occurrence of coeliac disease in children with Down's syndrome in north Moravia, Czech Republic. *Eur J Pediatr.* 162:207–8.

Korsager, S., Chatham, E. and Ostergaard Kristensen, H.P. (1978). Thyroid function tests in adults with Down's syndrome. *Acta Endocrinol.* 88:48–54.

Kurjak, A. and Kirkinen, P. (1982). Ultrasonic growth pattern of fetuses with chromosomal aberrations. *Acta Obstet Gynecol Scand.* 61:223–5.

Lamb, N.E., Feingold, E., Savage, A., Avramopoulos, D., Freeman, S., Gu, Y., Hallberg, A., Hersey, J., Karadima, G., Pettay, D., Saker, D., Shen, J., Taft, L., Mikkelsen, M., Petersen, M.B., Hassold, T. and Sherman, S.L. (1997). Characterization of susceptible chiasma configurations that increase the risk for maternal nondisjunction of chromosome 21. *Hum Mol Genet.* 6:1391–9.

Laurent, A.M., Li, M., Sherman, S., Roizes, G. and Buard, J. (2003). Recombination across the centromere of disjoined and non-disjoined chromosome 21. *Hum Mol Genet.* 12:2229–39.

Lejeune, J. (1979). Investigations biochimiques et trisomie 21. *Ann Génét.* 22:67–75.

Loudon, M.M., Day, R.E. and Duke, E.M.C. (1985). Thyroid dysfunction in Down's syndrome. *Arch Dis Child.* 60:1149–51.

Mackey, J., Treem, W.R., Worley, G., Boney, A., Hart, P. and Kishnani, P.S. (2001). Frequency of celiac disease in individuals with Down syndrome in the United States. *Clin Pediatr* (Phila). 40:249–52.

Martinez-Frias, M.-L., Pérez, B., Desviat, L.R., Castro, M., Leal, F., Rodriguez, L., Mansilla, E., Martinez-Fernandez, M.-L., Bermejo, E., Rodriguez-Pinilla, E., Prieto,

D., Ugarte, M. and ECEMC Working Group. (2006). Maternal polymorphism 677C-T and 1298A-C of MTHFR, and 66A-G MTRR genes: is there any relationship between polymorphisms of the folate pathway, maternal homocysteine levels, and the risk for having a child with Down syndrome? *Am J Med Genet.* 140A:987–97.

Massin, A., Frendo, J.L., Guibourdenche, J., Luton, D., Giovangrandi, Y., Muller, F., Vidaud, M. and Evain-Brion, D. (2001). Defect of syncytiotrophoblast formation and human chorionic gonadotropin expression in Down's syndrome. *Placenta.* 22, *Suppl. A, Trophoblast Research,* S93–S97.

Murdoch, J.C., Ratcliffe, W.A., McLarty, D.G., Rodger, J.C. and Ratcliffe, J.G. (1977). Thyroid function in adults with Down's syndrome. *J Clin Endocrinol Metab.* 44:453–8.

Myrelid, A., Gustafsson, J., Ollars, B. and Annerén, G. (2002). Growth charts for Down's syndrome from birth to 18 years of age. *Arch Dis Child.* 87:97–103.

Nisihara, R.M., Kotze, L.M., Utiyama, S.R., Oliveira, N.P., Fiedler, P.T. and Messias-Reason, I.T. (2005). Celiac disease in children and adolescents with Down syndrome. *J Pediatr* (Rio J). 81:373–6.

O'Leary, V.B., Parle-McDermott, A.P., Molloy, A.M., Kirke, P.N., Johnson, Z., Conley, M., Scott, J.M. and Swanson, D.A. (2002). MTRR and MTHFR polymorphisms: link to Down syndrome? *Am J Med Genet.* 107:151–5.

Papatreu, C., Lynch, S.A., Burn, J. and Edwards, Y.H. (1996). Methylenetetrahydrofolate reductase and neural tube defects. *Lancet.* 348:58.

Piro, E., Pennino, C., Cammarata, M., Corsello, G., Grenci, A., Lo, Giudice, C., Morabito, M., Piccione, M. and Giuffre, L. (1990). Growth charts of Down syndrome in Sicily: evaluation of 382 children 0–14 years of age. *Am J Med Genet Suppl.* 7:66–70.

Pueschel, S.M. (1993). Growth hormone response after administration of l-dopa, clonidine, and growth hormone releasing hormone in children with Down syndrome. *Res Dev Disabil.* 14:291–8.

Pueschel, S.M. and Pezzullo, J.C. (1985). Thyroid dysfunction in Down syndrome. *Am J Dis Child.* 139:636–9.

Pueschel, S.M., Romano, C., Failla, P., Barone, C., Pettinato, R., Castellano, Chiodo, A. and Plumari, D.L. (1999). A prevalence study of celiac disease in persons with Down syndrome residing in the United States of America. *Acta Paediatr.* 88:953–6.

Ragusa, L., Valetto, M.R., Proto, C., Alberti, A., Romano, C., Rossodivita, A., Corneli, G., Baffoni, C., Lanfranco, F., Aimaretti, G., Colabucci, F. and Ghigo, E. (1998). IGF-I levels in prepubertal and pubertal children with Down syndrome. *Minerva Endocrinol.* 23:31–6.

Rubello, D., Pozzan, G.B., Casara, D., Girelli, M.E., Boccato, S., Rigon, F., Baccichetti, C., Piccolo, M., Betterle, C. and Busnardo, B. (1995). Natural course of subclinical hypothyroidism in Down's syndrome: prospective study results and therapeutic considerations. *J Endocrinol Invest.* 17:35–40.

Rumbo, M., Chirdo, F.G., Ben, R., Saldungaray, I. and Villalobos, R. (2002). Evaluation of coeliac disease serological markers in Down syndrome patients. *Dig Liver Dis.* 34:116–21.

Sara, V.R., Gustavson, K.H., Annerén, G., Hall, K. and Wetterberg, L. (1983). Somatomedins in Down's syndrome. *Biol Psychiatry.* 18:803–11.

Sare, Z., Ruvalcaba, R.H. and Kelley, V.C. (1978). Prevalence of thyroid disorder in Down syndrome. *Clin Genet.* 14:154–8.

Sciberras, C., Vella, C. and Grech, V. (2004). The prevalence of coeliac disease in Down's syndrome in Malta. *Ann Trop Paediatr.* 24:81–3.

Sharav, T., Collins, R.M. and Baab, P.J. (1988). Growth studies in infants and children with Down's syndrome and elevated levels of thyrotropin. *Am J Dis Child.* 142:1302–6.

Simila, S. and Kokkonen, J. (1990). Coexistence of celiac disease and Down syndrome. *Am J Ment Retard.* 95:120–2.

Stegmann, K., Ziegler, A., Ngo, E.T., Kohlschmidt, N., Schroter, B., Ermert, A. and Koch, M.C. (1999). Linkage disequilibrium of MTHFR genotypes 677C/T-1298A/C in the German population and association studies in probands with neural tube defects (NTD). *Am J Med Genet.* 87:23–9.

Styles, M.E., Cole, T.J., Dennis, J. and Preece, M.A. (2002). New cross sectional stature, weight, and head circumference references for Down's syndrome in the UK and Republic of Ireland. *Arch Dis Child.* 87:104–8.

Swigonski, N.L., Kuhlenschmidt, H.L., Bull, M.J., Corkins, M.R. and Downs, S.M. (2006). Screening for celiac disease in asymptomatic children with Down syndrome: cost-effectiveness of preventing lymphoma. *Pediatrics.* 118:594–602.

Toledo, C., Alembik, Y., Aguirre, Jaime, A. and Stoll, C. (1999). Growth curves of children with Down syndrome. *Ann Genet.* 42:81–90.

Ueland, P.M., Hustad, S., Schneede, J., Refsum, H. and Vollset, S.E. (2001). Biological and clinical implications of the MTHFR C677T polymorphism. *Trends Pharmacol Sci.* 22:195–201.

Uibo, O., Teesalu, K., Metskula, K., Reimand, T., Saat, R., Sillat, T., Reimand, K., Talvik, T. and Uibo, R. (2006). Screening for celiac disease in Down's syndrome patients revealed cases of subtotal villous atrophy without typical for celiac disease HLA-DQ and tissue transglutaminase antibodies. *World J Gastroenterol.* 12:1430–4.

van der Put, N.M., Steegers-Theunissen, R.P., Frosst, P., Trijbels, F.J., Eskes, T.K., van den Heuvel, L.P., Mariman, E.C., den Heyer, M., Rozen, R. and Blom, H.J. (1995). Mutated methylenetetrahydrofolate reductase as a risk factor for spina bifida. *Lancet.* 346:1070–1.

van der, Put, N.M., van der, Molen, E.F., Kluijtmans, L.A., Heil, S.G., Trijbels, J.M., Eskes, T.K., Van Oppenraaij-Emmerzaal, D., Banerjee, R. and Blom, H.J. (1997). Sequence analysis of the coding region of human methionine synthase: relevance to hyperhomocysteinaemia in neural-tube defects and vascular disease. *QJM.* 90:511–17.

van der Put, N.M., Gabreels, F., Stevens, E.M., Smeitink, J.A., Trijbels, F.J., Eskes, T.K., van den Heuvel, L.P. and Blom, H.J. (1998). A second common mutation in the methylenetetrahydrofolate reductase gene: an additional risk factor for neural-tube defects? *Am J Hum Genet.* 62:1044–51.

Van Heel, D.A. and West, J. (2006). Recent advances in coeliac disease. *Gut.* 55:1037–46.

Van Trotsenburg, A.S., Kempers, M.J., Endert, E., Tijssen, J.G., de Vijlder, J.J. and Vulsma, T. (2006). Trisomy 21 causes persistent congenital hypothyroidism presumably of thyroidal origin. *Thyroid.* 16:671–80.

Wang, X., Thomas, P., Xue, J. and Fenech, M. (2004). Folate deficiency induces aneuploidy in human lymphocytes in vitro-Evidence using cytokinesis-blocked cells and probes specific for chromosomes 17 and 21. *Mutat Res.* 551:167–80.

Yang, Q., Rasmussen, S.A. and Friedman, J.M. (2002). Mortality associated with Down's syndrome in the USA from 1983 to 1997: a population-based study. *Lancet.* 359:1019–25.

Zachor, D.A., Mroczek-Musulman, E. and Brown, P. (2000). Prevalence of celiac disease in Down syndrome in the United States. *J Pediatr Gastroenterol Nutr.* 31:275–9.

Zitouni, M., Gharbi, Yermani, M., Laadhar, Kharrat, L., Kallel, Sellami, M., Gandoura, N. and Makni, S. (2003). [Prevalence of serologic markers in celiac disease in trisomy 21 in Tunisia]. *Ann Biol Clin* (Paris). 61:673–7.

# 4 Medical Therapies in the Lifespan

**ALBERTO RASORE QUARTINO**

## SUMMARY

Down syndrome is associated with cognitive impairment, congenital malformations, immune deficiencies, and early and sometimes pathological ageing. It is therefore understandable that therapies are sought for the improvement of the life and of the cognitive abilities of the affected people. Rehabilitation strategies and social integration have greatly contributed to the welfare of people with Down syndrome. As for pharmacological treatments, symptomatic therapies can correct malformations and cure or prevent the diseases that are associated in varying frequency with these people. Proposed health-care guidelines are also of great value to spread the knowledge of the therapeutic possibilities for improving health and offering a better quality of life to affected people. The prevention and treatment of ageing and of its pathological aspects are the major challenge confronting current medical care, because an increasing number of DS people are now growing older, and this ageing occurs some twenty years before that of the general population. Pharmacological therapies are under study, and some of them seem promising. Beyond these rational approaches to the pharmacological treatment of DS people, many unconventional therapies have been advocated with the object of remedying their intellectual impairment. These treatments, which are often without any scientific basis, do not lead to any improvements in the cognitive or behavioural aspects of the condition. On the contrary, they can have negative effects on patients and be the cause of severe disappointment in their relatives. Basic research has opened new routes towards the modification of the primary causes of trisomy. Interesting possibilities have been revealed, both in the field of genetic and molecular therapies and in the specific one of pharmacological treatments, although without any immediate practical applications up to the present. It is not unrealistic to believe that in some near future treatments will become available that may be effective for the improvement of the mental and physical development of people with Down syndrome.

*Therapies and Rehabilitation in Down Syndrome.* Edited by Rondal
© 2007 John Wiley & Sons Ltd

## INTRODUCTION

Down Syndrome (DS) is the most common autosomal anomaly in man, since it occurs in approximately 1/1000 normal newborns and is caused by the trisomy of chromosome 21. Its DNA sequence has recently been completed, and it is thought to contain about 300 genes. The well-known phenotype is characteristic: it shows many individual variations, but neuromotor anomalies and cognitive and language impairment are constant. Congenital malformations are frequent, as are immunological deficiency and autoimmune diseases. Precocious normal or pathological ageing is a constant. Survival is reduced.

Mechanisms determining DS phenotypic manifestations are still poorly understood. Genetic imbalance following trisomy is at present considered responsible, either directly or through complex genetic interactions (Antonarakis *et al.* 2004).

Genetic influences, already operating in prenatal life, cause physical and neurological abnormalities that are present at birth and continue their action throughout the lifespan. Therefore, many defects that appear late are combined results of the actions of genes and of environmental factors and may shorten life and interfere with the ability to live as well as possible.

The central question is whether there are therapies to avoid the appearance of anomalies or to reduce their effect on the developing organism.

A thorough knowledge of the diseases commonly associated with DS has enabled us to elaborate preventive and therapeutic strategies that have shown great value in the prolongation of life and the enhancement of its quality. Meanwhile the changes that have occurred in society in relation to social integration within the family, the school and employment, have also significantly contributed to this progress. Lastly, the innovative rehabilitation strategies offered to DS people provided an essential support for their development.

As for aetiological or causal therapies, i.e. those related to the possibility of preventing the birth of individuals with DS or to correct the genetic errors, we are still at the research stage, which is currently working on approaches that are of great interest, but without any practical results up to the present day.

By contrast, symptomatic therapies, which can correct malformations and cure diseases affecting people with DS, are routinely available.

## AETIOLOGICAL THERAPIES

Basic research currently envisages very promising lines of investigation. I shall mention only some up-to-date research on the possible prevention of the birth of at least a proportion of children with DS.

Recent investigations into polymorphisms in the methylenetetrahydrofolate reductase (MTHFR) gene (MTHFR 677C → T) and in the methionine synthase reductase (MTRR) gene (MTRR 66A → G) showed that the presence of these variant genotypes increases the risk of having a DS child, the increase ranging from 1.91- to 4.08-fold (Hobbs *et al.* 2000). An Irish follow-up study (O'Leary *et al.* 2002) also found an increased risk of DS associated with the MTRR polymorphism, while other investigations evaluating Italian (Guéant *et al.* 2003), French (Chango *et al.* 2005), Turkish (Boduroglu *et al.* 2004) and Gujarati Indian women could not demonstrate this association. Bosco *et al.* in 2003 suggested that in Sicily homocysteine and MTR polymorphisms are risk factors for DS. Despite the differences, the published studies agree upon the common theme of abnormal folate metabolism as an increased risk factor for having a DS child. These observations also suggest the existence of geographic variation in gene polymorphism. Moreover, the increased homocysteine present in all study groups raises the hypothesis of genetic–nutritional–environmental factors involved in a higher frequency of meiotic non-disjunction. To identify these relationships transnational and multinational study design is needed (Sheth and Sheth 2003). As these studies suggest that abnormal folate metabolism is associated with increased risk of giving birth to a DS child, periconceptional supplementation of the diet with folic acid has been advocated in the hope of reducing the prevalence of DS; but at present there is no clear evidence of its efficacy. In the USA since 1998 fortification of grain products with folic acid in order to reduce the prevalence of neural tube defects has been mandatory. Two recent studies confirm a decreased prevalence of spina bifida and, to a lesser degree, of other congenital defects. For DS however, the decrease was either absent (Canfield *et al.* 2005) or not statistically significant (Simmons *et al.* 2004). In other studies, neither folic acid food fortification nor periconceptional multivitamin use was found to be associated with a reduction in the occurrence of trisomy 21 (Botto *et al.* 2004; Goh *et al.* 2006; Ray *et al.* 2003).

These examples indicate both the complexity of research and the difficulties in the practical application of scientifically accurate and reliable studies.

## SYMPTOMATIC THERAPIES

### GROWTH RETARDATION

In DS short stature is almost a constant. Its origin is multifactorial. Besides genetic influences, it may sometimes depend on hypothyroidism or coeliac or renal diseases, or on nutritional deficiencies; but in most cases its cause cannot be definitely detected. Growth hormone (GH) deficiency is not commonly found, although suboptimal endogenous production, resulting from hypothalamic dysfunction, has been demonstrated. On the other hand a deficiency of insulin–growth–factor–I, but not of insulin–growth–factor–II, has been described (Barreca *et al.* 1994).

Therapy with human recombinant GH (hrGH) to DS children increases growth velocity and stature, but after cessation of treatment, growth velocity slows down. The risk of complications related to long-term administration (hypertension, diabetes mellitus, intracranial neoplasia) (Monson 2003) has not been sufficiently evaluated (Lanes 2004). At present hrGH treatment has no indication as routine therapy in DS children without GH deficiency (Annerén et al. 2000), even if more recent studies seem to exclude significant side-effects after long-term treatment (Pallotti et al. 2002).

## IMMUNOLOGY AND AUTOIMMUNE DISEASES

In DS anomalies of the immune system are constant and complex.

Historically a substantial increase in infectious diseases has been described, although extended antibiotic treatment and prophylactic vaccination have reduced the risk, which at present seems only slightly higher than that observed in non-trisomic people.

Non-controversial immunological defects are the presence of a small thymus, with numerous structural anomalies and lymphocyte depletion, increased antibody levels, altered maturation of T lymphocytes with CD4/CD8 rate reversal and an elevated number of functionally deficient NK cells.

On the premise of immune deficiency in DS, several tentative therapies for enhancing organic defences have been proposed over the years. Zinc supplementation for DS children showed a positive influence on some immune parameters and a reduction of recurrent infections (Franceschi et al. 1988; Licastro et al. 1994). Selenium supplementation would also reduce the rate of infections in DS children. According to Annerén et al. (1990), the action of selenium on the organism would be of the immuno-regulatory type. Further investigations are needed before using these substances as routine therapy in young DS persons.

Recent studies have shown that a rare disease, the autoimmune polyendocrine syndrome type I (APS-I) is caused by a mutation of the AIRE (autoimmune regulator) gene, mapping on chromosome 21q22.3 (Meyer and Badenhoop 2002). The high incidence of autoimmune diseases in DS could be due, at least in part, to disregulation of the AIRE gene.

The most frequent autoimmune diseases in DS are: thyroiditis (15 per cent), coeliac disease (6 per cent), diabetes mellitus type I (1 per cent), juvenile idiopathic arthritis (1 per cent), thrombocytopenia, and chronic active hepatitis.

Hypothyroidism, both congenital and acquired, is very frequent in DS, although most people are actually euthyroid.

Primary persistent congenital hypothyroidism affects 0.07–0.10 per cent of newborns with DS, versus 0.015–0.020 per cent of normal newborns. For acquired hypothyroidism, reported data vary between 3 per cent and 54 per cent, versus values for the general population ranging from 0.8 to 1.1 per cent. Increased values of thyroid antibodies are also found in 13–34 per cent of DS people. Autoimmune thyroiditis is uncommon before school age, but is more frequent after the age of 8 (Karlsson *et al.* 1998). Pathogenesis of hypothyroidism in DS seems related to a combination of thyroid autoimmunity and progressive gland hypoplasia. Generally, at the beginning of the disease increased thyroid stimulating hormone (TSH) values are observed, while the levels of thyroid hormones (T3 and T4) are within normal limits. Then, with the progressive decrease of hormone values, clinical symptoms appear. In DS they are often unspecific and of difficult diagnosis, because they can be confused with some neurological and behavioural characteristics of the syndrome, mainly in adolescents and adults. So slowing down of growth velocity and weight increase are generally preceded by other signs such as easy fatigue, reduction of attention, poor educational development, mood changes, and depression.

Since hypothyroidism negatively interferes in normal neuronal metabolism and, on the other hand, early diagnosis is not particularly easy, periodic laboratory tests are earnestly recommended, in order to ensure timely intervention with the necessary substitutive hormonal therapy (thyroxine).

The possibility of pharmacological treatment of cases with increased TSH alone without hormone deficiency is still controversial, since such cases chiefly represent a phase preceding a clinically evident hypothyroidism. It must be pointed out that in DS increased TSH is often transient and reversible.

Some authors have found significantly reduced IQ levels in people with elevated TSH and normal T3 and T4. One-third of people with persistent increased TSH and positive thyroid antibodies will in time develop true hypothyroidism. It is therefore possible that substitutive treatment in these cases may have a protective effect on thyroid and also prevent, or at least slow down, the occurrence of the disease.

Coeliac disease is relatively uncommon: it is caused by intolerance to gluten (Marsh 1992). In normal population its frequency ranges from 0.012 per cent to approximately 1 per cent (Lee & Green, 2006), while in DS it is much higher: 6.2 per cent (Bonamico *et al.* 2001).

The pathogenesis of coeliac disease is still not clear. Current studies ascribe the responsibility for the progressive intestinal mucosal damage to an abnormal immune response to gliadin (Marsh 1992). Gluten is a component of wheat, rye and barley, but not of maize and rice. In the condition's classic form, now very rare, symptoms appear with the introduction into the diet of gluten-containing foods after weaning, and consist of severe diarrhoea, bulky stools, abdominal distension, pallor and stunted growth. More commonly, atypical forms appear, mainly in adolescents and adults. They manifest with variable symptoms, not necessarily related to the gastrointestinal system, and often consist of growth failure, lack of appetite, iron deficiency anaemia, and hypoproteinaemia. Silent cases exist as well. Late complications, such as lymphoproliferative malignancies of the intestinal tract (non-Hodgkin lymphomas), are seldom observed. Diagnosis is made by intestinal biopsy. IgG and IgA gliadin antibody dosage is the available screening test. In DS the antiendomysium immunofluorescence test and the antiglutaminase antibody dosage test are more specific and more sensitive.

Treatment consists of the elimination of gluten from the diet, which brings complete recovery; but the gluten-free diet must be kept up for an indefinite period. High levels of commitment and continuous surveillance are required from patients and their relatives, since compliance is often difficult to obtain.

## LEUKAEMIA

DS children account for approximately 3 per cent of children with acute lymphoblastic leukaemia (ALL) and 5–8 per cent of children with acute myeloid leukaemia (AML). Among these, the majority of cases fall within the acute megakaryoblastic leukaemia (AMKL) subtype. The incidence of AMKL in DS children is 1 in 500, with a median age presentation of 2 years (Lange 2000). By contrast, solid tumours of childhood and adult non-haematological cancers seem to be less frequent in individuals with DS than in age-matched controls, except for testicular cancer (Goldacre et al. 2004). While in DS a 20-fold increased risk of leukaemia is observed, an increased sensibility to chemotherapy is recognized (Ravindranath 2003). Epidemiological data confirm that in ALL therapeutic results are similar to those obtained in children without DS. Great attention should be paid to methotrexate dosage in ALL treatment, since its toxicity is higher in DS. A reduced clearance from the organism and an increased intracellular transport are the main causes of its toxicity and therefore of enhanced sensitivity to therapy of DS ALL cells.

It is surprising that children with DS and AML and in particular AMKL have extremely high event-free survival rates (80–100 per cent) and lower relapse rates (<15 per cent) compared with non-DS children with AML (Taub and Ge 2005). This better outcome of AML in DS children is multifactorial in origin, and can be related to increased sensitivity of DS leukaemia cells to a large panel of chemotherapy drugs utilized in AML therapy, particularly ARA-C and other anthracyclines, and also to the increased spontaneous apoptosis that occurs in many cellular systems of DS (Taub and Ge 2005).

DS infants are also predisposed to a related myeloid disease named transient myeloproliferative disorder (TMD) or transient leukaemia (TL), which is characterized by accumulation of immature megakaryoblasts in peripheral blood, liver and bone marrow (Zipursky 2003). It has been suggested that TL originates in fetal liver (Taub et al. 2004). It occurs in approximately 10 per cent of DS newborns, and is associated with a high incidence of spontaneous remissions. In some cases, however, the disease is severe and life-threatening, manifesting as hydrops foetalis, multiple effusions and liver and multi-organ system failure (Isaacs 2003). Approximately 30 per cent of patients with TL within the first 4 years of life will develop AMKL, which, if untreated, rarely shows spontaneous regression a second time (Massey 2005). Pathogenesis of

TL and AMKL has recently been related to acquired mutations of the GATA1 gene (mapping to chromosome X), which are found almost exclusively in DS patients. This gene is indispensable for the normal growth and maturation of erythroid cells and megakaryocytes. The mutations that generally occur in the prenatal stage can be considered an early step in an otherwise multistep process of leukaemogenesis (Rasore Quartino 2006).

It is not clear whether patients with particularly severe TL should be treated how. Repeated courses of low-dose ARA-C have been used effectively to cure a small number of DS infants with TL (Cominetti et al. 1985; Zipursky 1996), so highlighting the appealing possibility that such a treatment could also prevent the further occurrence of AMKL (Ravindranath 2005).

## CONGENITAL MALFORMATIONS

Nearly 50 per cent of DS newborns have congenital heart disease, versus 0.5–1.0 per cent of non-trisomic infants. The prevailing anomaly is atrioventricular canal defect or endocardial cushion defect: approximately 70 per cent of cases are associated with DS. In newborns with chromosomal mosaicism the prevalence of congenital heart disease is reduced (30 per cent) and less severe (Marino and De Zorzi 1993). Atrioventricular canal defect is the most frequent (36–47 per cent), followed by interventricular septal defect (26–33 per cent), patent ductus arteriosus (8–10 per cent), interatrial septal defect and tetralogy of Fallot. Early diagnosis is very important, since almost all forms are treatable by surgical correction. In DS cardiac anomalies with increased pulmonary flux are the most common. Symptoms begin early, and pulmonary artery hypertension develops rapidly, causing cardiomegaly, hepatic cirrhosis and heart failure. The affected children have stunted growth and develop recurrent respiratory infections. A severe complication is the obstructive pulmonary vascular disease that in DS occurs earlier than in other children and prevents surgical correction of the underlying defect. It is therefore essential that surgery be performed as early as possible. In recent years surgical mortality has greatly declined, and the long-term prognosis is good (Marino and Pueschel 1996). Furthermore, it must be pointed out that congenital heart disease in children with DS is less severe and more predictable than in other children, and that often surgical results are more favourable than those obtained in patients with the same disease, but without DS (Marino et al. 2004).

Gastrointestinal malformations also have a higher incidence in DS than in non-trisomic newborns. Duodenal stenosis (4–7 per cent) represents approximately half of all the congenital duodenal stenoses. Hirschsprung's disease occurs in 3–4 per cent of DS newborns, versus 0.02 per cent of other newborns. Relatively frequent are also pancreas annulare and anal imperforation.

Malformations of the urinary tract (congenital hydronephrosis, obstructive uropathy) can be present.

For all these malformations diagnosis must be precocious (echography) and surgical correction appropriate.

## ORTHOPAEDIC DISORDERS

The commonest orthopaedic disorders of DS (flatfoot, patella instability, genu valgum, etc.) are chiefly the consequence of ligamentous laxity. Amongst them, atlanto-axial instability has received notable attention in current years. Its prevalence is high: from 10 per cent to 15 per cent, according to Pueschel and Schola (1987); from 15 per cent to 20 per cent, according to Menezes and Ryken (1992). Atlanto-axial instability is generally asymptomatic, but an elevated dislocation risk exists after cervical traumas or sudden and rough head movements: the ensuing compression of the cervical medulla causes neurological complications such as staggering gait, paraplegia, quadriplegia and urinary incontinence, often preceded by head deviation. The value of various instrumental diagnostic methods (X-rays, high-resolution CT scans, magnetic resonance imaging) is still debatable (Selby *et al.* 1991). An accurate neurological observation is very useful to diagnose the earliest symptoms.

Prevention is important too: children at risk of dislocation should not practise dangerous sport activities (diving, boxing, soccer, etc.). In symptomatic cases surgical stabilization (vertebral fusion or transarticular fixation with screws) has given positive results (Toussaint *et al.* 2003).

## SENSORY DEFECTS

Sensory defects, either visual or auditory, have great significance in the mental development of DS children, since their presence can reduce the effectiveness of rehabilitation programmes in the acquisition of new abilities. This is mainly true in the first periods of life. Although ocular abnormalities are more frequent than in other children, it is necessary to point out the clinical importance of strabismus, of refractory defects and of cataract, which can be observed both in newborns and in adults. These abnormalities can decrease the normal vision, adding in that way an organic defect to the pre-existing cognitive impairment. Early diagnosis is crucial, in order to correct the anomaly in time, preventing the impending deterioration. Spectacles are well tolerated even by small children, if they receive a real benefit from them. When necessary, the possibility of surgical correction should be taken into account.

Hearing abnormalities can reduce the cognitive development of DS children, who are not able to use the necessary strategies to make up for their deficiency. Although the data from the literature are controversial, it is thought that up to 78 per cent of DS people suffer from a total or partial hearing defect, mainly a conductive one (Mura and Medicina 2004). There is an excess of middle ear pathology; and the typical serous otitis begins early, in the first year of life. Owing to its scarce and mainly aspecific symptoms it almost constantly persists in childhood and even in adulthood. Actually all the medical and surgical treatments of ear infections have a low success rate, and often hearing defects are the unwanted consequence. A preventive approach to hearing problems in DS children is therefore of utmost importance, with periodic checks, in order to help them maintain a good communication ability and a satisfying socialization.

## DENTAL ANOMALIES

Dental anomalies are a common problem in DS, which is often underestimated, owing to the objective difficulties met with in visiting people with intellectual impairment. Treatment too can encounter almost insurmountable difficulties without the exercise of great patience by the dentist. Peculiar oral and dental anatomy, developmental anomalies and malocclusion are prevalent in DS children. By contrast, caries seems to be less frequent than in other children. When oral hygiene is poor, it generally leads to gingivitis, periodontal disease and early and total tooth loss. Dental checks should be constant from infancy and throughout life. Good compliance for dental hygiene should be obtained early, in order to avoid the depressing consequences of dental decay (Lowe 1990). Accurate orthodontic help should be available as well, for aesthetic and functional purposes.

## NORMAL AND PATHOLOGICAL AGEING

An important issue to be discussed in DS is ageing. In the last decades survival has greatly increased in the general population and in DS as well. Life expectancy, which for DS in 1929 was only 9 years, increased to 12 years in 1947, to 54 years in 1970 and to 65 (and more) in 2006. The causes of these extraordinary changes are multiple and complex, as has already been said. It should be generally noted that this increase in life expectancy has brought to light new medical problems, many of which are not yet resolved. Actually, most healthcare guidelines for DS people give only generic recommendations for older persons. Experiences with elderly DS people not living in communities are not yet frequent. It is common knowledge that precocious ageing is a constant in DS adults, who may show physical signs of senescence as much as 20 years earlier than other people (Service and Hahn 2003). Evidence has recently been found that the observed age-related functional changes are related to a rather normal chemical process (Devenny *et al.* 1996).

Chronic oxidative stress in individuals with DS has been demonstrated both *in vitro* and *in vivo*. Oxygen free radicals are involved in the ageing process, and are present in higher quantities in DS. Defence mechanisms produced by the organism are multiple: antioxidant enzymes are necessary to neutralize oxygen free radicals. Superoxide dismutase (SOD), catalase (Cat) and glutathione peroxidase (Gpx) participate in the conversion of noxious superoxide radicals to water. An imbalance in the ratio of SOD to Gpx and Cat results in the accumulation of peroxide, causing the formation of harmful hydroxyl radicals, which may damage DNA, proteins and lipids. Since in DS the SOD/Gpx + Cat ratio is altered in all tissues, this may contribute to premature ageing (de Haan *et al.* 1995). AD lesions may also originate from the progressive increase in oxidative stress that occurs with advancing age.

Neurological and psychological problems become more frequent with age. A consistent, intellectual decline is observed, although it is variable in its extent. A reduction in the ability to elaborate thought, mainly in the field of abstract thought and logic, appears earlier than in normal people. Mental status, short- and long-term memory, psychomotor function and visuospatial organization show slight progressive decreases. Under 50 years of age there is no significant reduction in memory (Fromage and Anglade 2002). Approximately 30 per cent of DS people will show a form of dementia that has been identified with Alzheimer disease (AD), which combines disorders of cognitive functions and behaviour, modifying the personality. Affected people show a deterioration of mental and emotional responses, apathy or abnormal excitation, irritability, temper tantrums, and loss of previously acquired vocabulary. Autonomy in everyday life deteriorates, affecting in particular the skills necessary to carry out common daily tasks, such as personal hygiene, dressing, feeding, etc. The course of the disease is generally more rapid than in non-Down people.

Late-onset epilepsy seems to show an age-related increase in DS, being present in approximately 80 per cent of people with AD after the age of 50 years. Some authors consider epilepsy an initial sign of dementia (Evenhuis 1990). Pueschel *et al.* (1995) reported a marked increase of epilepsy in the third decade of life. According to the literature, epilepsy in DS shows a bimodal distribution of age at onset, with a peak in developmental age and another during adulthood (Puri *et al.* 2001).

Recently, too, evidence has been unearthed for the premature ageing in DS people of numerous biological systems and the associated clinical features (Patterson 2006).

The pathological changes of AD are represented by two specific brain lesions: intraneuronal fibrillary tangles and extracellular plaques (Harman 2006). They appear very early in life in DS, but clinical signs of dementia are not apparent in most subjects before the age of 50 years. The frequent presence of AD in DS could be interpreted as a sign of more rapid ageing (Patterson 2006).

Prevention and treatment of premature normal and pathological senescence in DS is not an easy task. In the fields of cognition, autonomy and mental health, the ageing of DS subjects is very sensitive to their environment (Fromage and Anglade 2002), a fact that draws attention to the great value of the role played by families and care-givers in helping DS people to maintain or even to enhance their acquired abilities in adult life.

Nicotinamide and L-carnitine protect *in vitro* human cells from oxidative stress, and could be proposed as anti-ageing substances. Another suggestion might be that the prevention of early ageing might be achieved by specifically lowering brain oxidative stress levels with oral antioxidants that are capable of passing the blood–brain barrier, such as lipoic acid and dehydroascorbic acid (Harman 2006). Other antioxidant drugs and nutrients have been proposed as well, but the practical results often do not measure up to the theoretical possibilities.

Just recently important results have been obtained in the pharmacological treatment of AD in non-Down syndrome patients. The therapeutic approach is aimed at containing cognitive impairment through molecules that act on the cholinergic system, on the hypothesis that a functional deficiency in that system could be responsible for the cognitive defects seen in the disease (Coyle *et al.* 1983). Acetylcholinesterase inhibitors represent at the moment the most effective therapeutic approach, and could improve the cognitive function and behavioural disorders observed in AD (Farlow 2001). Acetylcholinesterase inhibitors nevertheless have a limited activity in time, and their use may cause in 7–30 per cent of patients side-effects that are of moderate intensity and mainly consist of nausea, vomiting, diarrhoea, and abdominal pain.

Several investigators started to treat DS subjects with AD with donepezil, which seems to show better therapeutic action and fewer side-effects than other acetylcholinesterase inhibitors. According to Lott *et al.* (2002), donepezil can be useful in reducing the symptoms of dementia during the early and middle stages of cognitive decline in DS. Heller *et al.* (2003) observed an improvement in expressive language performance in a 24-week clinical trial. Another study also showed an improvement in language among a group of DS patients without dementia (Johnson *et al.* 2003). Two patients with DS and severe cognitive impairment recovered verbal communication skills, but adverse effects also appeared, such as soft stools and urinary incontinence in one and transient agitation and muscle weakness in the other (Kondoh *et al.* 2005).

At present we can conclude that donepezil appears to have some effect in the treatment of cognitive and behavioural disturbances associated with the dementia of DS (Boada-Rovira *et al.* 2005). Other drugs, such as rivastigmine and galantamine (anticholesterase drugs) and memantine (a low-affinity antagonist to glutamate NMDA receptors) play an important role in treating dementia in adults with intellectual disability (Prasher 2004). Even if the results obtained in DS seem promising, the samples studied are still limited, and therefore wider multicentric research is required in order to evaluate the nature and degree of the response of DS to these drugs.

## NUTRITIONAL PROBLEMS AND OBESITY

The nutritional aspects of DS have gained much attention over at least three issues: first, the tendency to obesity; second, possible dietary intolerances or allergies; and third, possible vitamin and mineral deficiencies. All these aspects are complicated by genetic and environmental differences. Changes in the environment have contributed in recent years to an increase in life expectancy, both in the general population and in DS. Moreover, an overall improvement in the life conditions of DS was brought about by the abolition of institution-alization, better medical assistance and progressive social integration.

Obesity, formerly affecting approximately 50 per cent of children and young people with DS, is now greatly reduced, because of better feeding, a more active life and more widespread sports activities.

In a recent investigation, the body composition of a group of DS children was found to be not statistically different from that of a control group. Reported energy intake was lower in DS subjects, and several micronutrients were consumed at less than 80 per cent of the recommended dose. The authors pointed out the risk of further diminishing the intakes of vitamins and miner-als as a result of using diets that have been worked out with the aim of reduc-ing obesity (Luke *et al.* 1996). In the Netherlands an investigation into infants and children with DS showed the adequacy of their energy and nutrient intakes, but a significant delay in the age at which solid food was introduced. This delay may be dangerous to oral–motor development (Hopman *et al.* 1998). The practical meaning of this and other studies is debatable, mostly because of the paucity of the samples investigated, and the heterogeneity of the subjects studied in terms of age, environmental conditions and nutri-tional habits, which all show wide variations over all the different regions. A combination of a balanced diet without energy restriction but with vitamin and mineral supplementation and increased physical activity must be consid-ered necessary for the prevention of obesity. As to what specific vitamin and mineral deficiencies are concerned, the literature is very rich, but at the same time contradictory. For a comprehensive review, see Pueschel and Pueschel 1992.

On the premise of real or supposed vitamin deficiencies, high-dose vitamin and mineral supplementation has been proposed for many years, not just to correct the deficiency, but still more to effect an improvement in the cognitive and behavioural situations of people with DS.

It is important to recall briefly that vitamins are organic compounds essen-tial in very small amounts to normal human metabolism. When, on the con-trary, they are used in high doses, they no longer act as vitamins, but rather as true drugs. It has been known for a long time that liposoluble vitamins (A, D, E, K) taken in excess can be toxic. Recent research has shown that the hydro-soluble vitamins are also associated with toxicity, and can furthermore inter-fere with the action of other vitamins or drugs.

- Vitamin A excess has been associated with coarse hair, partial hair loss, cracked lips, a dry, rough skin that may peel, severe headaches, general weakness, bone and joint pain, and liver and spleen enlargement. In infants it may cause increased intracranial pressure, vomiting and retarded growth. In pregnancy the risk of abortions and of birth defects (ear anomalies, fissured palate, congenital heart disease and central nervous system malformations) increases.

- Vitamin D excess can cause nausea, vomiting, loss of appetite, weakness, nervousness and hypercalcaemia with deposition of calcium in the kidneys as well as in other organs.
- The effects of Vitamin E excess are infrequent, but they may cause muscle weakness, fatigue and diarrhoea, impaired immunity, and increased risk of bleeding (interference with the metabolism of Vitamin K).
- Vitamin C is rarely toxic: an excessive intake has been implicated in the formation of oxalate stones. It may produce a false positive test for glucose in the urine and can also cause haemolytic crises in G6PD-deficient individuals. It could also interfere with the metabolism of Vitamin $B_{12}$.
- Excessive intake of vitamin $B_1$ may cause insomnia, general weakness, a rapid pulse, itching, pain, headaches and irritability.
- For Vitamin $B_2$ the risk of toxicity is very low: in some cases it may cause itching, numbness and sensitivity to sunlight.
- A high intake of Vitamin $B_6$ has been associated with peripheral neuropathy.
- A vitamin $B_{12}$ excess may interfere with other medications and cause intestinal dysfunction, malaise and irritability.
- Nicotinic acid excess produces a drug-like effect on the nervous system, on blood glucose and lipids. It may cause flushing, itching, peptic ulcer and liver damage.
- Minerals can also be dangerous if taken in high doses.
- Calcium can cause constipation and alterations of renal function.
- Iron can increase the risk of heart and liver damage (haemosiderosis).
- Zinc may interfere with the utilization of other minerals such as iron and copper.
- Selenium may cause hair and nail loss.

## NON-CONVENTIONAL THERAPIES

Around the middle of the twentieth century the first supporters of vitamin and mineral administration to treat behavioural and learning difficulties in children appeared in both Europe and the USA (Pueschel and Pueschel 1992).

In 1975 Turkel proposed for DS children the so-called 'U-series', a therapy consisting of dozens of different compounds, including vitamins, minerals, thyroid hormone, enzymes and medications, to be administered several times a day. The author claimed to have obtained in cases so treated an improvement in intellectual abilities and even in physical features.

In 1981 Harrel et al. claimed to have attained a substantial improvement in intellectual and linguistic abilities in a small group of children with cognitive disabilities, some of whom had DS, after administration of vitamin and mineral mixtures in very high doses (up to 333 times the recommended dose). Controlled studies in succeeding years were unable to reproduce the positive results claimed by these and other authors (Salman 2002). Furthermore, one study demonstrated that treatment with vitamins and minerals was associated with decreased developmental progress and unwelcome side-effects (Bidder *et al.* 1989).

Beyond vitamin and mineral supplementation, many therapies have been proposed over the years to enhance the cognitive performances of DS children. Only the most popular are mentioned here. Sicca cell therapy consists of injections of freeze-dried cells from various organs of fetal cattle and sheep, with the intention of revitalizing various target organs of the patients. While no benefits were found in controlled studies, several potential adverse effects were pointed out, including allergy and anaphylactic reactions.

In 2005 van Trotsenburg *et al.* published the results of a double-blind, 24-months trial in which they compared thyroxine administration with placebo in a large group of DS newborns (196), evaluating the effects on development. They demonstrated a smaller delay in motor developmental age and mental development and greater gains in length and weight in the treated infants versus the placebo-treated ones. Although these results seem positive, great caution must be used, because of possible adverse long-term effects of thyroxine treatment on mental, behavioural and physical performances. It should be pointed out overall that thyroid hormone treatment has been sporadically used since the end of the nineteenth century, and has not been found to improve mental functions in euthyroid DS children (Pueschel and Pueschel 1992).

Pituitary extract treatment, glutamic acid therapy, treatment with 5-hydroxytryptophan (a precursor of serotonin), dimethil-sulfoxide treatment (treatment with a solvent extracted from wood pulp), facial plastic surgery and surgical reduction of the tongue did not show any improvement of cognitive or other functions in children with DS, according to numerous controlled studies performed over the last few decades (Pueschel and Pueschel 1992; Salman 2002; Roizen 2005).

A recently advocated therapy for the cognitive improvement of DS children is the treatment with piracetam, a psychoactive drug, and a cyclic derivative of gamma-amino-butyric acid (GABA). On the basis of anecdotal experiences its use spread as an uncontrolled self-medication, thus raising scientists' concerns (Holmes 1999). In point of fact a controlled study (Lobaugh *et al.* 2001) showed no significantly improved cognitive performances over placebo use in a group of DS children. On the contrary, the drug was associated with CNS stimulatory effects in some of the patients (aggressiveness, agitation or irritability, poor sleep, and/or decreased appetite). Furthermore, the results of research on the mouse T65DN model of DS do not offer any biological support for the treatment of DS children with piracetam (Moran *et al.* 2002).

At present there are no medical therapies or vitamin and mineral supplementations that would significantly improve the cognitive achievements of children with DS (Salman 2002).

## CONCLUSIONS

DS lifespan has significantly increased of late years as a consequence of better adapted medical care and better environmental conditions. Early rehabilitation and social integration have contributed as well. The natural history knowledge of DS allows care-givers to diagnose correctly the associated diseases or abnormalities, and to treat them.

The practical results of advanced basic research are not yet available. So the possibilities of either preventing the conception of trisomic fetuses or correcting the effects of the supernumerary chromosome in early prenatal life are only foreseeable within the near future.

By contrast, however, almost all the associated congenital defects or diseases can currently be tackled and improved or definitely cured. This permits one to propose up-to-date rehabilitation and integration strategies that may allow DS people to live their lives to the fullest.

It is also noteworthy that an increasing number of DS people are growing older and showing an accelerated deterioration of mental and behavioural abilities and, sometimes, the signs of dementia. Prevention of ageing is a difficult task. It is possible that the rehabilitation strategies and the social integration that are employed today may have positive effects on the lifestyles of elderly DS people. The use of antioxidant agents is theoretically feasible, but there are no controlled studies demonstrating significant beneficial effects. Anticholinesterase drugs seem promising for the treatment of age-related dementia.

It is essential to remember that many unconventional therapies have also been proposed to improve the cognitive impairments of DS people. Although the proposers claim very positive results, up to the moment all controlled studies can show no evidence of any substantial effect on cognitive or behavioural activities. Interrupting the slow and difficult passage to rehabilitation in favour of these miracle therapies may lead to bitter disappointment and to decreased developmental progress.

## REFERENCES

Annerén, G., Magnusson, C.G.M. and Nordvall, S.L. (1990). Increase in serum concentrations of IgG2 and IgG4 by selenium supplementation in children with Down's syndrome. *Archives of Diseases in Childhood.* 65:1353–5.

Annerén, G., Tuvemo, T. and Gustafsson, J. (2000). Growth hormone therapy in young children with Down and Prader–Willi syndromes. *Growth Horm IGF Res.* 10 Suppl B:S87–91.

Antonarakis, S.E., Lyle, R., Dermitzakis, E.T., Reymond, A. and Deutsch, S. (2004). Chromosome 21 and Down syndrome: from genomics to pathophysiology. *Nat Rev Gen.* 5:725–8.

Barreca, A., Rasore-Quartino, A. and Acutis, M.S. (1994). Assessment of growth hormone insulin-like growth factor-I axis in Down's syndrome. *J Endocrinol Invest.* 17:431–6.

Bidder, R.T., Gray, P., Newcombe, R.G., Evans, B.K. and Hughes, M. (1989). The effects of multivitamins and minerals on children with Down syndrome. *Dev Med Child Neurol.* 31:532–7.

Boada-Rovira, M., Hernandez-Ruiz, I., Badenas-Homiar, S., Buendias-Torras, M. and Tarraga-Mestre, L. (2005). Clinical-therapeutic study of dementia in people with Down syndrome and the effectiveness of donepezil in this population. *Rev Neurol.* 41:129–36.

Boduroglu, K., Alanay, Y., Koldan, B. and Tuncbilek, E. (2004). Methylenetetrahydrofolate reductase enzyme polymorphism as maternal risk for Down syndrome among Turkish women. *Am J Med Genet.* 127:5–10.

Bonamico, M., Mariani, P., Danesi, H.M., Crisogianni, M., Failla, P., Gemme, G. and Rasore Quartino, A. et al. (2001). Prevalence and clinical picture of celiac disease in Italian Down syndrome patients: a multicenter study. *J Pediatr Gastroenterol Nutr.* 33:139–43.

Bosco, P., Guéant-Rodriguez, R.M., Anello, G., Barone, C., Namour, F., Caraci, F., Romano, A., Romano, C. and Guéant, J.L. (2003). Methionine syntase (MTR) 2756 (A→G) polymorphism, double heterozygosity methionine synthase 2756 AG/methionine synthase reductase (MTRR) 66 AG, and elevated homocysteinemia are three risk factors for having a child with Down syndrome. *Am J Med Genet.* 121:219–24.

Botto, L.D., Mulinare, J., Yang, Q., Liu, Y. and Erikson, J.D. (2004). Autosomal trisomy and maternal use of multivitamin supplements. *Am J Med Genet.* 125:113–16.

Canfield, M.A., Collins, J.S., Botto, L.D., Williams, L.J., Mai, C.T., Kirby, R.S., Pearson, K., Devine, O., Mulinare, J. and National Birth Defects Prevention Network. (2005). Changes in the birth prevalence of selected birth defects after grain fortification with folic acid in the United States: findings from a multi-state population-based study. *Birth Defects Res A Clin Mol Teratol.* 73:679–89.

Chango, A., Fillon-Emery, N., Mircher, C., Blehaut, H., Lambert, D., Herbeth, B., James, S.J., Rethoré, M.O. and Nicolas, J.P. (2005). No association between common polymorphisms in genes of folate and homocysteine metabolism and the risk of Down's syndrome among French mothers. *Br J Nutr.* 94:166–9.

Cominetti, M., Rasore, Quartino, A., Acutis, M.S. and Vignola, G. (1985). Neonato con syndrome di Down e leucemia mieloide acuta. Difficoltà diagnostiche fra forma maligna e sindrome mieloproliferativa. *Pathologica.* 77:625–30.

Coyle, J.T., Price, D.L. and DeLong, M.R. (1983). Alzheimer's disease: a disorder of cholinergic innervation. *Science.* 219:1184–90.

de Haan, J.B., Cristiano, F., Jannello, R.C. and Kola, I. (1995). Cu/Zn-superoxide dismutase and glutathione peroxidase during aging. *Biochem Mol Biol Int.* 35:1281–97.

Devenny, D.A., Silverman, W.P., Hill, A.L., Jenkins, E., Sersen, E.A. and Wisniewski, K.E. (1996). Normal ageing in adults with Down's syndrome: a longitudinal study. I *Intellect Disabil Res.* 40:208–21.

Evenhuis, H.M. (1990). The natural history of dementia in Down's syndrome. *Arch Neurol.* 47:263–7.

Farlow, M.R. (2001). Pharmacokinetic profiles of current therapies for Alzheimer's disease: implications for switching to galantamine. *Clin Ther.* 23 Suppl A:A13–24.

Franceschi, C., Chiricolo, M., Licastro, F., Zannotti, M., Masi, M., Moccheggiani, E. and Fabris, N. (1988). Oral zinc supplementation in Down's syndrome: restoration of thymic endocrine activity and of some immune defects. *J Ment Defic Res.* 32:169–81.

Fromage, B. and Anglade, P. (2002). The aging of Down's syndrome subjects. *Encephale.* 28:212–16.

Goh, Y.I., Bollano, E., Einarson, T.R. and Koren, G. (2006). Prenatal multivitamin supplementation and rates of congenital anomalies: a meta-analysis. *J Obstet Gynecol Can.* 28:680–9.

Goldacre, M.J., Wotton, C.J., Seagrott, V. and Yeates, D. (2004). Cancer and immune-related diseases associated with Down's syndrome: a record linkage study. *Arch Dis Child.* 89:1014–17.

Guéant, J.L., Guéant-Rodriguez, R.M., Anello, G., Bosco, P., Brunaud, L., Romano, C., Ferri, R., Romano, A., Candito, M. and Namour, B. (2003) Genetic determinants of folate and vitamin B12 metabolism: a common pathway in neural tube defect and Down syndrome? *Clin Chem Lab Med.* 41:1473–7.

Harman, D. (2006). Alzheimer's disease pathogenesis: role of aging. *Ann NY Acad Sci.* 1067:454–60.

Harrel, R.J., Capp, R.H. and Davis, D.R. (1981). Can nutritional supplements help mentally retarded children? *Proc Natl Acad Sci USA.* 78:574–8.

Heller, J.H., Spiridigliozzi, G.A., Sullivan, J.A., Doraiswamy, P.M., Krishnan, R.R. and Kishnani, P.S. (2003). Donepezil for the treatment of language deficits in adults with Down syndrome. A preliminary 24-week open trial. *Am J Med Genet.* 116A:111–16.

Hobbs, C.A., Sherman, S.L., Hopkins, S.E., Torfs, C.P., Hine, R.J., Pogribna, M., Rozen, R. and James, S.J. (2000). Polymorphisms in genes involved in folate metabolism as maternal risk factors for Down syndrome. *Am J Hum Genet.* 67:623–30.

Holmes, L.B. (1999). Concern about Piracetam treatment for children with Down syndrome. *Pediatrica.* 103:1078–9.

Hopman, E., Csizmadia, C.G., Bastiani, W.F., Engels, Q.M., De Graaf, E.A., Le Cessie, S. and Mearin, M.L. (1998). Eating habits of young children with Down syndrome in the Netherlands: adequate nutrient intakes but delayed introduction of solid food. *J Am Diet Assoc.* 98:790–4.

Isaacs, H. (2003). Foetal and neonatal leukaemia. *J Pediatr Hematol Oncol.* 25:348–61.

Johnson, N., Fahey, C., Chicoine, B., Chong, G. and Gitelman, D. (2003). Effects of donepezil on cognitive functioning in Down syndrome. *Am J Mental Retardation.* 108(6):367–72.

Karlsson, B., Gustafsson, J., Hedow, G., Ivarsson, S.A. and Annerén, G. (1998). Thyroid function in children and adolescents with Down syndrome in relation to age, sex, growth velocity and thyroid antibodies. *Arch Dis Childhood.* 79:242–5.

Kondoh, T., Amamoto, N., Doi, T., Hamada, H., Ogawa, Y., Nakashima, M., Sasaki, H., Aikawa, K., Tanaka, T., Aoki, M., Harada, J. and Moriuchi, H. (2005). Dramatic improvement in Down syndrome-associated cognitive impairment with donepezil. *Ann Pharmacother.* 39:563–6.

Lanes, R. (2004). Long-term outcome of growth hormone therapy in children and adolescents. *Treat Endocrinol.* 3:53–66.

Lange, B. (2000). The management of neoplastic disorders of haematopoiesis in children with Down's syndrome. *Br J Hematol.* 110:512–24.

Lee, S.K. and Green, P.H. (2006). Celiac sprue (the great modern-day impostor). *Curr Opin Rheumatol.* 18:101–7.

Licastro, F., Chiricolo, M., Mocchegiani, E., Fabris, N., Zannotti, M., Beltrandi, E., Mancini, R., Parente, R., Arena, G. and Masi, M. (1994). Oral zinc supplementation in Down's syndrome subjects decreased infections and normalized some humoral and cellular immune parameters. *J Intellect Disability Res.* 38:149–62.

Lobaugh, N.J., Karaskov, V., Rombough, V., Rovet, J., Bryson, S., Greenbaum, R., Haslam, R.H. and Koren, G. (2001). Piracetam therapy does not enhance cognitive functioning in children with Down syndrome. *Arch Pediatr Adolesc Med.* 155:442–8.

Lott, I.T., Osann, K., Doran, E. and Nelson, I. (2002). Down syndrome and Alzheimer disease: response to donepezil. *Arch Neurol.* 59:1133–6.

Lowe, O. (1990). Dental problems. In D.C. VanDyke, D.J. Lang, F. Heide (eds), *Clinical perspectives in the management of Down syndrome.* pp. 72–9. New York: Springer Verlag.

Luke, A., Sutton, M., Schoeller, D.A. and Roizen, N.J. (1996). Nutrient intake and obesity in prepubescent children with Down syndrome. *J Am Diet Assoc.* 96:1262–7.

Marino, B. and De Zorzi, A. (1993). Congenital heart disease in trisomy 21 mosaicism. *J Pediatr.* 122:500–1.

Marino, B. and Pueschel, S. (1996). *Heart disease in persons with Down syndrome.* Baltimore, MD: Paul H Brookes Publishing Co.

Marino, B., Assenza, G., Mileto, S. and Digilio, M. (2004). Down syndrome and congenital heart disease. In J.A. Rondal, A. Rasore Quartino, S. Soresi (eds), *The adult with Down syndrome. A new challenge for society.* pp 39–50. London: Whurr Publishers.

Marsh, M.N. (1992). *Coeliac disease.* Oxford: Blackwell.

Massey, G.V. (2005). Transient leukaemia in newborns with Down syndrome. *Pediatr Blood Cancer.* 44:29–32.

Menezes, A.H. and Ryken, T.C. (1992). Craniovertebral anomalies in Down's syndrome. *Pediatr Neurosurg.* 18:24–33.

Meyer, G. and Badenhoop, K. (2002). Autoimmune regulator (AIRE) gene on chromosome 21: implications for autoimmune polyendocrinopathy-candidiasis-ectodermal dystrophy (APECED), a more common manifestation of endocrine autoimmunity. *J Endocrinol Invest.* 25:804–11.

Monson, J.P. (2003). Long-term experience with GH replacement therapy: efficacy and safety. *Eur J Endocrinol.* 148 Suppl 2:S9–14.

Moran, T.H., Capone, G.T., Knipp, S., Davisson, M.T., Reeves, R.H. and Gearhart, J.D. (2002). The effects of piracetam on cognitive performance in a mouse model of Down's syndrome. *Physiol Behav.* 77:403–9.

Mura, A. and Medicina, C. (2004). The audiological diagnosis in subjects with Down syndrome. In J.A. Rondal, A. Rasore Quartino, S. Soresi (eds), *The adult with Down syndrome. A new challenge for society.* pp. 67–74. London: Whurr Publishers Ltd.

O'Leary, V.B., Parle-McDermott, A., Molloy, A.M., Irke, P.N., Johnson, Z., Conley, M., Scott, J.M. and Mills, J.L. (2002). MTRR and MTHFR polymorphism: link to Down syndrome? *Am J Med Genet.* 107:151–5.

Pallotti, S., Giuliano, S. and Giambi, C. (2002). Growth disorders in Down's syndrome: growth hormone treatment. *Minerva Endocrinol.* 27:59–64.

Patterson, D. (2006). Ageing and susceptibility to Alzheimer's disease in Down syndrome. In J.A. Rondal, J. Perera (eds), *Down Syndrome. Neurobehavioural specificity.* pp 35–51. Chichester (UK): John Wiley & Sons, Ltd.

Prasher, V.P. (2004). Review of donepezil, rivastigmine, galantamine and memantine for the treatment of dementia in Alzheimer's disease in adults with Down syndrome: implications for the intellectual disability population. *Int J Geriatr Psychiatry.* 19:509–15.

Pueschel, S.M. and Pueschel, J.K. (1992). *Biochemical concerns in persons with Down's syndrome.* Baltimore, MD: Paul H Brookes Publishing Co Inc.

Pueschel, S.M. and Schola, F.H. (1987). Atlantoaxial instability in individuals with Down syndrome: epidemiology, radiographic and clinical studies. *Pediatrics.* 80:555–60.

Pueschel, S.M., Annerén, G., Durlach, R., Flores, J., Sustrova, M. and Verma, I.C. (1995). International League of Societies for Persons with Mental Handicap (ILSMH). Guidelines for optimal medical care of persons with Down syndrome. *Acta Paediatr.* 84:823–7.

Puri, B.K., Ho, K.W. and Singh, I. (2001). Age of seizure onset in adults with Down's syndrome. *Int J Clin Pract.* 55:442–4.

Rasore Quartino, A. (2006). Down syndrome specificity in health issues. In J.A. Rondal, J. Perera (eds), *Down syndrome. Neurobehavioural specificity.* pp. 53–65. Chichester (UK): John Wiley & Sons, Ltd.

Ravindranath, Y. (2003). Down syndrome and acute myeloid leukaemia: the paradox of increased risk for leukaemia and heightened sensitivity to chemotherapy (Editorial). *J Clin Oncol.* 21:3385–7.

Ravindranath, Y. (2005). Down syndrome and leukaemia: new insights into the epidemiology, pathogenesis and treatment. *Pediatr Blood Cancer.* 44:1–7.

Ray, J.G., Meier, C., Vermeulen, M.J., Cole, D.E. and Wyatt, P.R. (2003). Prevalence of trisomy 21 following folic acid food fortification. *Am J Med Genet.* 120:309–13.

Roizen, N.J. (2005). Complementary and alternative therapies for Down syndrome. *Ment Retard Dev Disabil Res Rev.* 11:149–55.

Salman, M.S. (2002). Systematic review of the effect of therapeutic dietary supplements and drugs on cognitive function in subjects with Down syndrome. *Eur J Pediat Neurol.* 6:213–19.

Selby, K.A., Newton, R.W., Gupta, S. and Hunt, L. (1991). Clinical predictors and radiological reliability in atlantoaxial subluxation in Down's syndrome. *Arch Dis Child.* 66:876–8.

Service, K.P. and Hahn, J.E. (2003). Issues in aging. The role of the nurse in the care of older people with intellectual and developmental disabilities. *Nurs Clin North Amer.* 38:291–312.

Sheth, J.J. and Sheth, F.J. (2003). Gene polymorphism and folate metabolism: a maternal risk factor for Down syndrome. *Indian Pediatr.* 40:115–23.

Simmons, C.J., Mosley, B.S., Fulton-Bond, C.A. and Hobbs, C.A. (2004). Birth defects in Arkansas: is folic acid fortification making a difference? *Birth Defects Res A Clin Mol Teratol.* 70:559–64.

Taub, J.W. and Ge, Y. (2005). Down syndrome, drug metabolism and chromosome 21. *Pediatr Blood Cancer.* 44:33–9.

Taub, J.W., Mundschau, G., Ge, Y., Poulik, J.M., Qureshi, F., Jensen, T., James, S.J., Matherly, L.H., Wechsker, J. and Crispino, J.D. (2004). Prenatal origin of GATA 1 mutations may be an initiating step in the development of megakaryocytic leukaemia in Down syndrome. *Blood.* 104:1588–9.

Toussaint, P., Desenclos, C., Peltier, J. and LeGars, D. (2003). Transarticular atlanto-axial screw fixation for treatment of C1–C2 instability. *Neurochirurgie.* 49:519–26.

Turkel, H. (1975). Medical amelioration of Down's syndrome incorporating the ortho-molecular approach. *J Orthomolecular Psychiatry.* 4:102–15.

van Trotsenburg, A.S., Vulsma, T., van Rozenburg-Marres, S.L., van Baar, A.L., Ridder, J.C., Heymans, H.S., Tijssen, J.G. and de Vijlder, J.J. (2005). The effect of thyroxine treatment started in the neonatal period on development and growth of two-year-old Down syndrome children: a randomized clinical trial. *J Clin Endocrinol Metab.* 90:3304–11.

Zipursky, A. (1996). The treatment of children with acute megakaryoblastic leukaemia who have Down syndrome. *J Pediatr Hematol Oncol.* 18:59–62.

Zipursky, A. (2003). Transient leukaemia – A benign form of leukaemia in newborn infants with trisomy 21. *Br J Haematol.* 120:930–8.

# 5 Language Rehabilitation*

JEAN-ADOLPHE RONDAL

## SUMMARY

Down syndrome (DS), as one of the most prevalent conditions of moderate and severe mental retardation of genetic origin, has been the object of intensive studies for a number of years. In respect of major aspects such as language, we are now in a position to sketch the greater lines of development according to a life-span perspective, i.e., from the beginning of life to the attainment of adult years. Of course, many questions remain without a clear answer (for instance in relation to communicative and prelinguistic development in the first year of life and the later difficulties and problems in the elderly), but a relatively comprehensive view of the nature of the acquisitions, stumbling blocks, plateaux, and relative strengths and weaknesses in speech and language profiles is becoming available. On the basis of this knowledge, it is increasingly possible to define sounder remediation principles for attempting to improve language functioning in persons with DS. Key aspects of language development in DS are identified (pointing out also areas in which knowledge is still insufficient) following a chronological perspective and dealing with major language components (i.e., phonology and articulation, vocabulary, grammar, pragmatics, and discourse). For each of these components, relevant principles of corrective treatment are specified.

In my view, language rehabilitation (or remediation) with individuals with Down syndrome should be based on several basic principles and take account of the set of interrelated dimensions illustrated in Fig. 5.1 (Rondal 2003).

Intervention must be developmental in the sense of the term used by Rondal and Edwards (1997) and (more generally – in other words, outside the language domain) in that of Cicchetti and Beeghly (1990). Research increasingly shows that development and functioning in individuals with intellectual disabilities (ID) are as organized, purposeful, and adaptive as in typically developing (TD) individuals and individuals with ID are viewed as variations in basically similar processes or as pathological distortions of otherwise normal phases of development.

*Therapies and Rehabilitation in Down Syndrome.* Edited by Rondal
© 2007 John Wiley & Sons Ltd

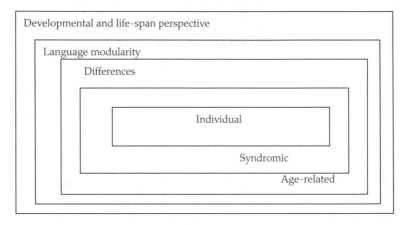

**Figure 5.1.** Major dimensions of language intervention with MR subjects.

Numerous observations (cf. Rosenberg and Abbeduto 1993; Rondal and Edwards 1997 for systematic reviews) suggest that language development in individuals with ID, including those with DS, proceeds, in major ways, as it does in TD individuals. Similar sequences of steps are documented until final plateaux are reached. Development in individuals with ID is slower and remains in many respects incomplete. There are no clear indications, however, that the basic mechanisms involved in each domain of language development radically differ. This suggests that intervention programmes should follow typical development as closely as possible. More specifically, programmes that closely follow the indications on the sequences of development within the various language components are likely to be more effective. Graduated sequences of training for prelinguistic, cognitive-semantic, phonological, lexical, morphosyntactic, pragmatic, and discursive skills can be implemented with children and adolescents with DS. The general objective of the intervention programmes can be summarized as follows: to enable persons with DS to master as quickly and as completely as possible the sequences of skills characteristic of normal development. It is believed that early and continuous intervention, when conducted adequately, carries the best chances of reducing further disabilities, given the cumulative nature of the developmental process.

Language intervention should be age-related. Language difficulties and obstacles vary considerably from the baby to the ageing person with DS. Age-appropriate intervention can and should be implemented.

Quite clearly, language development is a dynamic, interactive, and social process as well as an individual, brain-based, and cognitively dependent process; therefore families, schools, and communities matter considerably in any intervention perspective. In fact, an early intervention perspective cannot be effective outside the family setting and without the active participation of the parents or care-givers of the DS child. Schools and communities ought to be more closely associated with the remediation intervention perspective in ID, and DS in particular. Whatever the merits of a given intervention strategy, it will have only a limited effect in furthering development and functioning if the attitudes and opportunities of the inclusive educational or community setting are less than appropriate. This, of course, should come as no surprise. We do not develop skills, whether physical, cognitive, linguistic, or social, just for the sake of private personal satisfaction, but rather, at least partially, for use in social settings and with socio-functional aims.

Language organization is basically (but not exclusively) modular, meaning that language is not, despite appearances, a unitary phenomenon. It results from the appropriate integration of various components (such as its phonological, lexical, morphosyntactic, pragmatic, and discursive aspects) that are to a large extent autonomous, as numerous pathological observations indicate. The specificity of these major language components is such that attempts to implement multipurpose remediation procedures are bound to generate only mediocre effects.

The diverse modalities of language functioning also need to be taken into account. Spoken language, of course, is of the utmost importance. And this raises the problem of the particular speech difficulties that are common in DS individuals. There is no good reason to exclude DS children from written language learning and literacy training, as was generally the case even in the recent past. The idea that children with DS can achieve functional levels of literacy, when properly taught, is gradually gaining ground. Moreover, it is becoming clear that reading and writing may be beneficial for overall language acquisition. This may be particularly true for DS children, who have better visual perceptual and visual memory abilities than auditory ones.

Language can also be developed using non-verbal systems of communication. A number of such systems are available, from manual sign languages, such as the American or the British sign language, mainly used by deaf people, or simplified versions of these, to numerous visual systems relying on pictographic logographs and multimodality approaches. The potential benefits of the different systems have to be evaluated for each individual. Alternative and augmentative systems of communication may have a role in facilitating effective communication in people with ID. They can create a pathway to speech, setting improved communication contexts for better interpretation and more accurate use of the sounds of spoken language. In children whose spoken language is seriously delayed, they can complement the speech that these subjects have already learned or are learning. Alternative and augmentative systems of communication can also provide a substitute for speech in individuals with little possibility of acquiring vocal fluency for organic reasons. For this reason, and with regard to the communication difficulties of profoundly deaf people, it would be a good idea if those in charge of administering the schools in our countries were to recommend teaching and learning sign language as a second or third language from an early age for all children. Expressing oneself in a 'space language' is great fun. The children would enjoy it. It could be cognitively fruitful in promoting a sort of linguistic 'decentration' by exposing the children to a three-dimensional language system in addition to the strictly linear spoken and written codes. And last, but not least, it would be extremely beneficial for people who rely on non-verbal language systems for their communication, increasing the possibilities for their participation in school and in the community.

There is no *a priori* reason why DS children should be prevented from developing bilingual or even multilingual repertoires, even if it is unlikely that the levels of functioning eventually reached in the additional languages would be any different from those in the maternal tongue. Nor is it likely, as is sometimes believed by some people – in our view naïvely – that bilingualism *per se* could alleviate some of the cognitive limitations inherent in Down syndrome. In other words, bilingualism may probably be encouraged in children with DS with some caution when it is part of the family or community situation, but it is neither a cognitive nor a language therapy.

Quite clearly, language intervention must be planned in an age-related manner. Early intervention (from birth, as we shall argue) is an absolute necessity. It carries the best hopes for lasting effects from prelinguistic skills on the later linguistic structures. It can meaningfully be carried out in close collaboration with the family of the infant and young child with DS. Continued intervention during schooling should be organized in association with the schools (see Beveridge 1996). As language development occurs over time, particularly in DS individuals, a series of linguistic structures to be improved can be proposed, in parallel with typical language acquisition, at each school level. Parents will often need to be advised on how to help their children effectively during the school years and how to make appropriate choices regarding curricular options (Rynders 1994).

Another topic of importance relates to the peer relations of DS children in mainstreamed groups. There one has children with Down syndrome and typically developing children at different developmental levels interacting with each other in classroom and play activities (see Guralnick 1996; Guralnick *et al.* 1996).

Intervention should also be recommended in late adolescence and early adult years, particularly with regard to the lexical, pragmatic, and discursive aspects of language, which do not seem to exhibit critical period characteristics, as opposed to the phonological and morphosyntactic abilities, which do seem to be affected by critical periods (cf. Rondal and Edwards 1997 for a full-scale discussion). Attention to these areas is highly advisable as a means of enhancing sociocultural and work integration in DS individuals (Rosenberg and Abbeduto 1993). Lastly, language intervention with ageing persons with DS is not only possible but necessary. It should adapt current programmes with the elderly in the typical population. This may also provide a way to slow down language deterioration in the early stage of Alzheimer disease in some people with Down syndrome.

When designing language intervention programmes, individual differences have to be taken into account. Unfortunately, the study of these differences in ID (or in DS) is still little advanced. Current intervention work and programmes include nothing or only a little of this important dimension, despite lip service sometimes being paid to the issue. Exceptional cases of language development in DS and other ID individuals have been specified in recent research (cf. Rondal 1994, 1995), suggesting that the variance may be quite large. Those working in the field of intellectual disabilities still have fully to incorporate the data on the range of individual differences and adapt their approaches accordingly.

It seems clear that interventions that take into account aetiological characteristics have more chance of being effective. This claim was already formulated by Gibson (1981; see also Gibson 1991 for additional specifications in the area of cognitive remediation). Dykens *et al.* (1994), Turk *et al.* (1994), and Dykens and Hodapp (2001) insist that patterns of development in ID individuals may be, at least partly, syndrome-specific. Professionals should try to tailor intervention to specific aetiological groups. Regarding speech and language, Rondal and Comblain (1999) and Rondal (2004) have analysed the language profiles of twelve ID syndromes of genetic origin. This analysis reveals considerable partial specificity across syndromes. Intervention programmes might work better when the child's aetiology is among several important characteristics taken into account in designing remediation. The present work concentrates on Down syndrome and therefore axiomatically draws upon this specificity argument (cf. Rondal, in press, and the contributions gathered and edited by Rondal and Perera, in press).

## THE EFFECTIVENESS ISSUE

Evaluating the effectiveness of an intervention, particularly a language intervention, is clearly a difficult task. The goal is to enhance the individual's learning of better linguistic structures and behaviours. Having acquired these, individuals ought to be able not only to produce or understand specific exemplars involving the learned structures but also to exhibit generalized changes in terms of given aspects of language (Rusch and Karlan 1983).

Studies that evaluate the effectiveness of language intervention are still too rare. At the end of their comprehensive review, Snyder-MacLean and MacLean (1987) suggested that language intervention may be only moderately effective in modifying the course of language development. Their somewhat negative position at the time (also relayed by Hauser-Cram 1989 and Price 1989) was largely motivated by considerations of the many difficult methodological, evaluative, and even ethical problems (for example, who should be assigned to the experimental and/or the control groups?) in assessing remediation work – and by the fact that few of the published intervention studies at the time had provided systematic longitudinal data and/or data regarding the maintenance and the generalization of treatment effects to real-world communicative contexts. Warren and Kaiser (1988) argued that proper generalization and transfer of language intervention is rarely systematically explored and that it might even be considered that it is not usually achieved. According to these authors, proper generalization would be manifested as an increased rate of developmental progress after the intervention has reached a stringent criterion.

It is my opinion, indeed, that remediation programmes offered to children with moderate or severe intellectual disabilities have not met with sufficient success yet, particularly in fostering phonological, morphosyntactic, and discourse development. However, the areas of basic semantics and pragmatics, being more accessible and more easily accessed by language therapists and teachers, have begun to yield clearer gains and more stable ones, though of course within the cognitive limits of individuals. Critical time-periods for development in the conceptual aspects of language do not appear to exist, as they do in phonology and morphosyntax (Rondal and Edwards 1997). This permits additional time and degrees of freedom for intervention. The areas of phonology and morphosyntax (the so-called computational aspects of language) are technically more complex, demanding additional knowledge and professional skills from the therapist.

Yet the general opinion of professionals in the field regarding at least the short- and middle-term efficiency of their practices with DS individuals (particularly children) is generally positive, contrasting with the scepticism expressed in the judgements of the authors mentioned above. Beyond any undue naïveté it may be the case that more recent, methodologically sound, intervention strategies are yielding more positive outcomes. For example, programmes based on sound principles and involving parents or care-givers collaborating with professionals seem promising. Salmon *et al.* (1998) have reported a positive impact of adult prompting in facilitating prelinguistic communication in toddlers with DS. Explicit prompting by interacting adults (as opposed to minimal prompting) had a marked effect in promoting higher overall rates of intentional communication in the children. Iacono *et al.* (1998) had preschool children with Down syndrome and their mothers collaborating with a speech pathologist and special educator who acted as consultants within a collaborative consultation process aiming at defining and controlling the application of language-intervention strategies. Comparisons with a multiple baseline design demonstrated the efficiency of the intervention procedure for three out of the five children involved. Descriptive analyses of mothers' communicative behaviours indicated that, following treatment, they tended to direct more utterances to their children, model more, use more language-teaching strategies, ask fewer questions and produce fewer directives. That these improvements, although quite interesting, were not sufficient for progress was indicated by the fact that two out of the five target children failed to exhibit significant language improvement over time. Girolametto *et al.* (1998) have reported success in fostering expressive vocabulary development in young DS children, relying on parental involvement that promoted interaction and encouraged modelling and imitation of vocabulary (see also Girolametto 2000).

Another promising aspect of recent intervention programmes is the increased attention devoted to prelinguistic communication as a way to prepare and positively affect the emergence of receptive and productive language in DS infants. Yoder and Warren (2001) have conducted a study on the treatment effects of prelinguistic communication interventions on language in toddlers with developmental delays. Only some of these children had Down syndrome. Others were premature with medical complications, or had macrocephaly, neonatal meningitis, tuberous sclerosis, fetal alcohol syndrome, or no identifiable aetiology or diagnosis other than serious developmental delay. Yoder and Warren (2001) report positive treatment effects on children's language development extending 6 and 12 months after the end of prelinguistic intervention (conducted four times a week for 6 months) and affecting important aspects of early language development, such as comprehension of semantic relations, global measures of expressive and receptive language, and lexical density (the average rate of non-imitative vocabulary words used). The treatment outcomes, however, varied significantly as a function of pre-treatment maternal responsiveness and educational level.

In a 25-chapter review, covering more than 35 years of research and practice in early intervention, Guralnick (1997) shows how far this field has come in solidifying the science of early intervention. This makes it clear that the efficiency of early intervention depends on complex and delicate interactions between programme objectives and features, and child and family characteristics. In the introduction to the book, Guralnick distinguishes 'first generation (i.e., till the late 1980s)' and 'second generation' early intervention research. The former is described as a period in which there was much concern about whether early intervention was indeed effective and worth doing and subsidizing. Second-generation work extends beyond this question towards specifying empirically what characteristics of intervention are effective (or more effective) with particular pathological entities and particular groups of children and families, and understanding the mechanisms through which interventions operate. Of course, interventionists do not claim to cure children with intellectual disabilities, and therefore achieve therapy in the strict sense. Rather they aim to use the necessary knowledge and technological tools needed to give these children an advantage that might not have existed without intervention and to foster better development, particularly if intervention starts sufficiently early. It may indeed be considered that the work accomplished since the early 1970s provides the foundation for the next generation of intervention and prevention programmes and research, with the general objective of specifying effective remediation activities more precisely and increasing their long-term effects. In the same way, it is clear that future improvements in programme efficiency and the generalizability and durability of gains will also depend on increased knowledge of the mechanisms and sequences characteristic of language development in the various entities causing intellectual disabilities.

## LANGUAGE COMPONENTS

As has been indicated, language components should receive specific attention in view of the modular organization that is prevalent within the linguistic system and its neurobehavioural correlates. Accordingly, I shall deal separately, in what follows, with the lexical, phonological, morphosyntactic, and pragmatic aspects of rehabilitation as it relates to DS individuals.

However, basic to everything is prelinguistic development. Witness the numerous recent studies on prelinguistic development in TD infants; we now understand better the relationship between early sensorimotor development, sound discrimination, babbling and infraphonological development and the subsequent language acquisition. As a result of prenatal and perinatal speech exposure, TD babies display early discrimination of their mother's voice and its prosodic characteristics. Research has shown that young TD infants perceive language sounds in a categorical way, just as adults do. By one month of age, and probably before, they can be shown to be acutely sensitive to the acoustic contrasts between many (virtually all the) sounds existing in natural languages (for example, discriminating between consonants on the basis of place of articulation (such as p, t, k) and mode of articulation (such as p, f), and between oral vowels (such as a, i, u). The neonate's overall discriminative ability for speech sounds gradually decreases over the first year of life, except, most importantly, for the phoneme sounds characteristic of their community language. For example, Japanese babies are able to distinguish r and l sounds whereas older Japanese children and adults can no longer do this, as this phonemic discrimination does not exist in the Japanese language.

Regarding productive infraphonological development, before approximatively 6 months of age, the community language only minimally influences TD infants' babbling. Sounds that do not belong to maternal language are produced. Between 6 and 12 months, a gradual influence of the community language on the prosodic and segmental characteristics of infants' babbling is observed. Phonetically naïve adults can reliably recognize prosodic and segmental features of their language (for example, French, English, Cantonese, or Algerian Arabic) from babbling samples taken from 8 to 10-month-old infants.

Data are still largely missing on prelinguistic development in DS babies, but some indications have been proposed. Dodd (1972) and Smith and Oller (1981) have suggested that the sounds of babbling are mostly similar in types and tokens in TD and DS infants. Reduplicated babbling, a distinct precursor to the onset of speech (observed around 7–8 months in TD infants), is delayed by several months already in DS infants.

Despite the limited amount of information available, a number of activities have the potential to improve prelinguistic development in DS infants, and, given the importance of reducing the early delays for further language development, they should be given particular attention in any early rehabilitative programme. These strategies are: (1) installing a reciprocal relation with the DS infant as early and as systematically as possible; (2) stimulating auditory perception and discrimination; (3) fostering non-verbal communication and gestural imitation; (4) stimulating babbling and its evolution from vocalic to syllabic, reduplicated, interactive, and symbolic babbling; (5) fostering practical knowledge of the immediate environment; and (6) promoting symbolic games and behaviour (for details as to the particular objectives and rehabilitative strategies, see Rondal 1986, 1987, 1998, 2003).

Motor development in DS is closely associated with the degree of generalized hypotonia (Poo and Gassio 2000). The motor component of speech, therefore, can be expected to be problematic in this syndrome. Several techniques have been designed in order to reduce buccal (particularly lingual) hypotonia. The best-known one is that of Castillo-Morales *et al.* (1984), relying on a palatal plate equipped with mechanical stimulators. The average length of treatment is 18 months. Placement of the plate is advised from 2 or 3 months of age. Reported success varies from 50 per cent to 80 per cent. De Andrade *et al.* (1998) have designed a modified plate like the Castillo-Morales one but with the clever adjunct of a pacifier tied to the plate. This device allows a longer and safer positioning of the plate in the baby's mouth permitting greater efficiency in the improvement of buccal hypotonia, lingual protrusion, labial hypotonia, and permanent mouth opening, particularly when this technique is combined with orofacial stimulation.

In some (rare) cases of excessive macroglossia, the above treatment may not suffice. A surgical treatment consisting of removing a part of the lingual mass may be advised (Lemperle 1985). Correctly performed, it may improve the lingual-buccal apparatus laying the foundations for facilitated speech training.

## SPEECH TRAINING

Phonological intervention involves three steps (Stoel-Gammon 1981, 2003): (1) assessing the child's phonological system; (2) setting the intervention goals;

and (3) determining the most appropriate method for achieving those goals. Efficient programmes focus on increasing the phonetic repertoire and reducing the number of errors, using techniques similar to those for non-DS children with phonological delay or disorder (e.g. Cholmain 1994). The programmes are designed to encourage the child to recognize the basic structures of the adult's phonological system, insisting on listening and production practices focused on particular phonemes and phonological processes, with therapies occurring in the clinic and at home. Another type of therapy programme centres on the variability of word production by DS children (Dodd *et al.* 1994). The units of treatment, here, are whole words, and parents serve as the agents of therapy, being instructed to accept only one pronunciation for a set of words selected for their child. Pronunciation errors are accepted as long as they reflect developmental rather than deviant patterns.

## LEXICAL TRAINING

As explained by Mervis (1990) and Mervis and Becerra (2003), intervention concerned with early vocabulary acquisition should have three interrelated goals: (1) the child and the adult who interacts with him or her should develop patterns of interaction that are comfortable and effective for all of them; (2) the child should learn as many words as possible; and (3) the child should be encouraged to use the words he or she knows spontaneously, both to express ideas and to attempt to control the environment. Establishing and maintaining joint attention is crucial for facilitating children's lexical development (Kaiser *et al.* 2001). The most effective form of joint attention involves the adult following in on the focus of the child's attention and then labelling that focus multiple times within the same interactive episode as well as across different episodes. This strategy is particularly important for young DS children whose verbal memory weaknesses greatly increase the difficulty of encoding and remembering new labels and their referents (Jarrold and Baddeley 1997).

The onset of expressive oral language is often extremely delayed for DS children, and the rate of progress after the child begins to talk is typically very slow. To increase the rate at which children learn to communicate linguistically, sign language may be introduced in conjunction with oral language, in a sort of total communication strategy. An input composed of simultaneous speech and sign is provided, and may favour significantly larger expressive vocabularies in the children (Clibbens 2001).

It is important in lexical training to choose carefully the labels that will be used and the exemplars to be labelled. Objects may be labelled at a variety of different hierarchical levels. Children learn basic-level names for objects (e.g., dog, car, table, apple) much more easily than superordinates (e.g., animal, automobile, furniture, fruit) or subordinates (e.g., Collie, Peugeot, chess-table, Golden Delicious). At this stage, children need to hear a word multiple times, on multiple occasions, in various contexts with the referent clearly identified (and stressed), before they are able to map it to the appropriate referent and keep the association in semantic memory. It is also important that the initial exemplars be labelled good specimens (archetypes) of the category (for example, for bird, a robin rather than a penguin or a chicken) and that they are real objects or realistic replicas or pictures, rather than stylistic or abstract objects or pictures.

Once the child begins to produce labels, it is likely that the range of referents to which he or she applies a given label will not be identical to that used by an adult (in the direction of over- or undergeneralization most often; for example, calling a cat bow-wow or doggie, or refusing to label a car any car but the family one). Such steps are normal ones in the process of lexical acquisition. In these cases, it is best to accept the child's label until the adult thinks the child is able to appreciate the attributes (semantic features) that differentiate the object from other members of its child-basic category. At that time, the adult-basic label may be introduced, using the label plus verbal description and concrete illustration of differentiating attributes.

## MORPHOSYNTACTIC TRAINING

Comprehension (receptive) training should always precede production (expressive) training for any structure to be taught. Regarding expressive training, in the first stage, the child should be encouraged to repeat short utterances, phrases, and sentences presented orally in the appropriate situation. Once the child has started producing multiword utterances, the expansion technique should be used systematically. Expansions can be produced at high rates quite naturally in interactive sessions with the DS child, exactly as they are used spontaneously by parents of TD children (Rondal 1985). They consist in supplying the missing obligatory components in the utterance just produced by the child (e.g., child: cat sleeping; adult: Yes, the cat is sleeping). Semantic extensions can also be used profitably (i.e., elaborating on the meaning supplied by the child in his or her utterance (e.g., child: Cat sleeping; adult: Yes, the cat is sleeping on the mat). It is not necessary that the child correctly repeats at once the expanded and/or extended forms proposed by the adult, not even that he or she tries to repeat it in any way. In the longer term, however, expanding children's utterances into more complex syntactico-semantical structures will pay off in the sense that the child, including the DS child, will gradually incorporate the grammatical material into his or her spontaneous productions. Direct and explicit corrections should be avoided, particularly with the younger child. Only with the older child, adolescent, or young adult, could more direct explicit modelling and corrections be used as a secondary way for helping to promote better grammatical language in persons with DS.

The following indications (adapted, modified, and extended from Rondal 1986, 1997) will be useful in guiding the professional trainer to follow and foster grammatical development in DS children.

## MAJOR ACQUISITIONS IN MORPHOSYNTACTIC DEVELOPMENT

### THE ACQUISITION OF MAJOR SEMANTIC RELATIONS

The semantic relational basis of a given language (originating in general cognition) comprises a set of properties and relations between entities represented lexically in the language that are coded formally in the morphosyntax of this language. The semantic basis, therefore, is central for morphosyntactic development and functioning. Sentences are only rule-governed formalizations of networks of semantic relations. Understanding a sentence (linguistically) amounts to moving backward from its surface to the array of semantic relations and lexical meanings that may be plausibly supposed to have been at the starting-point of the sentence-construction process in the speaker's head, using relevant grammatical knowledge. Expressing a sentence involves the same operations but the other way around, moving from communication motivations and non-linguistic ideas on to semantic relations and their lexical and grammatical expression.

### Two-word Stage

At first, children use single words to communicate, and then they begin to put two words together to convey more information, usually according to the following semantic relations. No exact grammatical sequential order or inflexional marking of the lexemes matters at this stage. What is important is the understanding and expression of lexicalized semantic relations.

- Possession (for example: <u>mummy car</u>)
- Location-position (<u>in box</u>)
- Qualitative attribution (<u>blue ball</u>)
- Temporal (<u>go now</u>)
- Existence notice (<u>that biscuit</u>)
- Non-existence, denial, rejection, disappearance (<u>no banana</u>; <u>all gone juice</u>)
- Recurrence (<u>more biscuit</u>)
- Conjunction (<u>cup plate</u>)
- Instrument (<u>with brush</u>)
- Accompaniment (<u>with daddy</u>)
- Ambient (<u>rain fall</u>)

- Agent–action (<u>mummy push</u>)
- Agent–object (<u>drink juice</u>)
- Agent–object (<u>daddy shoe</u>, as he puts his shoe on, for instance).

**Three-word Stage**

Extending his or her two-word utterances, the child will gradually produce three-keyword utterances modelled after the following major semantic relations (other combinations may be observed, however) either in declarative or yes–no interrogative form (a question form based on the intonation of the utterance).

- Agent–action–object (<u>Daddy hit ball</u>)
- Agent–action–locative (<u>Mummy go store</u>)
- Action–object–locative (<u>Take shoe bathroom</u>)
- Prepositional relation (<u>car in box</u>)
- Experiential utterance (<u>Baby want biscuit</u>)
- Phrase with modifier (<u>Want more cheese</u>).

**Utterances with four or five words (and more) will then become possible by the recombination of the preceding structures.**

BUILDING UP PHRASES

Phrases are the building-blocks of sentences. They are formed of particular lexemes disposed in specific orders around a syntactic head. As a consequence, at this level of development sequential ordering matters but not, instead, the appropriate use of morphological inflections for marking grammatical concord. The major phrases in the English language for my limited purpose here are: nominal, verbal, attributive, and prepositional. I shall leave aside the adverbial and the conjunction phrases (see Halliday 1985, for example, for more details).

**Phrases**

*Noun phrases* (NPs) centre around a semantic core and syntactic head that may be either a common noun, a proper noun, or a personal pronoun; preceding or following the head, one may have one or several modifiers (for example, articles, qualifiers, quantifiers, classifiers, deictics).

- Article + common noun (<u>the ball</u>; <u>a pencil</u>)
- Article + qualifier + noun (<u>a red ball</u>)
- Quantifier + noun (<u>two balls</u>)
- Article + noun + classifier [<u>the house</u> (of) <u>the doggie</u>]
- Deictic + noun (<u>my house</u>; <u>that house</u>)

- Linear combinations of the preceding structures [the little house (of) the doggie]

*Verb phrases* (VPs): are constituted by a conjugated verb, as head of phrase, followed by one (or several) NPs.

- Verb + NP [(Mummy) cooks the meal]

*Prepositional phrases* (PPs) are composed of a preposition (head of phrase) followed by a NP.

- Prepositional + NP [(ball) under the car]

*Attributive phrases* (APs) are preceded by an auxiliary verb and have an attribute (of the grammatical subject) as head, which may be accompanied by a modifier (e.g., adverb). Most of the time, the attribute is an adjective.

- Auxiliary-Be + AP + adjective [(The house) is red]
- Auxiliary-Be + AP + modifier + adjective [(The doggie) is all black]

**Function Words**

As the examples in the first section above show, early combinatorial language is mostly deprived of function (or grammatical) words such as articles, pronouns, auxiliaries, and prepositions. The following steps in development will concern the comprehension and the production of these structures. This development is quite complex linguistically and cognitively and, as a consequence, is usually spread over a longer period of time even in the TD child.

*Articles*

The correct use of the articles the and a may be difficult because they are not stressed in normal talk and therefore identifying and processing them are more delicate operations. Strictly speaking, their contrastive use adds little to the meaning of the phrase, only permitting one to distinguish between specific and non-specific reference.

*Pronouns*

Pronouns are also delicate structures, replacing nouns in discourse. Some are dialogic entities (for example, I, you, we, me) referring to the speaker or the person spoken to. Others (for example, they, it, them, their) refer to entities outside the dialogic context. For these third-person personal pronouns, co-reference with the noun replaced by the pronoun must be established for the sentence to be intelligible. Most often, coreference is formally indicated by agreement in gender and number between pronoun and noun (for example, The little girl, she wore a red hat). Pronominal coreference takes some time to be mastered by typically developing children. It may be expected to cause a particular problem in comprehension and production for younger DS children.

*Auxiliaries*

In the same way as the articles, the auxiliary verbs such as <u>is</u> and <u>are</u> may be difficult because they are not usually stressed in talk and because they add little or no meaning to the sentence. They are mostly connecting structures. DS children often have difficulty learning to use them in their language.

*Prepositions*

The most common prepositions are those related to spatial localization, temporal succession, instrumentation, and accompaniment. Within spatial prepositions, the easiest to master are the topological ones, marking relations of vicinity (for example, <u>in</u>, <u>on</u>, <u>under</u>, <u>next to</u>). The projective prepositions (e.g., <u>above</u>, <u>below</u>, <u>ahead of</u>, <u>at the front</u>, <u>at the back</u>, <u>on the left</u>, <u>on the right</u>) are more difficult (cognitively). The latter demand that some sort of rule-governed projection be made on the designated entities in order to decide what part of them is front, back, left, and so forth. Temporal prepositions (for example, <u>before</u>, <u>after</u>) require that at least some minimal time-structuring be in place for their appropriate use.

## MARKING NUMBER CONCORD AND POSSESSION WITHIN PHRASES

The use of /s/ on the end of a word to indicate a plural is a grammatical rule that is learned early in typical development. A number of words have irregular plurals (such as <u>foot</u>–<u>feet</u>, <u>tooth</u>–<u>teeth</u>). These have to be learned individually, for there are no simple ways to tell them apart in advance from the words that form regular plurals.

The use of /s/ following the end of a word to indicate possession (the so-called Saxon genitive) is also learned relatively early by TD children. It is preceded by the acquisition of the possessive pronouns of the first and second persons and occurs alongside the regular use of the third-person possessive pronouns.

## INTEGRATING PHRASES INTO BASIC SENTENCES

Basic sentences (i.e., simple declarative affirmative actives) may be classified according to some of their most frequent structural compositions (full correct inflectional markings on verbs do not matter at this stage).

- NP–VP–NP (Simple transitive structures, for example: <u>The dog chases the cat. The man drives his car.</u>)
- NP–VP (Simple intransitive structures, for example: <u>The dog barks. Baby sleeps.</u>)
- NP–VP–NP–PP (More complex transitive structures, for example, <u>The dog chases the cat in the yard.</u>)
- NP–VP–PP (More complex intransitive structures, for example, <u>The dog barks in the yard.</u>)
- NP–Aux–Attribute (Simple attributive structures, for example, <u>The dog is big. The man is tall.</u>)
- Transitive or intransitive structures modified by an adverb (For example, <u>The man drives his car fast. The dog barks loudly.</u>)

'ing forms' (progressive forms) may be substituted for the non-progressive forms in some of the above combinatorial structures (for example, <u>The dog is barking. The man was driving his car fast</u>).


## DIFFERENT SYNTACTIC-PRAGMATIC TYPES OF SENTENCES

Expressing the most basic functional types of sentences (declaring, negating, questioning) is, of course, of the utmost importance in interpersonal communication. From quite early on, children understand and can use <u>no</u> when they do not want something or to do something. However, the proper formulation of negative sentences comes substantially later. To achieve this, a negative adverb has to be positioned within the sentence to perform the negating function, which additionally requires dealing properly with the auxiliary verb (for example, compare the following declarative and negative forms: <u>The cat is awake. It does not sleep. The man drives his car. He does not eat. The dog is small. It is not big</u>).

In a similar way, the typically developing child will display understanding of (unanalysed) question forms such as <u>What's that? Who's coming?</u> from quite early, and they will sometimes ask questions at the one-word stage by pointing or using something sounding like the interrogative word '<u>What?</u>'. However, the proper formulation of question sentences will come later. Two subtypes of questions may be distinguished: the 'yes–no' and the 'wh' questions. The first ones are based either on a particular intonation pattern (raising intonational level at the end of the sentence instead of lowering it, as is normally the case for declarative sentences) – for example, <u>John went there?</u> – or inverting the subject–verb order canonical for declarative sentences (for example, <u>Was John there?</u>). The 'wh' questions are constructed in such a way that a particular type of information is requested from the responder through the use of specific interrogative pronouns or adverbs – for example, a question such as <u>Who was there?</u> with an agent word, or <u>When did that happen?</u> with a time-referring word, or <u>What did you do?</u> with an object word or phrase, and so forth.

## MORPHOLOGICAL INFLECTIONS ON VERBS

Inflectional markings of three (non-orthogonal) types are effectuated on main verbs and auxiliaries. They are concerned with the person and the number of the grammatical subject (of the verb) and with the temporal aspectual relationships holding for the sentence.

Person and number markings are made on main and auxiliary verbs using particular inflections (for example, I sleep; She sleeps; I am; You are; He is; We are; They are) and personal subject pronouns. The forms for the first two persons are dialogue forms, and the third-person forms are exophoric.

Basic temporal organization is made around tenses referring to past, present, and future events (and relationships between events) in relation to the locutor's situation in time. To form many tenses properly, an auxiliary verb is needed (for example, He will be going; He has been there). The past tense of verbs comes in two forms, regular and irregular. The regular form is the 'ed'-form (for example, jumped, pushed). The irregular forms are all different, and as a consequence have to be learned individually (for example, slept, ran, made, came, had). Irregular verbs are among the most frequently used entities in the English verbal system (actually, historically, this is the major reason why they have become irregular). A number of irregular past tense forms are often learned by TD children before they learn the 'ed' form. Development regarding this verbal structure is often 'U-shaped' – children learn the irregular (most frequent) past forms first; then they learn some 'ed' forms; they then tend to generalize the 'ed rule', often extending it (wrongly) to the irregular verbs (productions such as comed, eated, drinked, are observed at these times); and eventually, they stabilize the correct dichotomy between regular and irregular verbal forms. Aspectual characteristics of the events referred to call for additional specifications justifying the existence of alternative 'tenses' in the grammar. Referring to past events, for instance, it is often the case that at least two aspectual tenses are distinguished. The so-called 'aorist' tense refers to events that are completely finished and have no important impact on the current locutory situation [for example He moved (years ago)] and, by contrast, the 'perfect' or composite past tense form (for example He has moved) is used when the event referred to may be considered as having some impact on the current locutory situation. The imperfect tense is used to refer to an event that lasted for some time in the past (for example, He was moving when we came).

## MORE ADVANCED FORMAL STRUCTURES

There are a number of more complex structures, either mono-propositional, such as the comparatives (for example, the series big, bigger, biggest; or forms such as Daddy is taller than Mummy), or bi-propositional (for example, John is taller than Bob but smaller than Robert). More complex sentence constructions mastered later by typically developing children include:

- 'X but not Y' sentences (for example, <u>It is windy but not raining</u>).
- Sentences with a relative clause derived to the right of the main clause (for example, <u>The man waited for a taxi that never came</u>). Also sentences with a relative clause embedded within the main clause (for example, <u>The man to whom I spoke this morning was waiting for a taxi</u>). Embedded relatives are notoriously more difficult to process, everything else being equal, than right-derived ones. Relative pronouns may function either as subject or object of the main verb of the main clause (for example, <u>The man who waited for a taxi wore a white hat. The man I spoke to wore a white hat. The man waited for a taxi that arrived after two hours. The man took a taxi for which he never paid</u>).
- Reversible passives (for example, <u>The black cat is chasing the white cat</u>) – as opposed to non-reversible passives (sentences such as <u>The operation was performed by the surgeon,</u> whose reversed passive would be implausible or unintelligible), the former being more difficult to understand and produced correctly later by TD children.
- Sentences with circumstantial clauses (causal, consequential, and temporal ones, in particular). They may be produced with an order matching the order in which the (real or imaginary) events have happened, will happen, or are happening, or not (the latter being more difficult and being acquired later by TD children). Similarly, the sentences may follow the natural order cause–effect or consequence, or not (the latter again being more difficult and acquired later). Contrast, for instance, the following formulations: <u>The man had breakfast and left. The man left after he had had breakfast. He was hit by the car and fell on the ground. The man fell on the ground because he had been hit by the car.</u>

## READING INSTRUCTION

The opportunity to learn to read and to be involved in reading activities is important in itself to acquire a useful level of literacy skills in a world forever more and more dependent on written and visual symbols; but also, and this is much less known, in order to improve spoken language. A number of studies conducted in the last twenty years demonstrate the feasibility and usefulness of teaching reading skills to children, adolescents, and even adults with Down syndrome (Pieterse and Center 1984; Buckley 1985; Irwin 1989; Buckley and Bird 1993; Buckley et al. 1996; Kotlinski and Kotlinski 2002). The levels reached by the DS individuals may be quite variable, however. Some subjects will achieve functional levels of literacy (8 years and above), while others will achieve a level of literacy skill that will allow them to record work in the classroom and to read with assistance. Some may not achieve any useful level of independent reading skills, but their speech and language may still benefit from literacy activities.

Regarding the benefits of literacy instruction for speech and language, Buckley (2003) reports case studies showing that DS children introduced to reading activities designed to teach spoken language as early as at 3 years of age show significantly advanced speech, language, literacy and verbal short-term memory skills in their childhood and teenage years. They show more advanced speech, language and literacy skills as teenagers than children introduced to reading after 5 or 6 years of age. Limited evidence of the benefits of ordinary literacy instruction in school based on group data is also available (Laws *et al.* 1995). The gains were approximately equivalent to two years of typical developmental progress.

Most authors consider that the principles for teaching DS children are the same as for TD children (Farrell and Gunn 2000). There is indeed no evidence that DS children of school age learn to read any differently from other children, but they may rely on a logographic strategy for longer than other children (Kay-Raining Bird *et al.* 2000). They do reach a stage when they can use alphabetic strategies for reading and for spelling. Data collected by Fletcher and Buckley (2002) indicate that DS children with reading ages of about 7 years and above can use an alphabetic strategy to decode words.

Considering the information available, the following principles (drawn from Buckley 2003, p. 148, with minor modifications) should inform the teaching of reading to DS children:

(1) Start reading activities when child (a) comprehends 50 to 100 spoken words and says or signs some, so is ready to combine words, and (b) can match and select pictures (usually at around 2:6 to 3:6 years of chronological age);
(2) Teach whole words first – 'look and say';
(3) Select words as appropriate for the child's language comprehension level and interests, starting with words the child already understands;
(4) Choose words to make sentences from the start – two-word- and three-word sentences for children under 4 years, but grammatically complete short, simple sentences for all children over 4 years;
(5) Make books using pictures of the child's own world and interests to illustrate the sentences;
(6) Always read the words and sentences with the child while he or she is learning – that is, use errorless learning techniques to prompt success;
(7) Once the child is enjoying the reading activities with familiar vocabulary, introduce new vocabulary into the reading;
(8) Always encourage the child to repeat the words and sentences with you;
(9) Practise writing alongside reading from the start, as this will draw attention to letters and help handwriting; and
(10) Teach phonics once the child has a sight vocabulary of 30 to 40 words; learning to write and spell rhyming sets of words helps.

## DISCURSIVE TRAINING

Discursive functioning in persons with Down syndrome is often lacking in macrostructure organization and in cohesion. I take macrostructure here to mean the larger discursive framework in opposition to the semantic propositional and the morphosyntactic levels (discursive or textual microstructure). Discourses vary as to their basic organization. At this level it is possible to distinguish between, at least, four major type of texts: narrative, argumentative, descriptive, and theoretical or explanatory (less relevant in the present context). Narratives are organized typically in chronological order. It is permissible to modify that order, but the interlocutor must be duly warned (so-called markedness of the expression). By default, one will expect the speaker to start the story at the beginning and go through it chronologically, optionally terminating with a personal comment or 'moral'. Argumentative texts are not necessarily organized according to a particular chronology (although they may be). The key object here is coherence (connectedness and absence of self-contradiction). A good argument is one that is relevant and does not contradict itself. Argumentative discourses may contain several arguments. It is essential not only that they do not contradict each other but also that they each contribute to bolster the case. Descriptive texts are not typically chronologically ordered (although, of course, they may be) and they do not need to be fully coherent (but, of course, they cannot be incoherent). Descriptive texts must obey referential adequacy – they must correspond in major ways with the objects or the events under description. The macrostructures mentioned above are clearly cognitive in nature, and as such can be expected to make problems for people with intellectual disabilities. Such is also the case most often for textual cohesion. According to Halliday (1985), textual cohesion is realized in four major ways:

- *Reference:* a participant or circumstantial element introduced at one place in the text can be taken as a reference point for something that follows (for example, the boy . . . he . . . him – pronominal use, in such cases, implies correct application of the coreference rule between noun and pronoun).
- *Ellipsis:* a clause or part of a clause once formulated may be presupposed and omitted at a subsequent place in text.
- *Lexical cohesion:* discursive continuity may also be established by the choice of words, which may take the form of word repetition, the presence of key words, or the choice of words that are related semantically to previous ones.
- *Conjunction:* a clause or some longer portion of text may be related to what follows by one of a set of particular words (adverbs, conjunctions) carrying relational or hierarchical meaning (for example, then, in such a way as, therefore, but, because, for).

*The above cohesive devices are often found insufficiently developed, and when they are produced are not always correctly used by persons with Down syndrome.*

## PRAGMATIC AND COMMUNICATION TRAINING

There is empirical evidence that DS individuals can improve their pragmatic language and language-tied social skills through participation in adequately designed intervention programmes (Abbeduto and Hesketh 1997; Abbeduto and Keller-Bell 2003). These interventions embody one of the following two approaches: either a more naturalistic one or one centring on the use of particular behavioural techniques to increase the frequency of specific pragmatic skills.

Several principles underlie the naturalistic approaches. They require the creation of an environment providing opportunities and motivations to communicate efficiently (Warren and Yoder 1998). The interaction style as controlled by the adult should be non-directive. Non-directivity implies following the child's lead by providing him or her with a more developmentally advanced or pragmatically effective linguistic means of achieving the desired interpersonal goal he or she just attempted to address. The most well-suited naturalistic approach is the 'milieu approach' (Warren 1991). Milieu intervention is typically conducted in a child's school or home, and it involves responding to naturally occurring teaching opportunities created by the child's attempts at communication.

Behavioural approaches have been used successfully for teaching particular communicative strategies to the intellectually disabled child, for example, increasing the number of verbal requests during a social episode (e.g., a meal), or improving topic initiation and maintenance in the child's conversation (Schloss and Wood 1990). But their overall usefulness as well as generalization to non-experimental contexts has still to be investigated.

## BILINGUALISM

Many parents living in bilingual or multilingual societies ask whether they should expose their DS child to two or several languages or whether it would be better, given their children's expected language delays and difficulties, to restrain the educational opportunities to monolingualism. The question is indeed a serious and a delicate one, and one that, unfortunately, the paucity of systematic data and research makes it difficult to answer. There mostly exists anecdotal evidence suggesting that a number of children and adults with ID and DS are able to learn two, sometimes three languages, to a certain extent (rarely, if ever, specified with precision, however). The levels of achievement seem to vary considerably between individuals. One systematic study has been conducted in Canada by Kay-Raining Bird *et al.* (2005). They compared the language abilities of 8 children with DS being raised bilingually with those of 3 control groups matched on developmental level (measured with the toddler form of the MacArthur Communicative Development Inventories) and an MLU of 3.5 or less (for the DS children): monolingual children with DS, monolingual TD children, and TD children raised bilingually. The bilingual children were learning English and one other language and were either balanced bilinguals or English-dominant. Results provided evidence of a similar profile of development and abilities in bilingual children to that which has been documented for monolingual children with DS. There was no evidence of a detrimental effect of bilingualism at these early stages of development although there was considerable diversity in the language abilities demonstrated by the DS individuals.

It seems reasonable to hypothesize that DS children learning a second language (L2) will meet with the same difficulties that they typically encounter in L1 learning (cf. Rondal and Edwards 1997).

On the basis of the current, admittedly scarce, knowledge of the capacities of students with ID and DS for L2 learning (either simultaneously with L1 or in succession), one would recommend the following general strategy, at least provisorily:

(1) Insist that intensive L2 exposure and/or training, in graduated immersion programmes or otherwise, be postponed for a few years (the precise delay remaining to be established from future particular developmental data). Most immersion programmes for TD children start at 4 or 5 years of age. These ages are generally considered to correspond to the period when these children have learned enough of their maternal tongue to have stabilized it in respect of the various basic receptive and productive repertoires (phonology, lexicon, and morphosyntax). Adapting to the child with moderate or severe ID, one is speaking of roughly 6 or 7 years of chronological age. What I am talking about is systematic and intensive L2 learning, not occasional or limited functional exposure. The thing that probably matters is limiting L2 influence so long as some strong basis in L1 is not yet established – and that establishment takes more time in ID children than in TD children. Acting otherwise could put the ID child at risk of having his/her first-language acquisition process additionally retarded or disturbed. The major problem may not be vocabulary exposure and learning in several languages, but rather morphosyntactic development and stabilization, which is already notoriously arduous for monolingual children with DS.

(2) In familial bilingual situations, one should try, as far as possible, to select the language of the school and the community to be privileged as the basic

language for daily use and therapy (not to the exclusion of the other familial tongue, however). Later, when this selected L1 is stabilized to a sufficient extent, L2 exposure may be attended with fewer risks of putting L1 development at risk.

(3) Of course, L2 learning (even more than L1) will have to be functionally oriented in individuals with moderate and severe intellectual disabilities.

(4) In ID individuals, L2 learning will extend over longer periods of time than in TD people for results that generally will not match those of non-disabled individuals. Beyond childhood and early adolescence, extrapolating from L1 development again (cf. Rondal and Edwards 1995), it is likely that the cost–benefit ratio in some aspects of L2 learning (particularly articulation, co-articulation, phoneme discrimination, and morphosyntax) will be less favourable. However, important learning benefits would still be expected regarding the lexical and pragmatic aspects of language.

## CONCLUSIONS

A great deal of relevant knowledge on language development in DS individuals and its difficulties exists that is of great help for guiding the work of therapists and teachers (cf. Rondal and Buckley 2003, for a full review). A major theme in this presentation has been the need to adopt a life-span perspective. This has clear implications. There is a need for language intervention to be age-appropriate and take account of the communication requirements of the individuals within their environment. It is important to stress that some aspects of language and communication skills may still improve into adult life and probably be maintained better with continued or renewed intervention at older ages. Also, recent evidence would lead one to advocate that interventionists should take seriously the importance of language learning in the first years, encouraging development as much as possible at those times. As for very early stimulation, although it is probably desirable, one should proceed with caution in the absence of precise knowledge regarding its effects on the neurogenesis of DS babies.

## REFERENCES

Abbeduto, L. and Hesketh, L. (1997). Pragmatic development in individuals with mental retardation: learning to use language in social interactions. *Mental Retardation and Developmental Disabilities Research Reviews.* 3:323–33.

Abbeduto, L. and Keller-Bell, Y. (2003). Pragmatic development and communication training. In J.A. Rondal and S. Buckley (eds), *Speech and language intervention in Down syndrome.* (pp. 98–115). London: Whurr.

Beveridge, M. (1996). School integration for Down's syndrome children: policies, problems, and processes. In J.A. Rondal, J. Perera, L. Nadel and A. Comblain (eds),

*Down's syndrome: psychological, psychobiological and socio-educational perspectives.* (pp. 207–18). London: Whurr.

Buckley, S. (2003). Literacy and language. In J.A. Rondal and S. Buckley (eds), *Speech and language intervention in Down syndrome.* (pp. 132–53). London: Whurr.

Buckley, S. and Bird, G. (1993). Teaching children with Down syndrome to read. *Down Syndrome Research and Practice.* 1(1):34–41.

Buckley, S., Bird, G. and Byrne, A. (1996). Reading acquisition by young children. In B. Stratford and P. Gunn (eds), *New approaches to Down syndrome.* (pp. 268–79). London: Cassell.

Castillo-Morales, R., Avalle, C. and Schmid, R. (1984). Possibilità di trattamento della patologia orofaciale nella sindrome di Down con la placa di regolazione motoria. *Pediatria Preventiva e Sociale.* 34:1–4.

Cholmain, C. (1994). Working on phonology with young children with Down syndrome. *Journal of Clinical Speech and Language Studies.* 1:14–35.

Cicchetti, D. and Beeghly, M. (1990). An organizational approach to the study of Down's syndrome: contributions to an integrated theory of development. In D. Cicchetti and M. Beeghly (eds), *Children with Down's syndrome: a developmental perspective.* (pp. 29–62). New York: Cambridge University Press.

Clibbens, J. (2001). Signing and lexical development in children with Down syndrome. *Down Syndrome Research and Practice.* 7:101–5.

De Andrade, D., Tavares, P., Rebello, P., Palha, M. and Tavares, M. (1998). Placa modificada para trattamento de hipotonia oro-muscular em crianças com i dade compreendida entre os 2 meses e os 2 ans. *Ortodontia.* 3(2):111–17.

Dodd, B. (1972). Comparison of babbling patterns in normal and Down's syndrome infants. *Journal of Mental Deficiency.* 16:35–40.

Dodd, B., McCormack, P. and Woodyatt, G. (1994). Evaluation of an intervention program: relation between children's phonology and parents' communicative behaviour. *American Journal of Mental Retardation.* 98(5):632–45.

Dykens, E. and Hodapp, R. (2001). Research in mental retardation: toward an etiologic approach. *Journal of Child Psychology and Psychiatry.* 42:49–71.

Dykens, E., Hodapp, R. and Leckman, J. (1994). *Behavior and development in Fragile X syndrome.* London: Sage Publications.

Fletcher, H. and Buckley, S. (2002). Phonological awareness in children with Down syndrome. *Down Syndrome Research and Practice.* 8(1):11–18.

Gibson, D. (1981). *Down's syndrome. The psychology of mongolism.* Cambridge, UK: Cambridge University Press.

Gibson, D. (1991). Down's syndrome and cognitive enhancement: not like the others. In K. Marfo (ed.), *Early intervention in transition: current perspectives on programs for handicapped children.* (pp. 61–90). New York: Praeger.

Girolametto, L. (2000). Participation parentale à un programme d'intervention précoce sur le développement du langage: Efficacité du programme parental de Hanen. *Rééducation Orthophonique.* 203:31–62.

Girolametto, L., Weitzman, E. and Clements-Baartman, J. (1998). Vocabulary intervention for children with Down syndrome: parent training using focused stimulation. *Infant–Toddler Intervention.* 8:109–26.

Guralnick, M. (1996). Future directions in early intervention for children with Down's syndrome. In J.A. Rondal, J. Perera, L. Nadel and A. Comblain (eds), *Down's syndrome: psychological, psychobiological and socio-educational perspectives.* (pp. 147–62). London: Whurr.

Guralnick, M. (ed.) (1997). *The effectiveness of early intervention.* Baltimore, MD: Brookes.

Guralnick, M., Connor, R., Hammoud, M., Gottman, J. and Kinnish, K. (1996). The peer relations of preschool children with communication disorders. *Child Development.* 67:471–89.

Halliday, M. (1985). *An introduction to functional grammar.* London: Arnold.

Hauser-Cram, P. (1989). The efficiency of early intervention. *Ab Initio.* 1:1–2.

Iacono, T., Chan, J. and Waring, R. (1998). Efficacy of a parent-implemented language intervention based on collaborative consultation. *International Journal of Language and Communication Disorders.* 33:281–303.

Irwin, K. (1989). The school achievement of children with Down's syndrome. *New Zealand Medical Journal.* 102(860):11–13.

Jarrold, C. and Baddeley, A. (1997). Short-term memory for verbal and visuo-spatial information in Down's syndrome. *Cognitive Neuropsychology.* 2:101–22.

Kay-Raining Bird, E., Cleave, P. and McConnell, I. (2000) Reading and phonological awareness in children with Down syndrome: A longitudinal study. *American Journal of Speech Language Pathology.* 9:319–30.

Kay-Raining Bird, E., Cleave, P., Trudeau, N., Thordardottir, E., Sutton, A. and Thorpe, A. (2005). The language abilities of bilingual children with Down syndrome. *American Journal of Speech Language Pathology.* 14:187–99.

Kotlinski, J. and Kotlinski, S. (2002). Teaching reading to develop language. *Down Syndrome News and Update.* 2(2):5–6.

Laws, G., Buckley, S., Bird, G., MacDonald, J. and Broadley, I. (1995). The influence of reading instruction on language and memory development in children with Down syndrome. *Down Syndrome Research and Practice.* 3(2):59–64.

Lemperle, G. (1985). Plastic surgery. In D. Lane and B. Stratford (eds), *Current approaches to Down's Syndrome.* (pp. 131–45). London: Cassell.

Mervis, C. (1990). Early conceptual development of children with Down syndrome. In D. Cicchetti and M. Beeghly (eds), *Children with Down syndrome: a developmental perspective.* (pp. 252–301). Cambridge: Cambridge University Press.

Mervis, C. and Becerra, A. (2003). Lexical development and intervention. In J.A. Rondal and S. Buckley (eds), *Speech and language intervention in Down syndrome.* (pp. 63–85). London: Whurr.

Pieterse, M. and Center, Y. (1984). The integration of eight Down syndrome children into regular schools. *Australia and New Zealand Journal of Developmental Disabilities.* 10(1):20.

Poo, P. and Gassio, R. (2000). Desarollo motor en niños con syndrome de Down. *Revista Medica Internacional sobre el Sindrome de Down.* 4(3):34–40.

Price, P. (1989). Language intervention and mother–child interaction. In M. Beveridge, G. Conti-Ramsden and I. Leudar (eds), *Language and communication in mentally handicapped people.* (pp. 185–217). London: Chapman and Hall.

Rondal, J.A. (1985). *Adult–child interactions and the process of language acquisition.* New York: Praeger.

Rondal, J.A. (1986). *Le développement du langage chez l'enfant trisomique 21. Manuel pratique d'intervention.* Brussels: Mardaga.

Rondal, J.A. (1987). *Faire parler l'enfant retardé mental. Un programme d'intervention psycholinguistique.* Brussels: Labor.

Rondal, J.A. (1994). Exceptional language development in mental retardation: natural experiments in language modularity. *Current Psychology of Cognition.* 13:427–67.

Rondal, J.A. (1995). *Exceptional language development in Down syndrome. Implications for the cognition–language relationship.* New York: Cambridge University Press.

Rondal, J.A. (1997). *Proposal for a computer-enhanced language intervention program: Cognitivo-semantical and morphosyntactic modules.* Manuscript, University of Liège, Laboratory for Psycholinguistics (unpublished).

Rondal, J.A. (1998). *Educar y hacer a hablar al niño Down. Una guia al servicio de padres y profesores.* Mexico, DF: Trillas.

Rondal, J.A. (2003). Prelinguistic training. In J.A. Rondal and S. Buckley (eds), *Speech and language intervention in Down syndrome.* (pp. 11–30). London: Whurr.

Rondal, J.A. (2004). Intersyndrome and intrasyndrome language differences. In J.A. Rondal, R. Hodapp, S. Soresi, E. Dykens and L. Nota, *Intellectual disabilities: genetics, behaviour and inclusion.* (pp. 49–113). London: Whurr.

Rondal, J.A. (in press). Language specificity. In J.A. Rondal and J. Perera (eds), *The neurobehavioral specificity of Down syndrome.* Chichester, UK: Wiley.

Rondal, J.A. and Buckley, S. (eds) (2003). *Speech and language intervention in Down syndrome.* London: Whurr.

Rondal, J.A. and Comblain, A. (1999). Current perspectives on genetic dysphasias. *Journal of Neurolinguistics.* 12:181–212.

Rondal, J.A. and Edwards, S. (1997). *Language in mental retardation.* London: Whurr.

Rondal, J.A. and Perera, J. (eds) (in press). *The neurobehavioral specificity of Down syndrome.* Chichester, UK: Wiley.

Rosenberg, S. and Abbeduto, L. (1993). *Language and communication in mental retardation. Development, processes and intervention.* Hillsdale, NJ: Erlbaum.

Rusch, J. and Karlan, G. (1983). Language training. In J. Matson and J. Mulick (eds), *Handbook of mental retardation.* (pp. 397–409). New York: Pergamon.

Rynders, J. (1994). *Supporting the education development and progress of individuals with Down's syndrome.* Communication to the Third Ross Roundtable on Critical Issues in Family Medicine, July, Washington DC.

Salmon, C., Rowan, L. and Mitchell, P. (1998). Facilitating prelinguistic communication: impact of adult prompting. *Infant–Toddler Intervention.* 8:11–27.

Schloss, P. and Wood, C. (1990). Effect of self-monitoring on maintenance and generalization of conversational skills of persons with mental retardation. *Mental Retardation.* 28:105–13.

Snyder-McLean, L. and McLean, J. (1987). Effectiveness of early intervention for children with language and communication disorders. In M. Guralnick and F. Bennett (eds), *The effectiveness of early intervention for at-risk and handicapped children.* (pp. 213–74). New York: Academic.

Stoel-Gammon, C. (1981). Speech development of infants and children with Down's syndrome. In J.K. Darby (ed.), *Speech Evaluation in Medicine.* (pp. 341–60). New York: Grune & Stratton.

Stoel-Gammon, C. (2003). Speech acquisition and approaches to intervention. In J.A. Rondal and S. Buckley (eds), *Speech and language intervention in Down syndrome.* (pp. 49–62). London: Whurr.

Turk, J., Hagerman, R., Barnicoat, A. and McEvoy, J. (1994). The fragile X syndrome. In N. Bonras (ed.), *Mental health in mental retardation: recent advances and practices.* (pp. 135–53). Cambridge, UK: Cambridge University Press.

Warren, S. and Kaiser, A. (1988). Research in early language intervention. In S. Docom and M. Karnes (eds), *Research in early childhood special education.* (pp. 89–108). Baltimore, MD: Brookes.

Warren, S. and Yoder, P. (1998). Facilitating the transition from preintentional to intentional communication. In A. Wetherby, S. Warren and J. Reichle (eds), *Transitions in prelinguistic communication.* (pp. 365–84). Baltimore, MD: Brookes.

Yoder, P. and Warren, S. (2001). Relative treatment effects of two prelinguistic communication interventions on language development in toddlers with developmental delays vary by maternal characteristics. *Journal of Speech, Language, and Hearing Research.* 44:224–37.

# 6 Cognitive Rehabilitation

GERALD MAHONEY

## SUMMARY

In this chapter, we describe an approach to rehabilitating the cognitive functioning of young children with disabilities that is associated with the cognitive strategy tradition. In this approach parents or primary care-givers are taught to use responsive interaction strategies as a means to promote their children's use of the pivotal behaviours that are the foundations for cognitive and other forms of developmental learning. This rehabilitation approach evolved from a research study we conducted that involved a large sample of children with Down Syndrome. Results indicated that children's rate of mental development was strongly associated with the degree to which parents engaged in responsive interactions with them. The Pivotal Behavior Model of Development is proposed to explain this effect. This model asserts that the influence of parental responsiveness on children's development is mediated by the impact that responsiveness has on children's use of the learning processes or strategies that are the foundations for developmental learning, which we refer to as pivotal behaviours. Finally we describe the Responsive Teaching curriculum that we developed to evaluate this approach to rehabilitation. A one-year evaluation of this curriculum indicated that it was highly effective at enhancing the cognitive and language development of children with a wide range of developmental disabilities including Down syndrome.

## COGNITIVE REHABILITATION OF YOUNG CHILDREN WITH DOWN SYNDROME: THE ROLE OF PARENTAL RESPONSIVENESS AND CHILDREN'S PIVOTAL BEHAVIOUR

At least three general approaches have been used to rehabilitate, or promote, the cognitive functioning of young children with Down Syndrome: the developmental stimulation approach; the behavioural approach; and the cognitive strategy approach. The developmental stimulation approach is one in which children are exposed to developmental and academic activities at a high level

*Therapies and Rehabilitation in Down Syndrome.* Edited by Rondal
© 2007 John Wiley & Sons Ltd

of intensity, often before the age at which such types of stimulation are normally provided to children who do not have disabilities. This approach is reflected in infant–toddler and preschool special education classrooms in which children with Down Syndrome and other disabilities are exposed to the types of developmental, pre-academic, and early academic experiences that typically developing children commonly experience in preschool settings and later. The behavioural approach is one in which children are systematically taught the skills and concepts that differentiate these children from children who have normal cognitive functioning. This approach relies on the use of highly structured instructional methods derived from applied behavioural analysis through which teachers or parents encourage children to repeat and/ or practise desired cognitive skills or concepts. The cognitive strategy approach is one in which children are provided with instructions and/or prompts to use cognitive strategies such as attention, rehearsal, practice, or planned action sequences as they participate in a variety of learning activities.

In this chapter, we will report on a series of research studies in which we first investigated how mothers influenced the cognitive development of children with Down Syndrome; next investigated the impact that responsive styles of parenting had on children's cognitive learning strategies; and finally, evaluated a curriculum in which parents were asked to accentuate responsive patterns of parenting to promote their children's use of the pivotal behaviours or learning strategies that are purported to be the foundations for early cognitive development. Results from this intervention point to a very promising approach to cognitive rehabilitation that is closely associated with the cognitive strategy tradition of rehabilitation.

## HOW PARENTS INFLUENCE CHILDREN'S COGNITIVE DEVELOPMENT

Several years ago we conducted a study to determine how parents influenced the rate of cognitive development of their young children with developmental disabilities (Mahoney et al. 1985). This study was based upon two assumptions. The first was that while children's level of cognitive functioning was undoubtedly affected by disabilities such as Down Syndrome, still the types of experiences children had in their early years of life also influenced their rate of cognitive growth. The second was that the primary environmental influence on children's early development was the information and support provided by their primary care-givers, who for most children were their mothers.

The sample for this study included 60 mother–child pairs in which all but 6 of the children had Down Syndrome. The sample included twenty children each within the 12-, 24-, and 36-month age-ranges. For the entire sample, the children's average chronological age was 24.7 months and their average Bayley Developmental Age (Bayley 1969) was 13.9 months.

We examined how mothers' style of interacting with their children was related to their children's general rate of cognitive development as measured by the *Bayley Scales of Mental Development* (Bayley 1969). Mothers were videotaped while they played with their children in their homes with a set of developmentally appropriate toys. The first 10 minutes of these videotapes were coded with a global rating scale referred to as the Maternal Behavior Rating Scale (MBRS: Mahoney *et al.* 1986). The 18 items on this scale assessed three dimensions of mothers' interactive style. These included responsiveness or child orientation, quantity of stimulation, and directiveness or performance orientation. Responsiveness/Child orientation included items such as sensitivity, responsiveness, reciprocity, enjoyment and playfulness. Quantity of stimulation included items that assessed how much social, physical and verbal stimulation mothers provided their children. Directiveness or Performance orientation included items that assessed how much mothers attempted to teach developmental skills and direct their children's play.

On a limited basis, this procedure allowed us to examine the potential merits of the competing approaches for rehabilitating the cognitive functioning of young children with disabilities. If children's cognitive development was influenced by the amount of developmental stimulation they received, then their Bayley Mental Development scores should be related to the Quantity of stimulation their mothers provided while interacting with them. If children's cognitive development was related to the types of 'structured skills teaching' commonly associated with the behavioural approach, then their Bayley Mental Development scores should be related to the their mothers' Directiveness or Performance orientation. However, if both developmental stimulation and structured teaching contributed to children's cognitive development, then both mothers' Quantity of stimulation and their Directiveness/Performance orientation should be positively associated with their rate of cognitive growth.

Consistently with the underlying assumptions made in this study, the way mothers interacted with their children accounted for 25 per cent of the variability in children's Bayley Mental Development scores. The cognitive functioning of this sample of children was clearly affected by their disabilities, as was indicated by the groups' average developmental quotients, which were in the moderate range of mental retardation. Nonetheless, even though all these children had disabilities that affected their cognitive functioning, their developmental quotients ranged from high scores that were within the average range of intellectual functioning to low scores that were within the severe range of mental retardation. The way mothers interacted with their children appeared to account for a substantial proportion, although clearly not all, of this variability.

The second set of findings was somewhat surprising given the predominant models of cognitive rehabilitation being used with young children with disabilities at that time (Bailey and Wolery 1984; Goodman 1992). Whether they were 12, 24 or 36 months of age, the children who had the highest rates of development were the children whose mothers were high in Responsiveness or Child orientation, and low in Directiveness or Performance orientation (Mahoney *et al.* 1985). The Quantity of stimulation that mothers provided during their interactions with their children was not statistically associated with children's rate of development.

In general, these findings were incompatible with the assumptions underlying the two major cognitive rehabilitation approaches being used at that time. On the one hand they contradicted the developmental stimulation approach in so far as they suggested that the amount of stimulation mothers provided their children had no impact on their children's rate of cognitive development. On the other hand, they also contradicted the behavioural approach by indicating that children whose mothers attempted to teach developmental behaviours by guiding and directing them had lower Bayley Mental Development scores than children whose mothers engaged interactions in which they focused on enjoying and responding to their children by encouraging and supporting the behaviours that the children themselves initiated. Yet despite the apparent inconsistency of these findings with contemporary cognitive rehabilitation approaches, the results were not surprising, owing to the fact that before this study was published similar findings had been reported from investigations of parent–child interaction that involved children who did not have disabilities (e.g., Ainsworth and Bell 1975; Elardo *et al.*1975; Stern *et al.* 1969; Lewis and Goldberg 1969).

## HOW DOES RESPONSIVENESS PROMOTE CHILDREN'S LEARNING AND DEVELOPMENT?

In contemporary cognitive rehabilitation, intervention objectives usually consist of the developmental behaviours and concepts that children have not yet mastered (Lynch and Beare 1990; Pretti-Frontczak and Bricker 2000; Weisenfeld 1986). This is based upon the idea that children who have cognitive delays will 'catch up' as they learn and use these higher-level cognitive skills. Directive instructional procedures are often used to help children perform and learn the skills that have been targeted as their intervention objectives, since children are unlikely to engage in these behaviours on their own.

However, the idea that children's development is accelerated by teaching them developmental skills that they do not know cannot be the way that responsive interaction promotes development. Parents who are responsive focus primarily on encouraging their children to say and do things they already know. They support their children by joining in their activity and doing or saying things that are similar to what their children are doing and saying (Mahoney and MacDonald 2007). The more parents encourage their children to engage in behaviours that they are not yet able to perform, the less responsive and the more directive they become. Thus, one must ask how responsive interaction promotes children's development if it does not help the children learn the targeted higher-level developmental skills. To attempt to understand this apparent paradox we conducted the following investigation.

This study included 45 infants and toddlers with developmental disabilities who were 25 months old and had a variety of developmental problems (Mahoney *et al.*, in press). These children were divided into two groups: children of High Responsive Mothers ($n = 28$) and children of Low Responsive Mothers ($n = 17$) on the basis of ratings of how mothers interacted with their children using the MBRS (Mahoney 1999). The manner in which these children interacted with their mothers was then measured using the Child Behavior Rating Scale (CBRS: Mahoney and Wheeden 1998). As is illustrated in Fig. 6.1, children of High Responsive mothers had higher ratings on each of the seven CBRS items than did children of Low Responsive Mothers.

Results from the comparison of these two groups of children suggested that the effects of maternal responsive interaction on children's development may be related to the impact it has on several critical child engagement behaviours. Most of the behaviours measured by the CBRS are considered by child development experts to be the processes or patterns of behaviour that children must engage in in order to learn. The amount children learn from a particular activ-

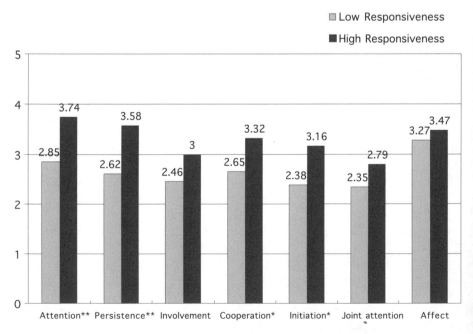

**Figure 6.1.** The relationship between mothers' and children's global pivotal behaviour.

ity or experience is thought to be highly dependent on how actively they are engaged in the activity. Many of the behaviours that are assessed by the Child Behavior Rating Scale reflect the critical processes that children utilize to initiate and maintain active engagement in their social and non-social activities.

To examine the idea that children's developmental learning may be influenced by the amount they use the engagement behaviours measured by the CBRS, we divided the 45 infants and toddlers described above into two groups, High Engagers and Low Engagers. High Engagers had composite CBRS scores that were above the midpoint, while Low Engagers had scores that were at the midpoint or lower. We then compared the average developmental age scores of these children on two developmental measures, the Vineland Adaptive Behavior Scale (Sparrow *et al.* 1984) and the Transdisciplinary Play Based Assessment (TPBA: Linder 1993), controlling for children's chronological age. As illustrated in Fig. 6.2, across the nine subscales of these two assessments, children who were High Engagers had higher developmental ages than children who were Low Engagers, and these differences were statistically significant.

Finally we conducted a series of regression analyses to determine whether the relationship between parental responsiveness and children's development

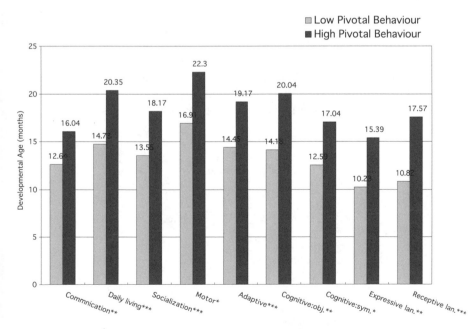

**Figure 6.2.** The relationship of children's pivotal behaviour level to their child development ages.

might be mediated by the impact that responsiveness has on children's engagement behaviours. Results indicated that maternal responsiveness had a significant relationship both with children's engagement behaviour and with 7 of the 9 child development subscale scores. However, when both children's pivotal behaviour and mothers' responsiveness were regressed on measures of children's development, the effect of children's engagement behaviour was nearly 3 times greater than the effect of maternal responsiveness. Furthermore, the effect of maternal responsiveness on children's development was no longer significant when the effect of children's engagement behaviour was controlled. This pattern of results provided strong evidence that children's engagement behaviour mediates the relationship between maternal responsiveness and their rate of development (Barron and Kenny 1986).

In general, these results suggest that the behaviours parents encourage when they interact responsively with their children are the learning processes that are the foundations for cognitive and other forms of developmental learning. Following the work of Koegel and his colleagues (Koegel *et al.* 1999), we refer to these as pivotal behaviours. That is, the child behaviours that parents promote by interacting responsively are pivotal to wide areas of functioning to the extent that improvements in these behaviours enhance children's ability to learn the skills and concepts that are the foundations for higher levels of cognitive and other domains of developmental functioning.

On the basis of this research, we proposed the Pivotal Behavior Model of Development to explain the early developmental learning of all children, including children with Down Syndrome (Mahoney *et al.*, in press). As indicated in Fig. 6.3, this model postulates that the behaviours that are most critical to children's developmental learning are the pivotal behaviours, or learning strategies, that are promoted through responsive interaction, rather than the discrete skills or behaviours that are commonly targeted in developmental interventions. By interacting responsively with children, adults influence chil-

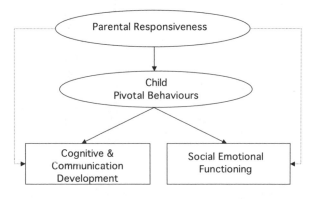

**Figure 6.3.** The Pivotal Behavior Model of Development.

dren's developmental learning *less* by teaching the skills and behaviours that are the benchmarks of higher levels of developmental functioning, and *more* by encouraging children to use the pivotal behaviours, or learning strategies, that children must use to learn from each of their daily, routine social and non-social activities. The more responsively adults interact with children, the more likely are children to use their pivotal behaviours, which in turn enhance the efficiency of their learning during their daily routines.

According to the Pivotal Behavior Model of Development the positive impact that parental responsiveness has on the cognitive functioning of children with Down Syndrome and other disabilities (Mahoney *et al.* 1985) is thus related to the long-term effects that responsiveness has on children's use of pivotal behaviour. Parents who interact with their children as little as one hour per day engage in more than 220,000 discrete interactions with their children each year (Mahoney and MacDonald 2007). In so far as parents' style of interaction transcends each of these interactions, highly responsive parents continually replicate the interactive effects on children's pivotal behaviours that are depicted in Fig. 6.1. Over time, this repetitive pattern of parent–child interaction helps children learn to become habitual users of pivotal developmental behaviours that increase their developmental learning efficiency in every social and non-social experience they have. Children's enhanced learning efficiency helps them attain their maximum level of developmental potential, which is reflected in higher Bayley Mental Development scores.

## REHABILITATING CHILDREN'S DEVELOPMENT THROUGH RELATIONSHIP FOCUSED INTERVENTION

The research reported above came from correlational studies in which we examined the relationship between parental responsiveness, children's mental development and children's use of pivotal behaviours as measured at the same point in time. While the results from these studies are consistent with the Pivotal Behavior Model of Development, they are inadequate for supporting the causal relationships that this model postulates. Many believe that the way that parents interact with their children is determined partly by effects that their children's behaviour has on them (Bell 1979; Sameroff and Fiese 2000). They have argued that parents tend to be more directive and less responsive with children who have significant developmental delays, because this type of interactive support is necessary to help these children participate more actively in both their play and social interactions (Roach *et al.* 1998; Tannock 1988). According to this position, the data reported above may not reflect the causal influences of parental responsiveness on children's development; rather, they reflect the necessary accommodations parents must make to help their children with significant developmental delays experience more appropriate developmental learning opportunities.

To conduct a more rigorous test of the causal relationships associated with the Pivotal Behavior Model of Development we conducted an evaluation of a Relationship Focused Intervention referred to as Responsive Teaching (Mahoney and Perales 2005). Relationship Focused Intervention (RFI) is the generic name of developmental interventions that are designed to encourage parents to use responsive strategies during routine interactions with their children. As many as 15 studies have been reported indicating that RFI can encourage parents to engage in more responsive interactions with their children, which in turn results in positive outcomes for children with developmental risks and disabilities (McCollum and Hemmeter 1986). These studies have included children between 2 and 60 months of age who have had social-environmental risks, moderate to severe developmental delays, and language delays, as well as children with cerebral palsy, autism and Down Syndrome.

The common element of RFIs is that they use responsive interaction strategies as a method of helping parents learn to interact more responsively with their children. These strategies are simple, concrete exercises or reminders that parents use to monitor their behaviour with their children and which help them to experience the effects of responsiveness on their children's behaviour. These strategies are designed to promote the various elements involved in responsive interaction, including: *Reciprocity* (e.g., Take One Turn and Wait); *Contingency* (e.g., Respond Quickly To My Child's Signals, Cries, or Nonverbal Requests); *Non-Directiveness* (e.g., Communicate Without Asking Questions; Expand To Show My Child The Next Developmental Step); *Affect* (e.g., Be Animated; Respond to my Child in Playful Ways); and *Match* (e.g., Request Actions that Match My Child's Developmental Level; Follow My Child's Lead). They help parents engage in responsive interaction before this is their routine style of interacting with their children. As parents use responsive interaction strategies, many discover the impact responsiveness has on their children's engagement and participation. These experiences help parents appreciate the implications this style of interaction has for all encounters with their children. It motivates them to incorporate these strategies into their spontaneous interactions, and eventually results in their instinctively using a responsive style of interacting with their children.

Responsive Teaching (RT) (Mahoney and MacDonald 2006) uses a similar rationale and similar intervention procedures to most of the existing RFIs, but has three features that distinguish it from these models. First, RT has incorporated most of the responsive interaction strategies that have been described in all the major RFI curricula currently being used [e.g., Hanen (Sussman 1999), ECO (MacDonald 1989), Floor Time (Greenspan and Weider 1998), and INREAL (Weiss 1981)]. It has 66 different strategies that promote 16 dimensions of responsive interactive behaviour.

Second, RT is based upon the Pivotal Behavior Model of Development and is explicitly designed to address a small set of 'pivotal behaviours' as intervention objectives. In this curriculum, pivotal behaviours consist of 16 behavioural processes that children use to learn developmental skills and competencies across the three developmental domains of cognition, communication and social emotional functioning. The pivotal behaviours included in Responsive Teaching were identified from contemporary theory and research in child development, including constructivist theories of cognitive development (Piaget 1963; Vygotsky 1978), communication theories of language develop-ment (Bates *et al.* 1979; Bruner 1975, 1983), and developmental theories of social-emotional development (Bowlby 1969; Goleman 1995). They are the developmental behaviours that parents and others promote by engaging in responsive interaction.

Third, RT is a fully manualized curriculum that uses three activities to help parents address concerns for their children: Responsive Teaching Strategies, Discussion Topics (Child Development Theory) and Family Action Plans (e.g., plans to incorporate RT into children's daily routine/natural environ-ment). For each pivotal behaviour intervention objective included in Responsive Teaching, there are 6 to 10 sets of Discussion Points. These describe in simple language the theories of development that are the basis for this curriculum. They explain how the pivotal behaviour that has been targeted as the interven-tion objective will both improve children's developmental learning and help parents attain the outcome they want for their child. Discussion Points have been designed so that parents can complete each intervention session having a few clearly defined ideas to think about that support the RT strategies that they have been asked to use with their children.

In our evaluation of RT we examined whether children who received this intervention made significant developmental and social emotional improve-ments, and whether the improvements they achieved were consistent with the Pivotal Behavior Model of Development. In other words, we were interested in determining whether the developmental improvements children made in intervention were related either to their parents' learning to interact more responsively or to improvements in children's use of pivotal behaviours.

Fifty mother–child pairs participated in this evaluation. The children's ages ranged from 12 to 54 months, with 85 per cent of the children being younger than 36 months when they began. The average age of the mothers was 32.6 years and most were Caucasian (89.1 per cent) and married (92.7 per cent). The sample included 20 children with Autism Spectrum Disorders (ASD) and 30 children with Developmental Disorders (DD). All these children had sig-nificant delays in cognition and communication.

RT intervention sessions were conducted individually with parents and their children either in homes or centre-based settings. Each session focused on one or two pivotal behaviours that were relevant to the needs of the child. For each pivotal behaviour, the interventionist introduced one or two sets of Discussion Points to provide parents with background information about the pivotal behaviours they are being asked to encourage their children to use throughout the daily routine. Sessions also helped parents learn and use one or two RT strategies that the curriculum recommends for promoting the pivotal behaviours being targeted.

Subjects received RT during weekly one-hour sessions. They received an average of 33 sessions over a one-year period of time. A comprehensive child development assessment was conducted at the beginning and end of intervention to evaluate the effects of this intervention. The Transdisciplinary Play Based Assessment (Linder 1993) was used to assess children's cognitive and language development. Mothers' style of interaction and children's pivotal behaviour were also assessed from a seven-minute videotaped observation of children and mothers playing together. The MBRS (Mahoney 1999) was used to assess mothers' style of interacting with their children, and the CBRS (Mahoney and Wheeden 1998) was used to assess children's pivotal behaviour.

As expected, pre/post comparisons indicated that Responsive Teaching strategies helped mothers make significant increases in their levels of Responsiveness and Affect while interacting with their children. In addition, over the course of intervention children made improvements in all seven of the pivotal behaviours assessed by the CBRS. To assess intervention effects on children's cognitive and language development a proportional change index (PCI: Wolery 1983) was computed. PCIs compare children's rate of development during intervention to their rate of development before intervention as measured by the TPBA. PCIs indicated that children's rate of development during intervention was 109 per cent greater than it was before intervention. Specifically children made a 64 per cent increase in their rate of cognitive development, a 167 per cent increase in their rate of expressive language development and a 138 per cent increase in their receptive language development.

To determine whether Responsive Teaching was truly responsible for these improvements, analyses were conducted to examine if the changes in mothers' responsiveness and children's pivotal behaviour that were promoted through Responsive Teaching were related to the developmental improvements children made. If the children who made the greatest improvements were the ones whose mothers' changes in responsiveness resulted in the improvements in their pivotal behaviour, then there would be a strong reason to believe that Responsive Teaching is a highly effective developmental intervention (Shadish *et al.* 2002).

Results from these analyses produced the following findings. First, changes in mothers' responsiveness during intervention accounted for 20 per cent of the variance in changes in children's pivotal behaviour. There was a linear relationship between the degree to which mothers changed their level of responsiveness and changes in children's pivotal behaviour. When mothers did not change their responsiveness, children made negligible increases in their pivotal behaviours. However, when mothers became more responsive, the degree that children increased their pivotal behaviour was directly related to the degree to which mothers changed their responsiveness. The more responsive mothers became during intervention, the more children increased their pivotal behaviour.

Second, changes in children's pivotal behaviour accounted for an average of 10 per cent of the variability in improvements in children's rate of cognitive and communication development. In other words, how much children's pivotal behaviour changed during intervention was related to the magnitude of the improvements they made in their cognitive and language Developmental Ages. Children who did not change their pivotal behaviour during intervention attained Developmental Age scores at the end of intervention that were comparable to their expected Developmental Age scores. However, children who increased their pivotal behaviour attained Developmental Ages that were greater than their Expected Developmental Ages.

Overall, results from this evaluation indicated that children made remarkable developmental improvements when their parents used Responsive Teaching with them. The magnitude of the improvements we observed is comparable to, and in most cases far greater than, the level of improvements that have been reported for most other early intervention procedures (cf. Guralnick 1997). While there was no control group in this study, the analyses we conducted suggested that the intervention effects we observed were indeed causally related to Responsive Teaching. Approximately one-third of the parents who participated in this project were not very successful in using RT strategies. This was indicated by the fact that the RT strategies had no impact on these mothers' level of responsiveness with their children. Children of these mothers made no improvements in either their pivotal behaviour or their rate of cognitive and language development during intervention. However, for the remaining two-thirds of the sample, the picture was the opposite. RT strategies were effective at helping these mothers learn to interact more responsively with their children. How much these mothers improved their responsiveness was related both to increases in their children's pivotal behaviour and to improvements in their children's rate of cognitive and language development.

## IMPLICATIONS FOR THE COGNITIVE REHABILITATION OF YOUNG CHILDREN WITH DOWN SYNDROME

There are several important implications that this evaluation of Responsive Teaching has for the cognitive rehabilitation of children with Down Syndrome. First, RT is as likely to be effective with children with Down Syndrome as it is for children with other developmental disabilities. In this regard, it is important to note that children with Down Syndrome were the starting-point for this curriculum. We developed this curriculum because of our research findings, which suggested that parental responsiveness played a major role in fostering the cognitive functioning of young children with Down Syndrome and other disabilities.

In addition, the overall results from this evaluation indicated that RT can enhance the developmental status of children with a wide range of disabilities, including children with Down Syndrome. Although only one child with Down Syndrome participated in this evaluation, this child made developmental gains that were comparable to those of the other children. He made a 113 per cent improvement across all developmental domains and an 84 per cent improvement in his rate of cognitive development. While these results are encouraging, clearly they are not sufficient for claiming that RT is an effective intervention for all children with Down Syndrome. To make such a claim, RT would need to be validated with a larger, more representative sample of children with Down Syndrome, and the intervention outcomes would need to be examined for more than one year.

Second, results from this evaluation provide support for the notion that children's pivotal behaviour is a critical mediator of the developmental improvements they make in intervention. Consistent with the Pivotal Behavior Model of Development, the increased rates of cognitive and language development that occurred during intervention were significantly associated with improvements in children's pivotal developmental behaviours. In the area of cognitive functioning, the pivotal behaviours targeted in RT included social play, initiation, exploration, practice and problem-solving. Children's increased use of these behaviours appears to have resulted in improvements in the cognitive activities or processes that are the basis for constructive learning as described by Piaget (1963).

Third, the research findings reported in this paper are generally supportive of the strategic approach to cognitive rehabilitation that was described at the outset of this chapter. The cognitive strategy approach is based upon the theory that children can become more efficient learners when they increase their use of the strategies or processes that are required for various types of learning activities. While there is a long tradition of implementing this approach with older children who have various types of disabilities and learning challenges, the cognitive strategy approach has been far less popular for children under 6 years of age. It has been problematic with this age range of children because of the difficulty of identifying procedures for sustaining children's use of these strategies.

Perhaps the key to the effectiveness of Responsive Teaching is that the methods this intervention uses to sustain children's pivotal behaviours are responsive interaction strategies that any adult can integrate into their routine, spontaneous interactions with children. However, we believe that parents played a particularly crucial role in this regard, both because of the special relationship they have with their children and because of the overwhelming amount of time they are with their children compared to most other adults. In so far as parents constantly engage in responsive interactions with their children, they have a unique opportunity to help their children become habitual users of the pivotal behaviours that are the foundations for cognitive learning.

Fourth, one of the more interesting findings from this evaluation was that the same responsive interaction strategies that were used to promote children's cognitive functioning were simultaneously effective at promoting their communication. While the Responsive Teaching curriculum is designed so that it can address three different areas of child development, viz. cognition, communication, and social-emotional functioning, the evaluation indicated that children's progress in these domains had less to do with the extent to which intervention focused on these domains, and more to do with how responsive children's mothers became during intervention. Thus it appears that the instructional strategies that RT recommends to promote children's cognitive development also help to address children's communication, even when this is not the focus of intervention.

These findings are important for at least two reasons. First they point to a rehabilitation method that can be used across disciplines. In intervention programmes where different specialists are employed to address the cognitive and communication needs of children, Responsive Teaching provides a method that each of these professionals can use to address their own area of expertise in a way that complements the work being done by the other. This is particularly important when specialists work directly with parents, since parents are much more likely to follow through with recommendations from different professionals that are based upon a similar intervention philosophy and similar strategies. Second, these findings suggest that when only one interventionist is available to work with a child and her family, as often happens in the United States, even though the recommendations by this interventionist may be focused on only one domain of development, the strategies that parents are asked to use with their children are as likely to address developmental needs in other domains that are not being targeted directly.

## CONCLUSIONS

In this chapter we have described an approach to rehabilitating the cognitive functioning of young children with disabilities in which parents or primary care-givers are taught to use responsive interaction strategies as a means to promote their children's use of the pivotal behaviours that are the foundations for cognitive and other forms of developmental learning. We described how this rehabilitation approach evolved from a research study that involved a large sample of children with Down Syndrome. Results from this study indicated that children's rate of mental development in the first three years of life was strongly associated with the degree to which parents engaged in responsive interactions with their children. We proposed the Pivotal Behavior Model of Development to explain this effect. This model asserts that the influence of parental responsiveness on children's development is mediated by the impact that responsiveness has on children's use of the learning processes or strategies that are the foundations for developmental learning, which we referred to as pivotal behaviours.

Finally we described the Responsive Teaching curriculum that we developed to evaluate this approach to rehabilitation. This curriculum was designed to help parents become more effective at promoting their children's development by infusing Responsive Teaching strategies into their routine interactions with them. A one-year evaluation of this curriculum showed that it was highly effective at enhancing the cognitive and language development of children with a wide range of developmental disabilities. While only one child with Down Syndrome participated in this evaluation, the research findings that led to the development of this intervention point to the likelihood of its effectiveness with children with Down Syndrome.

## REFERENCES

Ainsworth, M.D. and Bell, S.M. (1975). Mother–infant interaction and the development of competence. In K.J. Connelly and J. Bruner (eds), *The growth of competence.* (pp. 97–118). New York: Academic.

Bailey, D.B. and Wolery, M. (1984). *Teaching infants and preschoolers with handicaps.* Columbus, OH: Merrill.

Barron, R. and Kenny, D. (1986). The moderator–mediator variable distinction in social psychological research: conceptual, strategic and statistical considerations. *Journal of Personality and Social Psychology.* 51:1178–81.

Bates, E., Benigni, L., Bretherton, L., Camioni, L. and Volterra, V. (1979). *The emergence of symbols: Cognition and communication in infancy.* New York: Academic.

Bayley, N. (1969). *Bayley Scales of Infant Development.* New York: The Psychological Corporation.

Bell, R.Q. (1979). Parent, child and reciprocal influences. *American Psychologist.* 34:821–6.

Bowlby, J. (1969). *Attachment and loss.* New York: Basic Books.

Bruner, J.S. (1975). From communication to language: a psychological perspective. *Cognition.* 3:255–87.

Bruner, J. (1983). *Child talk.* New York: Norton.

Elardo, R., Bradley, R. and Caldwell, B.M. (1975). The relation of infants' home environments to mental test performances from six to thirty six months: a longitudinal analysis. *Child Development.* 46:71–6.

Goleman, D. (1995). *Emotional intelligence.* New York: Bantam.

Goodman, J.F. (1992). *When Slow is Fast Enough.* New York: Guilford Press.

Greenspan, S. and Wieder, S. (1998). *The Child with Special Needs.* Reading, MA: Addison-Wesley.

Guralnick, M.J. (ed.) (1997). *The Effectiveness of Early Intervention.* (pp. 549–76). Baltimore, MD: Brookes.

Koegel, R.L., Koegel, L.K. and Carter, C.M. (1999). Pivotal teaching interactions for children with autism. *School Psychology Review*. 28(4):576–94. Baltimore, MD: Brookes.

Lewis, M. and Goldberg, S. (1969). Perceptual–cognitive development in infancy: a generalized expectancy model as a function of mother–infant interaction. *Merrill Palmer Quarterly*. 15:81–100.

Linder, T.W. (1993). *Transdisciplinary play-based assessment: A functional approach to working with young children*. Baltimore, MD: Brookes.

Lynch, E.C. and Beare, P.L. (1990). The quality of IEP objectives and their relevance to instruction for students with mental retardation and behavioral disorders. *Remedial and Special Education*. 11(2):48–55.

McCollum, J.A. and Hemmeter, M.L. (1997). Parent–child interaction intervention when children have disabilities. In M.J. Guralnick (ed.) *The Effectiveness of Early Intervention*. pp. 549–76. Baltimore: Brookes.

MacDonald, J.D. (1989). *Becoming Partners with Children: From Play to Conversation*. San Antonio, TX: Special Press.

Mahoney, G. (1999). *The Maternal Behavior Rating Scale–Revised (unpublished)*. Available from the author, Mandel School of Applied Social Sciences, 11235 Bellflower Rd., Cleveland, OH 44106-7164.

Mahoney, G. and MacDonald, J. (2007). *Autism and developmental delays in young children: The Responsive Teaching curriculum for parents and professionals*. Austin, TX: PRO-ED.

Mahoney, G. and Perales, F. (2005). A comparison of the impact of relationship-focused intervention on young children with Pervasive Developmental Disorders and other disabilities. *Journal of Developmental and Behavioral Pediatrics*. 26(2):77–85.

Mahoney, G. and Wheeden, C. (1998). Effects of teacher style on the engagement of preschool aged children with special learning needs. *Journal of Developmental and Learning Disorders*. 2(2):293–315.

Mahoney, G., Finger, I. and Powell, A. (1985). The relationship between maternal behavioral style to the developmental status of mentally retarded infants. *American Journal of Mental Deficiency*. 90:296–302.

Mahoney, G., Powell, A. and Finger, I. (1986). The maternal behavior rating scale. *Topics in Early Childhood Special Education*. 6:44–56.

Mahoney, G., Kim, J.M. and Lin, C.S. (in press). Parental responsiveness and children's pivotal behavior: The keys to intervention effectiveness. *Infants and Young Children*.

Piaget, J. (1963). *The psychology of intelligence*. Totowa, NJ: Littlefield, Adams and Co.

Pretti-Frontczak, K. and Bricker, D. (2000). Enhancing the quality of Individualized Educational Plan (IEP) goals and objectives. *Journal of Early Intervention*. 23(2):92–105.

Roach, M.A., Barratt, M.S., Miller, J.F. and Leavitt, L.A. (1998). The structure of mother–child play: young children with Down syndrome and typically developing children. *Developmental Psychology*. 34(1):77–87.

Sameroff, A.J. and Fiese, B.H. (2000). Models of development and developmental risk. In C. Zeanah (ed.), *Handbook of infant mental health*. (pp. 374–416). New York: Guilford.

Shadish, W.R., Cook, T.D. and Campbell, D.T. (2002). *Experimental and quasi-experimental designs for generalized causal influence*. New York: Houghton Mifflin.

Sparrow, S.S., Balla, D.A. and Cicchetti, D.V. (1984). *Vineland adaptive behavior scales*. Minneapolis, MN: American Guidance Services.

Stern, G.G., Caldwell, B.M., Hersher, T., Lipton, E.L. and Richmond, J.B. (1969). A factor analytic study of the mother–infant dyad. *Child Development*. 40:163–82.

Sussman, F. (1999). *More Than Words*. Toronto: Hanen Centre.

Tannock, R. (1988). Mothers' directiveness in their interactions with their children with and without Down syndrome. *American Journal of Mental Retardation*. 93(2):154–65.

Vygotsky, L. (1978). *Mind in society*. Cambridge, MA: Harvard University Press.

Weisenfeld, R.B. (1986). The IEPs of Down syndrome children. *Education and Training in Mental Retardation and Developmental Disabilities*. 21(3):211–19.

Weiss, R.S. (1981). INREAL intervention for language handicapped and bilingual children. *Journal of the Division of Early Childhood*. 4:40–51.

Wolery, M. (1983). Proportional change index: An alternative for comparing child change data. *Exceptional Children*. 50:167–70.

# 7 Psychomotor Rehabilitation in Down Syndrome

GIOVANNI MARIA GUAZZO

## SUMMARY

Motor abilities are the skills that allow us to manipulate, move around in, and explore the world. It is clear that the programming and the execution of movement schemas require the activation of a series of extremely complex and articulated processes, quite similar to those implemented by other types of cognitive learning processes. Children with Down Syndrome have problems with motor learning that are due to deficits in programming, execution and control. Young children with Down Syndrome tend to experience hypotonia (low muscle tone), hyperflexibility, and delays in the emergence and fading of reflexes and automatic patterns of movement (Haley 1986, 1987; Rast and Harris 1985).

Psychomotor Rehabilitation is commonly used as a component of motor intervention for children with movement dysfunction. Although psychomotor rehabilitation is widely used as a component of various therapeutic programmes, scientific studies have demonstrated the benefits of these therapies in young children with Down Syndrome (Guazzo 1990; Harris 1981).

## INTRODUCTION

During the first part of infancy, the child passes from nearly complete dependency on the adult to relative autonomy. She manipulates objects, moves in the environment, and explores the space around her. Unquestionably, the development of these abilities is connected with the interaction of several systems, among which, beyond the factors inherent in the individual nervous system, are the features of the environment (for example, the structuration of space, the degree of reinforcement, the force of gravity) and the biomechanical characteristics of the individual (for example, the inertial, static and dynamic forces involved in movements). Therefore the acquisition of a new motoric routine or pattern depends upon the continuous cooperation among

*Therapies and Rehabilitation in Down Syndrome.* Edited by Rondal
© 2007 John Wiley & Sons Ltd

the various factors (even the non-neurological factors) that contribute to that specific routine or pattern (Thelen 1989, 1994; Thelen *et al.* 1993; Thelen and Smith 1994). During the first two years of life, the child develops several major motor abilities. She become able to raises her head, to orient the upper limbs, and gradually to grab objects. She maintains the seated position and, if helped, the orthostatic one, crawls on all fours, walks if held by the hand, etc. More precisely, we can identify two lines of development. First, an ever-increasing mobility: this allows her to widen the range of action, to explore a progressively more extended environment, and to take up whichever object attracts her attention. The second line of development consists of a tendency to achieve the ability to walk. Indeed, walking allows her to know the environment and renders her exploratory capacities almost unlimited. Besides, it also facilitates the ability to represent her body as an independent object in space; it contributes to the localization and the representation of herself, and gives her a strong impulse towards achieving autonomy (Thelen *et al.* 2001; Cottini 2003).

Actually, these phases of development indicate a progression that is not the same in all children. Indeed, all children have their own rhythms of development and learn the various skills by choosing the times and the ways that are better adapted to their own styles of movement and to the goals that, from time to time, they try to achieve. The variability among individuals is greater when a new ability is emerging, while it decreases as soon as more effective and mature strategies are selected. Moreover, these strategies are essentially the same in all children. But this variability increases in individuals subject to developmental delay, such as children with Down Syndrome.

## MOTOR LEARNING

The programming and the execution of movement schemas require the activation of a series of extremely complex and articulated processes, quite similar to those implemented by other types of cognitive learning processes. It is clear that, in studying movement, it is necessary to focus not only on the body but also on the context in which movement takes place and the possible stages that may occur in the process of motor learning. Concerning these last, Fitts (1964) has distinguished three phases: (a) the cognitive phase, during which the student identifies the goal and takes the decisions that permit the earliest enactions of the movement – in other words, the first examples of the action that must be learnt, usually performed by the educator, allow the student, through an adequate focalization of attention, to perceive and to memorize the movement that must be developed; (b) the associative phase, in which, through several repetitions, the student attains the construction of a motor programme, i.e., organizes the subroutines of the previous phase, by also using the motor abilities already learnt; and (c) the automation phase, which characterizes the situation in which the movement, by now extensively practised, can be executed without any attentional control, transforming itself from a controlled process to an automatic process (Schmidt and Lee 1999; Summers 1999; Shiffrin and Schneider 1977). The fact that cognitive processes can occur in an automatic way as well as in a controlled way is of great importance in learning. Indeed, only what has been processed in the working memory can, later on, pass into the long-term memory, becoming a permanent acquisition. In other words, only the information elaborated in a controlled way can, if certain conditions occur, be elaborated in a stable way, so as to become available for subsequent use (Schneider et al. 1984; Smith et al. 1999).

Therefore, according to this model, when the movement is completed, several items of information related to the different phases (and the relations among them) are stored. The strength of the relations among the elements that compose the movement increases at each repetition of the same movement or of a similar one. In this way, the schema is gradually developed, and it will be the more complete and articulated the greater the variability during the phase of its formation (i.e., during the practice period) has been. Once the schema has been formed, the component motor abilities can be transferred to other new movements, and hence the process of motor learning becomes progressively easier. Of course, the transfer of motor abilities to new movements will be the greater the greater the similarity between the new movement and the movements already learnt; this happens because in both cases the same classes of movement are represented within the same abstract schema (Nicoletti, 1992; Cottini 2003).

The theory that is constructed on the basis of the existence of motor schemas permits us to resolve problems that were left unsolved by earlier theories, according to which each example of motor learning was determined by a specific mnestic trace (Adams 1971). Actually, it would be rather difficult to accept the existence of as many mnestic traces as there are possible movements: such an organization of memory would involve an enormous amount of work, both in the storing and in the recovering of any individual movement. The notion of the motor schema, by contrast, allows an interpretation of motor learning such that the effectiveness characteristics and the working economy of the central nervous system are alike preserved. Indeed, the schema implements a generative process that, starting from movements belonging to the same category, forms a rule that can be applied to all movements within the category. It is based on four types of motor information that the subject stores during the execution of movements (Schmidt 1975, 1982; Schmidt and Lee 1999): (1) the physical parameters that play a part in the execution of the movement (e.g. duration, force, direction, etc.); (2) the result that has been obtained after the movement: by storing these results, the correctness of the information about the values of the variables that need to be employed in the execution of the movement is increased; (3) the sensory consequences determined by the movement (proprioceptive and exteroceptive afferents); and (4) the starting conditions, such as, for example, the initial position of the body with respect to the object that is to be manipulated and to the environment in which one is moving.

In other words, in order to answer at the motor level the adequately elaborated requests coming from the environment, the individual must recover from the long-term memory an example of a schema through a mechanism of choice among the schemas. However, the selected schema is not always suitable to answer the demands of the environment completely or totally to satisfy the goal. Therefore, it may happen that a schema gets adapted or that some further schemas are combined with it (the programming of motor activity) on the basis of examination of input from the environment and from the situation of the individual. The adaptations of the motor schemas are structured on the interaction of three orders of processes: neurological, psychological and psychomotor (Spencer *et al.* 2001).

The term 'neurological processes' signifies the neurological morphofunctional substrate, in the absence of which no phenomena of any kind would be possible. In order to be able to give a comprehensive account of the motor translation of the schemas, it is necessary to emphasize that the fulcrum of all motor activity is represented by the central nervous system. Inside the central nervous system are contained the neuromotor models, which can be considered as motor formulae responsible for realizing every human motor activity, from the simplest to the most complex (Brooks 1986; Magall 1999). In other words, they represent the neurological equivalent of the mental schemas (Fig. 7.1).

By psychological processes we mean that tissue of cognitive, affective, motivational and associational-cultural factors that mould every human action and confer on it a purpose and a meaning. Among the psychological theories that have postulated various modalities of control over movement, there are two that have found a large measure of empirical confirmation: one based on the 'closed circuit' and one based on the 'open circuit' model. In the 'closed circuit' model control would be based on 'feedback' (peripheral control), while in the 'open circuit' model movement would be carried out on the basis of one of the abstract representations that are defined as 'motor programmes' (Nicoletti 1992; Cottini 2003).

The psychomotor processes are those specifically concerned with movement and that represent the main object of interest of this work: the body schema, general and segmentary co-ordination, balance, spatio-temporal organization, and the process of lateralization. In every problematic situation, all these processes give rise to an active interchange of values and together realize the implementation of the motor programme. In other words, the psychomotor adaptations of the schemas and/or the combination of several schemas stored in memory are such that the schemas selected become effectively suitable to resolving the motor problem for the individual at that determined moment (Aucouturier *et al.* 1986; Busacchi 1993; Coste 1981). More details on such psychomotor factors will be given in the next paragraph.

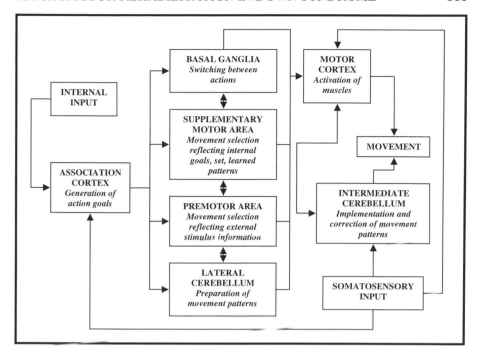

**Figure 7.1.** The schematic architecture of the motor nervous system.

## THE PSYCHOMOTOR PROCESSES OF HUMAN MOVEMENT

As we have pointed out before, psychomotor processes turn out to be of fundamental importance for the adaptation of motor schemas to the wide range of external situations, and, therefore, to promoting effective experiences of motor learning. In this perspective, walking, running, and jumping, as well as all the other possible different motor manifestations, acquire a special meaning that goes beyond the biomechanical and morpho-functional data, and assumes the meaning of an action in which the subject completely expresses him- or herself with respect to the external environment. In general terms, however, it can be asserted that the psychomotor approach substantially manifests its own peculiar character by placing the individual in situations of active search and relation in respect of space, time, objects and other people. In this conceptual picture, the following points assume particular importance (Bernardi *et al.* 1982; Calabrese 1974; Le Boulch 1974, 1979):

### BODY SCHEMA

The notion of 'body schema' is complex, and refers to studies and researches of a philosophical, psychological, neurological, and psychoanalytic order that constitute a rich web of theoretical-conceptual references, differing epistemo-logically among themselves, yet still, even though only in a far distant perspective, ultimately integrable into one single unitary conception (Schilder 1950). Indeed, some authors talk about 'body schema', others of 'self-image', others of 'somatognosy', identifying such terms with a mainly psychological or a mainly neurological vision, depending on their own principal sphere of interest, as if there could co-exist a neurological body schema and a new psychological awareness (De Ajuriaguerra 1974). In order to identify the notion at issue completely, however, it may be useful to make the following points: (1) on the neurological plane, the integration of visual, tactile, kinaesthesic and vestibular sensorial data concerned with the body and in accordance with the working out of the body schema happens at the cerebral level, in particular in the region of the parietal cortex; (2) motor experiences are fundamental for the formation of the body schema, which, in turn, as long as it goes on structuring itself, becomes an essential prerequisite for the organization and the control of movement, which therefore only in this way can assume the meaning of a totally integrated and active function in the complex psychic organization of the individual; (3) the body schema is composed of two psycho-physiological levels: the body as an object of perception or perceptive synthesis, and the body as a model of representation and therefore of symbolic, cognitive and intuitive knowledge, which thus gives rise to the so-called 'self-consciousness'; and (4) the 'body schema', as inner psychic 'truth', is the product of a complex mental processing in which the participating factors are both of a perceptive-cognitive order and of an affective-emotional-relational order. In conclusion, the expression 'body schema' denotes a variety of concepts; and such concepts are often clear only within the theoretical picture in which they have been defined – if used in any other framework, they can both lose their original theoretical value and create confusion at the metatheoretical level (Lurçat 1980).

## RELAXATION

Relaxation has the goal of producing effects on both the somatic and the psychic planes. Indeed, it provides a resolution of muscular tensions, better control, a refinement of gesture and a more detailed self-knowledge. The ability to control the degree of muscular contraction represents a basic condition for the execution of co-ordinated movements that are well adapted to achieving their ends (Jacobson 1948, 1957; Jarreau and Klotz 1960; Bernstein 1967; Bernestein and Borkovec 1973; Nanetti 1993). The problems are often connected with the difficulty of arriving at total or partial relaxation, that is, to a state of relaxation of the musculature, obtained through automatic and voluntary channelling, in order to avoid unintentional and involuntary secondary contractions during movement, rather than voluntary ones, and to place all the body in a state of rest. Various applied techniques are used, in both the clinical and the educational fields. In the latter, the main goal is to impel the individual to an active research into his own body knowledge: along with relaxation, the child, through attention to its own proprioceptive sensations, is progressively sensitized to a knowledge of and a more stable acquisition of 'corporal self-consciousness'. Moreover, relaxation is also a means to acquiring a good postural and respiratory training, over and above the positive repercussions it can have at the level of fostering fluidity, co-ordination and control of movement. In particular (Luthe 1965) it has positive effects on the intellectual faculties (better ability to concentrate, mental rehearsal, memorization and non-oral creativity), on scholastic learning (with improved capacities for study, for self-discipline, and for organization of work and lowered levels of anxiety) and on social anxiety (with better adaptation to responding to the environment, to interpersonal relations and to the overcoming of states of inhibition and fears) (Berges and Bounes 1978; Soubiran and Coste 1983).

## CO-ORDINATION AND BALANCE

By co-ordination of movement, we mean the execution of a finalized motor action by using the various structures of the body in a synergic way. In human activity, co-ordination means attuning all the partial processes of motor action to the goal that must be achieved through the movement (Gabbard et al. 1995; Michel 1991). There is segmentary co-ordination (which involves particular parts of the body, such as the hand, forearm and arm), intersegmentary co-ordination (which involves the co-ordinated action of various segments, as in cases of hand–eye co-ordination) and general co-ordination (which involves the entire body). The development of co-ordination is closely related to the development of the central nervous system and to the sum of the programmed and carried through motor experiences. The use of different motor schemas in various situations, indeed, leads the individual to refine his own general, intersegmentary and segmentary co-ordinations. It is of fundamental importance, therefore, to favour the greatest possible number of motor adjustments, suggesting a variety of different situations for experimentation: racing, climbing, wrestling, etc. (Sechi and Capozzi 1994; Morrison et al. 1991; Gagnon et al. 1998). The emphasis must be placed on favouring lived experience, more than on considering the result of the motor action in itself: on the improvement in co-ordination, obtained thanks to the practical staff, which teaches children how to use the body. In addition, the maintenance and regaining of balance can be considered as a form of motor co-ordination in relation to gravity. Balance is defined as the outcome of a search for the exactly correct position of the body in stasis and during movement, and depends, apart from biomechanical and physiological factors, on psychological factors not easily defined from the qualitative and quantitative points of view (Calabrese 1974). Indeed, these movements are the result of adaptations due to the interpretation of proprioceptive and exteroceptive sensations, which come from four principal sources of information: cutaneous, kinaesthetic, labyrinthine (propriocep-tivity) and visual sensations (exteroceptivity). The development of balance happens progressively, starting from the conquest of the various postures (control of the head from prone positions, of the trunk in seated position, etc.), and moving on to the more refined postures found in dynamic and in in-motion balance. It depends intimately on the quantity and quality of the motor experiences, which, facilitating the interpretation of a whole series of items of afferent information of both a proprioceptive and an exteroceptive nature, facilitate a better understanding of the relationships of the various segments of the body among themselves and with the external world.

## LATERALIZATION

Lateralization (cerebral asymmetry) represents a human characteristic, typically not found in experiments on animals, consisting of differences in the operation of the cortical areas involved. A greater tendency to use one hemisphere, or an equal tendency to use both, determines either a homolateral dominance (of one side of the body over the other) or mixed dominance. Various hypotheses have been formulated in order to explain the causes of lateral dominance. It can be said with certainty that genetic transmission plays a part, besides the pressure of the social environment, which unquestionably does nothing to favour left-handed people, who are not, as was believed in the past, mere mirror-images of the right-handed, but rather individuals having a cerebral dominance mechanism that is mainly attuned to ambidexterity (Boliek and Obrzut 1995; Nicoletti and Umiltà 1984, 1985; Trentin 1979).

## SPATIO-TEMPORAL ORGANIZATION

The body schema is also structured by the acquisition of time and space concepts. Every individual, when he or she acts, acquires the knowledge of spatio-temporal elements; and, at the same time, when he or she is engaged in the organization of spatio-temporal data, gets a more stable consciousness of the 'corporal self'. To have consciousness of one's body always presupposes a relationship with oneself, objects and other people in a space–time continuum. The basic knowledge of the dimensions 'within–outside', 'over–under', 'high–low', and 'right–left', 'before–after', etc. is realized primarily in relation to the body and through its relationship with the objects of the external world. Piaget (1936, 1945, 1946), linking the origins of the structures of thought to direct experience, has extensively illustrated the connections between the acquisition of spatio-temporal discriminations and the development of cognitive processes. Every form of thought activity, indeed, initially develops from the level of the sensory-motor period with the internalization of action outlines, which are indissolubly connected to spatio-temporal categories, and thus destined to influence the totality of scholastic learning (Malim 1994; De Loache and Todd 1988; Cohen 1983; Piaget and Inhelder 1947). Think about the genesis of numerical symbols, where it turns out in an obvious way that the basic operational structures, such as classification, serialization, and ordering, refer to interrelated forms of the elementary notions of space and time.

## MOTOR DIFFICULTIES IN CHILDREN WITH DOWN SYNDROME

Down Syndrome children will have problems in motor learning owing to deficits in the following processes: planning, execution and motor control (Table 7.1).

Analysis of stimuli from the environment is often difficult in individuals with Down Syndrome because of a deficit at the attentional level. Such problems can be related both to the focalization (in many cases the child pays more attention to stimuli irrelevant to the goals of the learning task) and the stability of the attention (some subjects continuously move their attention from one aspect of the situation to another, with serious repercussions for the quality of their learning) (Norman and Shallice 1986; Guazzo 2006).

In the literature we can also find plenty of experiments showing significant deficits at the level of working memory in children with Down Syndrome. These deficits affect both aspects of visual memory and sequential auditory memory, and, above all, the spontaneous use of memory strategies (Baddeley 1986, 1990; Bower and Hayes 1994; Bray *et al.* 1994; Brown 1975; Cornoldi 2004; De Beni 2004; Guazzo 1987, 1991, 2006). The Down students have significant difficulty during the phase of the adaptation of the motor schemas to the requirements of the particular situation. This is due to factors related to the deficiency of stored schemas as well as to problems in storing and recovering such schemas from the long-term memory (Ellis *et al.* 1989; Marcell and Weeks 1988; Ohr 1991; Vicari *et al.* 1995). Moreover, a consistent deficit in

**Table 7.1.** Summary of motor difficulties in Down Syndrome

| Processes | Motor difficulties |
|---|---|
| • Motor planning | • Difficulty with attention and memory |
| | • Difficulty in implementation of movement pattern |
| | • Difficulty with psychomotor abilities |
| • Motor execution | • Difficulty in nerve impulse transmission |
| | • Difficulty in the osteo-arthromuscular system |
| • Motor control | • Difficulty in feedback transmission |
| | • Difficulty in feedback decoding |
| | • Difficulty in corrective movement |

the structuring of the psychomotor factors of movement is always present. Therefore, there is a lack of relational references from the body to the spatio-temporal characteristics of the action to be completed. The execution of the movement shows difficulties because of some morpho-structural limitations that are sometimes associated with the various syndromes. This is the case, for example, with the muscular hypotonia and the slackness in the ligaments typical of Down Syndrome, or with the outcomes of cerebral lesions that have affected motor capacities more extensively than cognitive ones. And finally, also affecting motor control, deficiencies related both to the transmission of nervous impulses (afferent and/or efferent; sometimes it is difficult to tell owing to specific pathologies associated with the central nervous system) and to the decoding process have been recorded. The Down student is much more dependent than the normally intelligent student on exteroceptive input, owing to difficulties in interpreting feedback (Chamberlin and Magill 1992).

Table 7.2 gives a clear résumé of other difficulties, partially linked to deficits of a physical type and in neuromotor control, and partially correlated directly to the delay in cognitive development. Among the physical problems associated with Down Syndrome are slackness in the ligaments and muscular hypotonia, which hinder the attainment of the main developmental stages and the acquisition of the prerequisites for motor function (control of muscle tone and relaxation, co-ordination, balance, etc.). The hypothesis that muscular hypotonia and slackness in the ligaments play an important role in the causation of the delay in motor development is also confirmed from a study by Urlich and Urlich (1992). These authors have shown that in children with Down Syndrome not yet able to achieve independent ambulation, there exist, as in normal children, schemas whose presence can be demonstrated under particular conditions. The interpretation of these data is that the delay in motor development in children with Down Syndrome depends on muscular hypotonia and on lack of balance rather than on the simple absence of the motor schema. Sechi and Capozzi (1994) have estimated qualitatively the motor profile of children with Down Syndrome, putting in evidence generalized delays in all the components, extending from the gross-motor components (balance, postural ability, running, etc.), to the fine-motor components (co-ordination of the hands, visuo-motor control, etc.). Moreover, in the same study, they have drawn, based on their own data experiments and on a detailed analysis of the literature, the following general considerations about the quality and the nature of the motor and praxic difficulties of the children with Down Syndrome (Cunningham 1984; Dunst 1990):

- all the Down children show, even though in different measures, a difficulty in the development and the use of the praxic schemas. In some children the motor difficulty assumes the characteristics of a 'specific' difficulty, which seems selectively to compromise the implementation of executive programmes;

**Table 7.2.** Motor Development Milestones in Down Syndrome (DS) children and non-disordered (ND) children

| Motor skills | | Mean age | |
|---|---|---|---|
| Gross motor | Fine motor | ND children | DS children |
| • Balances the head | • Holds small object in hand | 3 months | 6 months |
| • Crawls | • Reaches and briefly holds toy | 5 months | 8 months |
| • Sits without support | • Transfers objects from one hand to the other | 7 months | 9 months |
| • Pulls self to standing position and stands unaided | • Starting to have ability to pick up small foods | 8 months | 14 months |
| • Walks with aid | • Drops and picks up toy | 10 months | 16 months |
| • Rolls a ball in imitation of adult | • Gives toy to care-giver when asked | 12 months | 20 months |
| • Walks alone | • Builds tower of two or three small blocks | 14 months | 21 months |
| • Walks backwards | • Puts four or five rings on stick | 15 months | 22 months |
| • Walks up and down stairs with hand held | • Uses both hands to play | 17 months | 24 months |
| • Moves to music | • Places three or four tiles in mosaic | 20 months | 30 months |
| • Picks up toys from floor without falling | • Paints with whole arm movement and shifts hands | 24 months | 36 months |
| • Stands on one foot with aid | • Snips with scissors | 26 months | 40 months |
| • Runs around obstacles | • Copies a circle | 30 months | 48 months |
| • Walks on a line | • Drives home nails and pegs | 34 months | 52 months |
| • Uses slide independently | • Manipulates plastic material (e.g. clay) | 36 months | 56 months |

- Down children show relevant deficiencies in their postural-kinetic development, probably related to their particular neuromotor executive difficulties (hypotonia, slackness in the ligaments, etc.) and to their basic cognitive deficit;
- all Down children, both those with specific praxic difficulties and those with praxic problems associated with cognitive organization, present typical and persistent difficulty in the independent and spontaneous use of the praxic schemas that they have mastered and in the integration of their praxic action within a map of meanings.

Further researches of a developmental-Piagetian type that have looked at the sensory-motor development of children with Down Syndrome, in order to pick out any possible atypical and heterochronous development, have demonstrated (Dunst 1990):

- a regular succession in the appearance of the various stages of sensory-motor development;
- a progressive slowing down of development with advancing age;
- a modality of integration among several different types of competences quite similar to that of normal children; and
- in Down Syndrome, a specific slowing down that occurs between one phase of development and the next.

## PSYCHOMOTOR REHABILITATION IN DOWN SYNDROME

The studies and the researches reported and discussed in the preceding paragraphs demonstrate that, even if there is an extreme variability in subjects with Down Syndrome, common factors exist in the consciousness, knowledge and use of the body. On this evidence, it is already possible to attribute an important role to psychomotor rehabilitation in the process of the development of the Down child, especially in the first developmental periods: pre-school age, nursery school and primary school (Guazzo 2006). To this consideration another must be added (surely no less important in emphasizing the primacy of motor activities), related to the necessity of privileging a practical education, centred mainly on doing, operating, and experimenting in concrete terms. Through an approach of this type, a manipulative one, especially if associated with play aspects, it is possible to make the development of abilities and competences easier for the student, and to guide her or him to a correct evaluation of her or his own abilities and limits. By contrast, a verbose and abstract type of instruction is not suitable for Down students. Indeed, the intellectual viscosity that marks the personality of these individuals is such that educational procedures of a traditional type often result in the accentuation of items that are void of significance, to a lowering of self-esteem and a reduction or refusal of new experiences. Another necessary component of the process of psychomotor rehabilitation, in order to facilitate a motivation to learning on the part of the student, is represented by play activities (Dweck 1986; Weiner 1990). When the difficulties are consistent, these activities do not appear spontaneously, and demand specific programmes to promote them. Teaching through play and also teaching to play mean offering the student the opportunity to exercise those motor and cognitive functions already demonstrated in the preceding paragraphs and, consequently, facilitating the processes of the development of the personality and its integration (Wehman 1977).

The importance of psychomotor rehabilitation to the educational plan for the Down subject is hard to question in the light of research and of the experiments conducted in several settings. That is, the approach must be to search out, in the common environment, learning strategies as similar as possible to those employed by non-delayed subjects. The long-term educational goal is to facilitate the maximum development of the motor function allowed by an individual's personal conditions, namely, to promote, through play activity, the formation of an extensive and finalized motor ability (the development and improvement of the basic motor schemas), and to research the development of the structural and functional prerequisites of movement. The emphasis must be placed on the condition of the individual pupil, on his residual and on his potential abilities, on his motivations, and on his emotional and relational characteristics. The operational goals of the educational programme, consequently, must be planned for the student with deficit in relation to his own individual situation, once this has been appropriately assessed. At the same time, the contents must be personalized, and they must be proposed with due regard for the appropriate time needed for learning, which may also be drastically retarded. This work of adaptation of the educational programme can be pursued exclusively by making reference to a system of motor abilities evaluation that takes into evidence not only the deficiencies, but also the patrimony of competences that the student has at the moment and those that he could acquire in a short space of time. Moreover, in Down children the knowledge of objects seems to assume a central position among the developmental data: competence in the use of objects integrates motor, cognitive, symbolic and affective factors alike (Ashman and Conway 1989; Guazzo 1990; Russell *et al.* 2001).

Therefore, the rehabilitation of the Down child must not only aim at the attainment of motor subroutines, but also at the systematization of this knowledge: action on objects and the repetition of experience allow the creation of codes and operations of coding/decoding of reality and 'accommodation' with respect to this. The learning of meaning (integrating perceptive, motor and affective-emotional information) seems to be a main deficit in these children: it is the sense of things that is altered, since it is not recognizable through its spatio-temporal and emotional characteristics. To give a meaning to an event means to recognize its cognitive value and its affective tonality in the moment in which it happens on the basis of a meaningful interaction: the object as a shared element of a meaningful interaction can be the pivot on which the existing developmental impulses are made to turn (Becci and Balducci 1990; Kreitler *et al.* 1990; Nanetti and Busacchi 1993).

The psychomotor therapy session then becomes the moment in which, on the interactive plane, dynamics, actions, and emotions are lived with the aid of an educational operator aware of the profile of that specific child and, therefore, of his or her specific difficulties. The therapeutic interaction has the goal of mediating the learning process to make it possible to decode some situations that have hitherto been perceived as irrelevant because they are not identifiable or cannot be integrated with the available information (Picq and Vayer 1968; Peck *et al.* 1990).

From the above analysis there clearly appear the indication for and the usefulness of an immediate and individualized therapeutic action. If early action is essential in order to avoid important dissociations and the consequent establishment of atypical behaviours, the individualization concept instead sends one back to look at school programmes that are not always profitable for the subject. However, the promptness and the individualization of the action taken are also important in order to prevent the establishment of behavioural disturbances or of frankly psychopathological developments (Zigler and Hodapp 1986).

Within psychomotor rehabilitation therapy, this integration (promptness/individualization of action) is surely possible. Think about all the work on the basic motor schemas, on the practices finalized to strengthen functional prerequisites, on the play situations that enable, through the methodology of creating strategies, every student to carry out motor activities in a personal way, as a result of predisposing conditions supplied by the educator. The use of play, then, can turn out to be a truly effective vehicle in facilitating integrated experiences. Experience shows that Down children are facilitated, through a natural ecological rather than an artificial context, in progressing at their own levels of learning and benefiting in the following points (Peck *et al.* 1990):

- improving one's self-concept;
- a greater ability to establish interpersonal relationships based on assertiveness and prosociality;
- a smaller fear of differences;
- greater tolerance;
- experience of genuine acceptance;
- acquisition of metacognitive competences in cooperative learning; and
- an increase in self-esteem.

This operating methodology meets the conditions of presenting a playful style of intervention and also offers the possibility of practically implementing the versatility principle (favouring the development of all the dimensions of the personality: morphological-functional, behavioural, cognitive, affective-emotional, communicative and socio-relational), multilaterality (choice of those contents and educational means that are more suitable to achieving an optimal motor development) and participation (structuring of the educator–student relation).

## CONCLUSIONS

Developmental psychology insists that the roots of conceptual thought and the highest abstractions and constructions are to be found in movements and perceptions. Indeed, the psychogenetic hypothesis propounded by Piaget postulates that every developmental phase, every intellectual construction, derives from the previous one and generates other more complex ones. The tight relation between the more elementary mental organizations and the advanced ones guarantees that the order of succession made up of the phases of development is constant. From the earliest motor manifestations (several movements in relation to the other people and objects, movement of objects towards and away from the person, search for hidden objects, etc.) it is possible to find the presence of a logic at the practical level (space relations, temporal relations, relations of causality, serialization and classification, etc.), that is prolonged and developed later on into a logic of thought. The co-ordination of actions and in more general terms of sensory-motor schemas is indispensable in order to scale the highest adaptive peaks (Steffens *et al.* 1987; Stewart and Deitz 1986).

During the developmental age it is not only the development of the intellectual area that comes to be influenced by the co-ordinated development of a functional motor activity. Indeed, the discovery and the use of the body is situated at the beginning of the development that leads to the representation of oneself as a personality and to the possibility of interacting with the world: the personality functions are only developed as a result of the activation of motor schemas. Indeed, the validity and the effectiveness of the motor schemas link positively with the development of the schemas of the individual functions of the person; it follows that movement is not only a basic attribute that dynamizes the biological substrate, but is the decisive function, because it supplies the life, development and conservation of all the areas and all the functions of the individual. The cognitive and perceptive–motor functions usually show a more or less serious delay in connection with the elementary motor functions, and this phenomenon is exacerbated with increasing age (heterochronous development). In any case, the difficulties and the insufficiencies in motor and neuromotor activities cannot have any other result than to disturb and to paralyse the manifestations of intelligence.

On the basis of the above discussion, it is possible, at this point, to try to delineate the role that psychomotor rehabilitation covers in Down Syndrome. The positive aspects of a psychomotor programme associated with an approach of a cognitive–behavioural type can be divided into three levels:

- *General*. Psychomotor action, early and individualized, represents a fundamental prerequisite for all learning.
- *Specific*. A customized motor activity directly affects the processing components of the cognitive system (perception, memory, attention, etc.).

• *Motivational*. Psychomotor action in a playful format emphasizes the use of natural reinforcement to favour and upgrade intrinsic motivation.

Through these three levels, the child with Down Syndrome can acquire knowledge and competences that will bring her to reconcilation with herself and the world, to becoming more independent, to being able to express her inner world, to becoming self-determined, and to conquering her own identity.

# REFERENCES

Adams, J.A. (1971). A closed-loop theory of motor learning. *Journal of Motor Behavior*. 3:101–50.
Ashman, A.F. and Conway, N.F. (1989). *Cognitive strategies for special education*. New York: Routledge.
Aucouturier, B., Darrault, I. and Empinet, J.L. (1986). *La pratica psicomotoria: rieducazione e terapia*. Rome: Armando.
Baddeley, A. (1986). *Working memory*. Oxford: Clarendon Press.
Baddelcy, A. (1990). *Human memory. Theory and practice*. Hove, E. Sussex: Erlbaum.
Becci, L. and Balducci, F. (1990). Proposte didattiche per lo sviluppo dei prerequisiti funzionali. In A. Fabi and L. Cottini (eds), *Educazione motoria e scuola*. (pp. 101–35). Urbino: Montefeltro.
Berges, J. and Bounes, M. (1978). *Il rilassamento terapeutico nel Bambino*. Milan: Masson.
Bernardi, E., Canevaro, A. and Ferioli, L. (1982). *Il comportamento psicomotorio a scuola*. Bologna: Il Mulino.
Bernestein, D.A. and Borkovec, T.D. (1973). *Progressive relaxation training: a manual for the helping professions*. Champaign, IL: Research Press.
Bernstein, N. (1967). *The coordination and regulation of movement*. Oxford: Pergamon.
Boliek, C.A. and Obrzut, J.E. (1995). Perceptual laterality in developmental learning disabilities. In R.J. Davidson and K. Hugdahl (eds), *Brain asymmetry*. pp. 637–58. Cambridge, MA: MIT Press.
Bower, A. and Hayes, A. (1994). Short-term memory deficits and Down's syndrome: a comparative study. *Down's Syndrome Res. Pract*. 2:47–50.
Bray, N.W., Saarnio, D.A., Borges, L.M. and Hawk, L.W. (1994). Intellectual and developmental differences in external memory strategies. *American Journal on Mental Retardation*. 99(1):19–31.
Brooks, V.B. (1986). *The neural basis of motor control*. Oxford: Pergamon.
Brown, A.L. (1975). The development of memory: knowing, knowing about knowing, and knowing how to know. In H.W. Reese (ed.), *Advances in Child Development and Behavior*. vol. 10. New York: Academic Press.
Busacchi, M. (1993). Aspetti metodologici dell'educazione motoria. In E. Nanetti, L. Cottini and M. Busacchi (eds), *Psicopedagogia del movimento umano*. pp. 105–14. Rome: Armando.

Calabrese, L. (1974). *L'apprendimento motorio dai cinque ai dieci anni*. Rome: Armando.

Chamberlin, C.J. and Magill, R.A. (1992). The memory representation of motor skills: a test of schema theory. *Journal of Motor Behavior*. 24:309–19.

Cohen G. (1983). *Psychology of cognitive processes*. London: Academic Press.

Cornoldi, C. (2004). I disturbi di memoria in età evolutiva. In G.M. Guazzo (ed.), *Disturbi dello sviluppo e strategie di intervento*. pp. 37–54. Nola, NA: IRFID.

Coste, J.-C. (1981). *La Psicomotricità*. Florence: La Nuova Italia.

Cottini, L. (2003). *Psicomotricità. Valutazione e metodi nell'intervento*. Rome: Carocci.

Cunningham, C. (1984). Down Syndrome. An introduction for parents. Cambridge: Brookline.

De Ajuriaguerra, J. (1974). *Manuel de psychiatrie de l'enfant*. Paris: Masson.

De Beni, R. (2004). Potenziale di apprendimento e strategie di memoria nel ritardo mentale. Caratteristiche e peculiarità di bambini con sindrome di Down. In G.M. Guazzo (ed.), *Disturbi dello sviluppo e strategie di intervento*. pp. 81–96. Nola, NA: IRFID.

De Loache, J.S. and Todd, C.M. (1988). Young children's use of spatial categorization as a mnemonic strategy. *Journal of Experimental Child Psychology*. 46:1–20.

Dunst, C.J. (1990). Sensory motor development of infants with Down syndrome. In D. Cicchetti and M. Beeghly (eds), *Children with Down syndrome*. pp. 233–51. Cambridge, MA: Cambridge University Press.

Dweck, C.S. (1986). Motivational processes affecting learning. American Psychologist. 41:1040–8.

Ellis, N.R., Woodley-Zanthos, P. and Dulaney, C.L. (1989). Memory for spatial location in children, adults, and mentally retarded persons. *American Journal on Mental Retardation*. 93(5):521–7.

Fitts, P.M. (1964). Perceptual–motor skills learning. In A.M. Melton (ed.), *Categories of human learning*. pp. 243–85. New York: Academic Press.

Gabbard. C., Hart, S. and Gentry, V. (1995). General motor proficiency and handedness in children. *Journal of Genetic Psychology*. 156:411–16.

Gagnon, I., Forget, R., Sullivan, S.J. and Friedman, D. (1998). Motor performance following a mild traumatic brain injury in children: an exploratory study. *Brain Injury*. 12:843–53.

Guazzo, G.M. (1987). Spontaneous formation of regions with different properties in neural nets. *Biosystems*. 20:237–41.

Guazzo, G.M. (1990). *Psicologia dell'handicap*. Salerno: Ripostes.

Guazzo, G.M. (1991). A formalization of Neisser's model. In T. Kohonen, K. Makisara and O. Simula (eds), *Artificial neural networks*. pp. 1423–6. Amsterdam: North-Holland.

Guazzo, G.M. (2006). Learning difficulties in Down syndrome. In J.A. Rondal and J. Perera (eds), *Down Syndrome: neurobehavioural specificity*. pp. 153–73. Chichester: Wiley.

Haley, S.M. (1986). Postural reactions in infants with Down syndrome: relationship to motor milestone development and age. *Physical Therapy*. 66(1):17–22.

Haley, S.M. (1987). Sequence of development of postural reactions by infants with Down syndrome. *Developmental Medicine and Child Neurology*. 29(5):674–9.

Harris, S.R. (1981). Effects of neurodevelopmental therapy on motor performance of infants with Down's syndrome. *Developmental Medicine and Child Neurology*. 23(4):477–83.

Jacobson, E. (1948). *Progressive relaxation*. Chicago, IL: University of Chicago Press.

Jacobson, E. (1957). *You must relax*. New York: McGraw-Hill.

Jarreau, R. and Klotz, H.P. (1960). Les paratonies cruciales en relaxation. *Revue de Médicine Psyco-somatique*. 2:194–8.

Kreitler, S., Zigler, E. and Kreitler, H. (1990). Rigidity in mentally retarded and nonretarded children. *American Journal on Mental Retardation*. 94(5):550–62.

Le Boulch, J. (1974). *Verso una scienza del movimento umano*. Rome: Armando.

Le Boulch, J. (1979). *Educare con il movimento*. Rome: Armando.

Lurçat, L. (1980). *Il bambino e lo spazio. Il ruolo del corpo*. Florence: La Nuova Italia.

Luthe, W. (1965). *Autogenic Training*. New York: Grune & Stratton.

Magall, R. (1999). *Motor control*. London: Human Kinetics.

Malim, T. (1994). *Cognitive processes*. London: Macmillan.

Marcell, M.M. and Weeks, S.L. (1988). Short-term memory difficulties and Down's syndrome. *Journal of Mental Deficiency Research*. 32:153–62.

Michel, G.F. (1991). Development of infant manual skills: motor programs, schemata, or dynamic systems? In J. Fagard and P.H. Wolff (eds), *The development of timing control and temporal organization in coordinated action: invariant relative timing, rhythms and coordination*. pp. 175–99. Amsterdam: North-Holland.

Morrison, C.D., Bundy, A.C. and Fisher, A.G. (1991). The contribution of motor skills and playfulness to the play performance of preschoolers. *American Journal of Occupational Therapy*. 45:687–94.

Nanetti, F. (1993). Il rilassamento. In F. Nanetti, L. Cottini and M. Busacchi (eds), *Psicopedagogia del movimento umano*. pp. 69–79. Rome: Armando.

Nanetti, F. and Busacchi, M. (1993). Psicopedagogia dell'azione motoria. In F. Nanetti., L. Cottini and M. Busacchi (eds), Psicopedagogia del movimento umano, pp. 11–29. Rome: Armando.

Nicoletti, R. (1992). *Il controllo motorio*. Bologna: Il Mulino.

Nicoletti, R. and Umiltà, C. (1984). Right–left prevalence in spatial compatibility. *Perception and Psychophysics*. 35:333–43.

Nicoletti, R. and Umiltà, C. (1985). Responding with hand and foot: the right–left preva-lence in spatial compatibility is still present. *Perception and Psychophysics*. 38: 211–16.

Norman, D. and Shallice, T. (1986). Attention to action: willed and automatic control of behavior. In R.J. Davidson, G.E. Schwartz and D. Shapiro (eds), *Consciousness and self relation*. pp. 165–201. New York: Plenum.

Ohr, P.S. (1991). Learning and memory in Down syndrome infants. *Dissertation Abstract International*. 51(10-B):505.

Peck, C.A., Donaldson, J. and Pezzoli, M. (1990). Some benefits nonhandicapped adolescents perceive for themselves from their social relationships with peers who have severe handicaps. *Journal of the Association for Persons with Severe Handicaps*. 15(4):23–35.

Piaget, J. (1936). *La naissance de l'intelligence chez l'enfant*. Neuchâtel: Delachaux et Niestlé.

Piaget, J. (1945). *La formation du symbole chez l'enfant*. Neuchâtel: Delachaux et Niestlé.

Piaget, J. (1946). *Le développement de la notion de temps chez l'enfant*. Paris: Presses Universitaires de France.

Piaget, J. and Inhelder, B. (1947). *La répresentation de l'espace chez l'enfant.* Paris: Presses Universitaries de France.

Picq, L. and Vayer, P. (1968). *Educazione psicomotoria e ritardo mentale.* Rome: Armando.

Rast, M.M. and Harris, S.R. (1985). Motor control in infants with Down syndrome. *Developmental Medicine and Child Neurology.* 27(5):682–5.

Russell, T.L., Peterson, N.G., Rosse, R.L. and Hatten, J.T. (2001). The measurement of cognitive, perceptual, and psychomotor abilities. In J.P. Campbell and D.J. Knapp (eds), *Exploring the limits in personnel selection and classification.* pp. 71–109. Mahwah, NJ: Erlbaum.

Schilder, P. (1950). *The image and appearance of the human body.* New York: International Universities Press.

Schmidt, R.A. (1975). A schema theory of discrete motor skills learning. *Psychological Review.* 82:225–61.

Schmidt, R.A. (1982). *Motor control and learning.* Champaign. IL: Human Kinetics Publisher.

Schmidt, R.A., Lee, T.D. (1999). *Motor control.* New York: Academic Press.

Schneider, W., Dumas, S.T. and Shiffrin, R.M. (1984). *Automatic and control processing and attention.* New York: Academic Press.

Sechi, E. and Capozzi, E. (1994). Le difficoltà di sviluppo motorio-prassico: disturbo prassico o deficit cognitivo? In A. Contardi and S. Vicari (eds), *Le persone Down. Aspetti neuro psicologici, educativi e sociali.* pp. 132–43. Milan: Angeli.

Shiffrin, R.M. and Schneider, W. (1977). Controlled and automatic information processing, II. Perceptual learning, automatic attending, and a general theory. *Psychological Review.* 84:127–90.

Smith, L.B., Thelen, E., Titzer, R. and McLin, D. (1999). Knowing in the context of acting: The task dynamics of the A-not-B error. *Psychological Review.* 106:235–60.

Soubiran, G.B. and Coste, J.C. (1983). *Psicomotricità e rilassamento psicomotorio.* Rome: Armando.

Spencer, J.P., Smith, L.B. and Thelen, E. (2001). Tests of a dynamic systems account of the A-not-B error: the influence of prior experience on the spatial memory abilities of two-year-olds. *Child Development.* 72:1327–46.

Steffens, K.M., Semmes, R., Werder, J.K. and Bruininks, R.H. (1987). Relationship between quantitative and qualitative measures of motor development. *Perceptual and Motor Skills.* 64(3):985–6.

Stewart, K.B. and Deitz, J.C. (1986). Motor development in children with Sotos' cerebral gigantism. *Physical and Occupational Therapy in Pediatrics.* 6:41–53.

Summers, J.J. (1999). Motor programs. In D.H. Holding (ed.), *Human skills.* pp. 49–69. New York: Wiley.

Thelen, E. (1989). Self-organization in developmental processes: can systems approaches work? In M. Gunnar and E. Thelen (eds), *Systems and development: the Minnesota Symposia on child psychology.* pp. 77–117. Hillsdale, NJ: Erlbaum.

Thelen, E. (1994). Three-month-old infants can learn task-specific patterns of interlimb coordination. *Psychological Science.* 5:280–5.

Thelen, E. and Smith, L.B. (1994). *A dynamic systems approach to the development of cognition and action.* Cambridge, MA: MIT Press.

Thelen, E., Corbetta, D., Kamm, K., Spencer, J.P., Schneider, K. and Zemicke, R.F. (1993). The transition to reaching: mapping intention and intrinsic dynamics. *Child Development*. 64:1058–98.

Thelen, E., Schoner, G., Scheier, C. and Smith, L.B. (2001). The dynamics of embodiment: a field theory of infant perseverative reaching. *Behavioral and Brain Sciences*. 24:1–86.

Trentin, G.C. (1979). *Le attività motorie di base*. Rome: Carocci.

Urlich, B.D. and Urlich, D.A. (1992). Alternating stepping patterns: hidden abilities of II-month-old with Down Syndrome. *Development and Child Neurology*. 34:233–9.

Vicari, S., Carlesimo, G.A. and Caltagirone, C. (1995). Short-term memory in persons with intellectual disabilities and Down syndrome. *Journal of Intellectual Disability Research*. 39:532–7.

Wehman, R. (1977). Research on leisure time and the severely developmentally disabled. *Rehabilitation Literature*. 38:98–105.

Weiner, B. (1990). History of motivational research in education. *Journal of Educational Psychology*. 82;4:616–22.

Zigler, E.F. and Hodapp, R.M. (1986). *Understanding mental retardation*. Cambridge: Cambridge University Press.

# 8 Families and Services

SALVATORE SORESI AND LEA FERRARI

## SUMMARY

The family has an essential role in the treatment and integration of children with disability. Parents' involvement in planning and realizing interventions is of fundamental importance not only in increasing the effectiveness of interventions, but also in improving the parents' own quality of life. This chapter examines the construction of the quality of life in the families of individuals with disability and the role that parents have to be admitted to in planning treatment for their children. Two tools will be introduced that can be used by experts in counselling the parents of children with disability.

## INTRODUCTION

Little doubt now exists about the importance that must be assigned to the family in the treatment and the social and educational integration of their children with disability: on the one hand, many studies of the specialized literature maintain the need for parental involvement and, on the other, recommendations along these lines come from international bodies, such as for instance the World Health Organization, and from laws on disability that have been issued in a number of nations (WHO 2001; Luckasson *et al.* 2002; Nota 2004; Nota and Soresi 2004; Soresi and Nota 2004).

The services and the experts in the sector must offer families two types of attention in a clear and reliably continuous way:

(a) the first, as Soresi, Nota and Ferrari (2006) have emphasized, concerns the personalized support that must be guaranteed to all family members to help them cope with the daily problems that they have to confront; and

(b) the second concerns the right to participate actively in the choice and implementation of treatments that are collaboratively considered suitable and collaboratively decided upon.

*Therapies and Rehabilitation in Down Syndrome.* Edited by Rondal
© 2007 John Wiley & Sons Ltd

In the pages that follow the importance that the construction of quality of life (QoL) has for the families of individuals with disability will be examined and two instruments will be proposed for the analysis of satisfaction and aspects associated with it that could be used by experts in their jobs as consultants to parents of children with disability. Also examined will be the role for families that must be recognized in planning the activities that are realized for their children and the way in which it is better to involve them if the quality of life of all family members is to be increased.

## SUPPORTS AND THE QUALITY OF LIFE OF PARENTS

The support that health and education services have to supply should be heterogeneous, both because the needs for help vary from family to family in accordance with the specific disabilities of their children, and also because over the lifespan the problems they have to face, albeit remaining complex, do change; these consist mainly of:

(a) communication of diagnosis (Fox et al. 2002);
(b) activities that have to be realized daily during the first months and years of the child's life (Mailick Seltzer et al. 2001); and
(c) difficulties typical of infancy and childhood and, in the course of time, of adolescence and adulthood (Soresi et al. 2006).

The main purpose of this support is essentially to prevent unmanageable forms of family discomfort and, through the reduction of negative effects deriving from the presence of a child with disability and the strengthening of positive ones, guarantee a fairly satisfactory quality of life (Summers et al. 2005). The most reliable measure of the adequacy of the help and the efficacy of the support provided will increasingly be the degree of the improvement in the family's quality of life (Soresi 2004).

Quality of life, as witness the copious literature on it (see Schalock 2004 for a review), is a particularly complex and multifaceted construct, which includes several different dimensions and conditions: experienced levels of well-being, quality and quantity of supportive social networks, work satisfaction, extent of self-determination, extent of realization of possibilities, quality of the settings frequented (Felce 1997; Nota et al. 2006; Schalock et al. 2002). Such dimensions describe not only the QoL of individuals with impairment, but also that of their family members and, not least, of disability professionals. In addition, choosing to analyse disability issues from the QoL perspective also allows one to deal with family involvement in a positive and 'normalizing' way (Summers et al. 2005).

After giving up the idea that being parents of children with disability is very likely to mean 'running into' psychopathological problems (Soresi et al. 2006; Wilgosh et al. 2004; Nota et al. 2003), the factors and the strengths that allow these families to function in an adaptive way and to maintain satisfactory levels of quality of life have been increasingly underlined (Cohen 1999; Dellve *et al.* 2000; Jokinen and Brown 2005; Patterson 2002; Thompson and Gustafson 1996; Wallander *et al.* 1989).

From this perspective, particular attention is paid to aspects such as the sense of coherence, cohesiveness, coping strategies, and efficacy beliefs of parents. Sense of coherence is characterized by propensity to consider one's own life context as sufficiently predictable and capable of providing reinforcements and supports to particularly serious demands. The perception of sense of coherence increases the probability that parents will see stressful situations as challenges that can be dealt with and managed; that they will make efforts to analyse and understand problems; that they will actively seek the available resources that they need; and that they will successfully cope with the problems they encounter (Antonovsky 1987). Cohesion and adaptability are two constructs that represent crucial elements in family functioning (Prage *et al.* 1992): the first reflects the degree to which family members feel near one another and reciprocally sustain one another; the second, instead, reflects the degree to which the family system is flexible and willing to change in function in the light of contextual variations (Olson 1986). Both these aspects are particularly important, given that cohesive, well organized and supportive families generally tend to promote child development and adjustment (Nelson 1984; Putallaz and Hope-Heflin 1990).

The possession of suitable coping strategies, and above all of those centred on positive knowledge and reformulations, helps parents of children with disability to reduce levels of stress experienced and individualize the quality of care they provide for their children (Chang 2002). In accordance with this belief, Scorgie and collaborators (Scorgie *et al.* 1998; Wilgosh *et al.* 2000) have devised a questionnaire, the Life Management Survey (LMS), that assesses to what extent a series of strategies to manage difficult situations and some personal characteristics – such as decisional abilities and a positive philosophy of life – are considered important by parents. This instrument was tested in Italy by Wilgosh *et al.* (2004), who obtained similar results to those found in the US and in Canada. The latter study, in particular, compared parents of children with Down Syndrome, autism, problems associated with growth hormone production dysfunction, and Turner's syndrome. Compared to the other parents, the parents of children with intellectual disability had the biggest problems in resorting to productive and adaptive coping strategies; however, they also showed the greatest changes in their life perspective, even managing to find surprisingly positive elements in their particular parental situation.

Parents of children with Down Syndrome and with autism interviewed by King *et al.* (2006) reported that they experienced changes in their way of viewing life and disability: such experience 'opened their eyes' and helped them to reconsider what is important in life, to appreciate little things and little successes; they started to emphasize their children's strengths rather than their deficits, also applying strategies of 're-languaging' and stressing their positive performances. Always working from a perspective that emphasizes the need to stress these parents' strengths, potentialities and resources, particular attention is today being devoted to the analysis and improvement of parents' self-efficacy beliefs.

As is well known, since its diffusion in the international psychological literature by Bandura (1997) the construct of self-efficacy has been repeatedly analysed in different settings (education, health, psychopathology, organizations, etc.). In this connection, Coleman and Karraker (1997, 2003) maintained that parents' belief that they could meet their parental tasks effectively was associated with the use of more efficacious coping strategies and with lower levels of stress and depression in difficult situations. Nota *et al.* (2003) involved 54 parents of children with visual disability, 40 with hearing disability, 28 with Down Syndrome and 55 without disability. As regards differences between groups, the parents of children with Down Syndrome were found to be the ones that experienced the lowest levels of quality of life. The path analyses conducted to determine the influence exerted on parents' quality of life by some personal factors (individual characteristics, strategies considered as more important, changes observed) and by educational self-efficacy allowed us to conclude that the 'influence' factors changed with parent typologies. The strong variability recorded has strengthened the conviction that both individuals and families are unique 'subjects', who express their levels of satisfaction in relation to personal values, needs and problems (Brown and Brown 2004; Schalock *et al.* 2002).

The variability that characterizes the parental world and the importance taken on by the dimensions mentioned above should also stimulate the services to pay greater attention to the strengths and weaknesses of families and to aim at setting up the conditions necessary to increase and maintain their empowerment and their positive characteristics. As regards assessment, the instruments to be used by professionals, rather than focusing on finding psychological dynamics or even psychopathological problems in parents, should concern dimensions associated with the good adjustment and functioning of family members, including those of quality of life and efficacy beliefs. The presence of these tools in the 'offices' of professionals, their use and the discussion of results with parents would see a change of course and the choice of a positive approach to 'taking on responsibility' for these families. It must not be forgotten that being able to resort to professionals and to specialized qualified services capable of effective interaction with parents and of encourag-ing and sustaining parents' expectations of success is a factor that more than others can enable parents to cope with stress and improve quality of life (Guralnick 2000; Iarocci *et al.* 2006; Minnes 1998; Virji-Babul 2004). For these reasons it is important that, besides addressing the evaluation of levels of autonomy, services for people with disability implement further operations of assessment of parents' quality of life and self-efficacy beliefs.

The instruments that we have devised to this purpose and that we shall shortly describe can be used with parents of children with either typical or atypical development, on the basis of the belief that such dimensions (QoL and Self-efficacy), in addition to their relevance for any typology of parent, are articulated over very similar factors (Schalock 1999).

The first tool, *My life as a parent* (Soresi *et al.* 2003, 2006), derives from a validation and standardization study that involved over 2000 parents.

Exploratory factor analyses with oblique rotations yielded a final structure composed of 7 factors that were able to explain 62.46 per cent of the total variance. Confirmatory factor analyses showed that the seven-correlated-factor solution was the best (GFI: 0.93; AGFI: 0.91; CFI: 0.93; RMSEA: 0.04); subsequent analyses in accordance with logistic models proved that each item represented the dimension it belonged to in an adequate manner (Andrich 1988; Rasch 1960/1980).

The results of our analyses led to a final 29-item version of the instrument (Fig. 8.1) making reference to the following 7 factors: Satisfaction with Family Relations, made up of 3 items (alpha: 0.78; items 11, 19, 20); Sense of Wellbeing, made up of 3 items on satisfaction for perceived levels of tranquillity and safety (alpha: 0.77; items 9, 14, 24); Job Satisfaction, made up of 5 items (alpha: 0.86; items 1, 3, 6, 16, 21); Satisfaction with Relations with One's Own Children, made up of 6 items (alpha: 0.87; items 2, 5, 7, 12, 13, 27); Satisfaction with Free Time, made up of 3 items (alpha: 0.83; items 15, 18, 23); Satisfaction with Provided Support and Back-Up, made up of 4 items (alpha: 0.78; items 4, 10, 17, 26); Satisfaction with Self-Determination Opportunities, made up of 5 items that investigate satisfaction with the possibility of making important decisions with some autonomy, with enjoying private spaces and with engaging in pleasant activities (alpha: 0.70; items 8, 22, 25, 28, 29).

In utilizing this instrument and the standardization norms, it must not be forgotten that perception of individuals' Quality of life seems to undergo a homeostatic control characterized by personality and cognitive factors that contribute to maintaining experienced satisfaction within certain, usually positive, levels (Cummins 2003). Recognizing that mere subjective evaluations do not constitute data able to safeguard weaker individuals and cannot be considered as valid measurement criteria for the evaluation of the social policies carried out (Felce 1997), and that this can be considered true also for parents (Jokinen and Brown 2005), we worked to establish a series of objective indicators (Fig. 8.2) that can be used for specific in-depth investigations.

To stimulate attention and reflection on individual levels of well-being, a personalized report for parents can be used (see Figs 8.3 and 8.4), which shows the values they recorded in filling out the instrument *My life as parent*. In drafting the report raw data are compared with the mean values of a standardization group and transformed into T points: in that way parents can reflect

### MY LIFE AS A PARENT

Instructions

This questionnaire shows different aspects of a parent's life. After reading carefully the sentences below please indicate how much they describe your current situation by bearing in mind that:

    1 = *does not describe* my current situation *at all*;
    2 = *describes* my current situation *a little*;
    3 = *describes* my current situation *fairly well*;
    4 = *describes* my current situation *very well*;
    5 = *describes* my current situation *perfectly well*.

In thanking you for your collaboration, we wish to remind you that in the questionnaire there are no right or wrong answers: the only important thing is for you to answer all the questions by giving your own viewpoint.

\* \* \*

| | | |
|---|---|---|
| 1. | I am happy with my job. | 1 2 3 4 5 |
| 2. | I am happy about how I am bringing up my children. | 1 2 3 4 5 |
| 3. | In my job I can give my best. | 1 2 3 4 5 |
| 4. | If necessary, there is always someone at home who can help me. | 1 2 3 4 5 |
| 5. | I feel comfortable with my own children. | 1 2 3 4 5 |
| 6. | I am satisfied about what I can provide financially. | 1 2 3 4 5 |
| 7. | I am happy about how my children are growing up. | 1 2 3 4 5 |
| 8. | The most important decisions in my life depend above all on myself. | 1 2 3 4 5 |
| 9. | I think things are going much better for me than for most people I know. | 1 2 3 4 5 |
| 10. | In times of need and misery, I know there are people outside my family who can help me. | 1 2 3 4 5 |
| 11. | I am happy about my relationship with my partner. | 1 2 3 4 5 |
| 12. | My children let me think I am a good parent. | 1 2 3 4 5 |
| 13. | I am happy about the education my children are receiving. | 1 2 3 4 5 |
| 14. | I consider myself happier than most people I know. | 1 2 3 4 5 |
| 15. | I am satisfied with the way I spend my free time. | 1 2 3 4 5 |
| 16. | All the jobs I do make me feel happy about what I am doing. | 1 2 3 4 5 |
| 17. | In times of need and misery, I know there is someone who can help me. | 1 2 3 4 5 |
| 18. | I am happy about the amount of time I can devote to myself. | 1 2 3 4 5 |
| 19. | At home I feel free to express my wishes and my worries. | 1 2 3 4 5 |
| 20. | I feel really comfortable in my own home. | 1 2 3 4 5 |
| 21. | All my working activities enrich my personal life. | 1 2 3 4 5 |
| 22. | I can decide on my own how and how much to spend. | 1 2 3 4 5 |
| 23. | The free time I have is enough for me. | 1 2 3 4 5 |
| 24. | I think I have fewer problems than other people I know. | 1 2 3 4 5 |
| 25. | I feel free to express my wishes and my worries outside my own home. | 1 2 3 4 5 |
| 26. | In times of need and misery, I know who to turn to. | 1 2 3 4 5 |
| 27. | I am satisfied with my relationship with my children. | 1 2 3 4 5 |
| 28. | I can say I am a free person and that I can organize my own life with full autonomy. | 1 2 3 4 5 |
| 29. | I think I would be able to deal clear-headedly with even the greatest difficulties. | 1 2 3 4 5 |

\* \* \*

**Figure 8.1.** *Questionnaire.*

on the levels of satisfaction that they experience and be encouraged to set the goal of increasing the quality of their own lives. The second instrument that we recommend, *How Much Confidence Do I Have in Myself? Parents' Questionnaire* (Soresi *et al.*, in press), is about parents' efficacy beliefs in their own abilities to carry out valid educational behaviours. The questionnaire is made up of 18 items that investigate Self-Efficacy Beliefs about One's Own Parenting Abilities (9 items; alpha: 0.89; e.g.: 'I am a parent who is capable of teaching my own children how they must behave'; 'I know when and how to reward my children adequately'); Self-Efficacy Beliefs about One's Own

*Objective indicators for the analysis of parents' quality of life*

| *Features of the dwelling* | | |
|---|---|---|
| 1. Does the dwelling have the rooms necessary to family life (kitchen, bathroom, at least two bedrooms, living room)? | yes ❑ | no ❑ |
| 2. Do you have personal spaces in which to carry out specific activities? | yes ❑ | no ❑ |
| 3. Does the dwelling have appliances that are useful to everyday life: telephone, washing machine, oven, etc? | yes ❑ | no ❑ |
| 4. Is the dwelling provided with heating and air-conditioning systems? | yes ❑ | no ❑ |
| 5. Does the dwelling have such comforts as a TV set, a radio, a stereo system, etc.? | yes ❑ | no ❑ |
| 6. Do you have a place to keep your own objects, clothes, materials, etc.? | yes ❑ | no ❑ |
| 7. Are there essential services near your dwelling (shops, a chemist's, a GP's surgery, meeting places, etc.)? | yes ❑ | no ❑ |
| *Availability of means of communication and transport* | | |
| 8. Do you have a cellphone? | yes ❑ | no ❑ |
| 9. Do you have a bicycle? | yes ❑ | no ❑ |
| 10. Do you have a moped or a car? | yes ❑ | no ❑ |
| 11. Do you have a pass for any means of transport (bus, train, etc.)? | yes ❑ | no ❑ |
| *Health* | | |
| 12. Is your health good? | yes ❑ | no ❑ |
| 13. Do you suffer from depression? | yes ❑ | no ❑ |
| 14. Do you suffer from any mental disorder? | yes ❑ | no ❑ |
| *Personal properties* | | |
| 15. Do you manage your own finances in an autonomous way? | yes ❑ | no ❑ |
| 16. Do you have a bank/post office current account? | yes ❑ | no ❑ |
| 17. Do you have a credit card or a bank card? | yes ❑ | no ❑ |
| 18. Is the dwelling your own property in full or at least in part? | yes ❑ | no ❑ |
| *Social relationships and social participation* | | |
| 19. Do you have at least one friend? | yes ❑ | no ❑ |
| 20. Do you have daily or at least weekly contacts with other family members? | yes ❑ | no ❑ |
| 21. Do you go to recreational places at least once a week? | yes ❑ | no ❑ |
| 22. Do you go to the cinema, pub, or other meeting places? | yes ❑ | no ❑ |
| 23. Do you actively participate (voice your opinion, affect decisions) in your family, in the groups you frequent, etc.? | yes ❑ | no ❑ |
| 24. Do you have a positive loving relationship with your partner? | yes ❑ | no ❑ |
| *Occupational situation* | | |
| 25. Do you have a regular work contract? | yes ❑ | no ❑ |
| 26. Is your salary above the poverty line? | yes ❑ | no ❑ |
| *Routine* | | |
| 27. On working days do you follow a routine similar to that of other people of your own age (wake up at the same time, wash and get dressed, go to work/school, go home for lunch, etc.)? | yes ❑ | no ❑ |
| 28. On your days off do you follow a routine similar to that of people of your own age (wake up later, do some hobbies, etc.)? | yes ❑ | no ❑ |
| 29. Every year do you have holidays with significant others (family members, friends, etc.)? | yes ❑ | no ❑ |
| *Support provided by the health, social and educational services* | | |
| 30. Do you have clear and unambiguous documentation of your child's diagnosis? | yes ❑ | no ❑ |
| 31. Do you know the characteristics of your child's disability? | yes ❑ | no ❑ |
| 32. Have you ever attended a Parent Training programme? | yes ❑ | no ❑ |
| 33. Do you know specific techniques of ability improvement? | yes ❑ | no ❑ |
| 34. Do you know specific techniques of maladaptive behaviour management? | yes ❑ | no ❑ |
| 35. Are you aware of concepts such as problem-solving, coping, assertiveness, etc.? | yes ❑ | no ❑ |
| 36. Do you have daily contacts with social and health-care providers? | yes ❑ | no ❑ |
| 37. Do you have at least weekly contacts with social and health-care providers? | yes ❑ | no ❑ |
| 38. Are you supported in actions of school/work integration (do providers work with teachers and classmates; do employers and colleagues work in favour of integration)? | yes ❑ | no ❑ |
| 39. Are you supported in actions of social/community integration (do providers work with neighbours, parishes, etc.)? | yes ❑ | no ❑ |

**Figure 8.2.** *Objective indicators for the analysis of parents' quality of life.*

---

*My life as a parent*
**Personalized REPORT**

Date_____

To_____

**Reference:** Personalized report

*What is written in the present report is bound by professional secrecy and protected by the law of confidentiality. None of the information reported here can be used without your authorization.*

The questionnaire 'My life as a parent' that you have filled out aimed at analysing the quality of life of parents, that is, to what extent they think they are satisfied with the different life situations they experience. Those considered focus above all on some 'psychological' and 'relational' aspects such as, for instance, how much the person feels really at ease in his/her own family and professional environment, the degree of satisfaction about his/her own relationships and the possibility of carrying out diversified activities and duties.

In examining the scores shown in the graph below, please bear in mind that values between 0 and 39 indicate that the person considered him/herself little satisfied with his/her life, those between 40 and 60 indicate that he/she considers him/herself fairly satisfied and those between 61 and 100 indicate that he/she considers him/herself very satisfied about his/her quality of life.

More in detail, the graph shows how the parent assesses:

- **Satisfaction with relationships with family members,** that is, with relationships established with children and partner and with positive feelings that are experienced within the family. In cases of dissatisfaction with relationships of this type, and with the aim of improving the situation, it has been useful at times to have positive behaviours toward the rest of the family, like trying to be helpful, showing interest and appreciation for what they do, and letting them know one's own    and opinions, what one wishes and feels, without resorting to aggressive and punitive action.
- **Level of well-being perceived,** that is, satisfaction with the safety and tranquillity of one's own life. In cases in which levels of dissatisfaction are experienced, it can be helpful to begin identifying the reasons why the person does not feel safe and fairly tranquil and try to do something that could improve the situation. If high levels of discomfort persist it may be a good thing to have a talk with a trusted person.
- **Level of satisfaction with one's occupation,** that is, with one's own working activities. In cases in which levels of dissatisfaction are experienced, it can be important to verify what factors in the professional setting can cause it and consider different hypotheses and options that may turn out to be more advantageous and useful.
- **Level of satisfaction with the educational relationship with the children,** that is, with the way the children have been brought up and with how they are growing. In cases in which levels of dissatisfaction are experienced, it can be helpful to establish some essential points to discuss with the children, trying to bear in mind their points of view and avoiding excessively punitive approaches that can stimulate equally aggressive and inadequate reactions.
- **Level of satisfaction with one's own leisure time,** that is, with the quality and quantity of leisure time available. In cases in which levels of dissatisfaction are experienced, it can be important to establish one's own needs and seek approaches that could improve the situation.
- **Level of satisfaction with the presence of perceived support and encouragement,** that is, with the awareness that, both inside and outside the family, there is someone that can be applied to for help. In cases in which levels of dissatisfaction are experienced, it can be important to strive to seek and maintain positive interpersonal relationships with these people, engaging in positive behaviours towards them.
- **Level of satisfaction with the possibility of self-determination,** that is, with the ability to make important decisions autonomously, to be able to have one's own 'space' within the family, and to engage in activities that one finds pleasing. Although it is true that everyone often has to come to terms with the demands and expectations of others, it is also important to state one's own autonomy by asking, without however resorting to an aggressive stance, for one's own space to be respected and for the recognition of one's own rights to privacy and independence.

---

**Figure 8.3.**

**MY LIFE AS A PARENT**

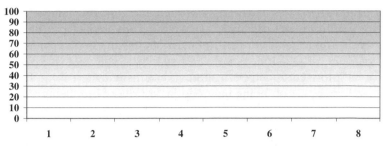

Legend
1. Relationships with family members
2. Perceived well-being
3. Occupation
4. Educational relationship with the children
5. Leisure time
6. Support and encouragement
7. Self-determination

**Figure 8.4.**

Ability to Handle Difficult Situations (4 items; alpha: 0.66; e.g.: 'I can criticize my children without losing my patience'; 'I consider myself capable of not imposing my ideas on my children'); and Self-Efficacy Beliefs about One's Own Ability to Support One's Children (5 items; alpha: 0.85; e.g.: 'I am capable of helping my children make important life decisions'; 'I am capable of making my children think about the appropriateness of their ideas and conduct').

## PARENTS' INVOLVEMENT IN TREATMENT PLANNING

Habilitation programmes should aim at the massive expansion of repertoires of abilities necessary to carry out daily life activities, should be implemented in normal life environments and should also plan for the systematic involvement of family members, with the purpose of guaranteeing the maintenance and generalization of what is achieved (Dunst *et al.* 2006).

Very clear indications in this respect have also been formulated by the World Health Organization when, in revising the classification of the consequences of impairments, it decided to replace the list of disabilities with classifications of daily life activities and to expressly mention participation and involvement. Before that, when speaking of disability reference was made to a disadvantaged life . . . now the focus is on restriction in participation in the life of environmental contexts and the health and social services are invited to consider the quantity and quality of the involvement that, in an essentially ecological behavioural perspective, individuals with disability and their relatives actually experience.

The need is for particularly sophisticated and sensitive analyses given that different environments can have a very different impact on the same individual with impairments or with activity limitations. An environment that offers barriers, or which does not offer supports, will decrease participation, while other, more equipped environments can instead increase it. Involvement can mean being part of, being included in an area of life, being accepted and having access to the necessary resources. All of this can favour satisfaction, realization and fun (WHO 2001).

Participation is certainly a complex construct which includes important and traditionally separate aspects, such as integration, adjustment, empowerment, self-determination and satisfaction. The involvement meant by the WHO implies, on one side, *being and operating with* and, on the other, *turning to, tending to . . . operating jointly* in order to reach shared goals and objectives. To favour that, not only competences, willingness and abilities are necessary, but also great flexibility and availability. Often, it is a matter of choosing and deciding on objectives and strategies . . . together with others in a mutual recognition of rights, expectations, and power. Not by chance, the construct of participation recalls also that of empowerment, which in recent years has been increasingly found in the sociopolitical and psychoeducational literature and also (at last!) in the literature on health and rehabilitation.

Empowerment could be defined, in Bruscaglioni's (1994, p. 124) words, as 'the process of extension (through the better use of one's own existing and potentially acquirable resources) of the possibilities that the individual can put into practice and make operational and among which he/she can then choose'. As far as it concerns us here, it deals with providing choice and decisional power, also in the planning of treatments to individuals with disability and their family members. In other words, parents should be recognized to have the power to significantly influence what is programmed and realized in favour of their children (for instance, as regards the hierarchy of rehabilitation goals, treatments, choice of contexts to frequent, value attributed to their levels of satisfaction, their self-evaluation, etc). However, this is not so straightforward: as Price (1993) maintains, power is not something that many people are prepared to surrender easily.

Furthermore, habilitation and rehabilitation programmes devised together with parents should be realized as early as possible (Guralnick 2000; Kasari and Hodapp 1996). Specifically as regards Down Syndrome and intellectual disabilities, early intervention and active parental involvement are today unanimously considered essential for children's psychosocial development (Rondal 2004). In this way interactions between children with Down Syndrome and their care-givers, that is those that can influence their social, affective and cognitive development, are guaranteed to be suitable and effective from the very beginning (Iarocci *et al.* 2006).

In addition, early interventions that aim at autonomy and privilege analysis of daily activities also represent occasions about which it is easier to gather consensus and collaborations between experts and parents. Ambits of comparison and collaboration can certainly be numerous and diverse. Dunst *et al.* (2000) list as many as 22: a) those typical of the family circle (family routines, parenting routines, child routines, literacy activities, physical play, entertainment activities, family rituals, family celebrations, socialization activities, gardening activities); b) those typical of the community (family activities, family outings, play activities, community events, outdoor activities, recreation activities, children's attractions, art/entertainment activities, church/religious groups, organizations/groups, sports activities/events).

Being able to 'transfer' adequate and shared treatment modalities to the family context increases the likelihood of educational success (Bennett 2001; Kibby *et al.* 1998; Ready *et al.* 2001). In this respect, Dunst *et al.* (2006) have verified the efficacy of two different forms of early intervention: the first was realized by experts in environments where certain activities were developed (for instance doing motor exercises in the bathroom while taking a shower) – activity setting; the second emphasized the use of daily life environments as learning opportunities in which the children interact with others and with the environment in a 'natural' way (using an activity setting as an everyday learning opportunity) (use the hose to water flowers or vegetables in the garden; position the children's hand on the glass and help them to drink; ask them to lift their arms when they are about to wear a shirt; take them to the park and let them play with the animals). The analyses carried out have shown that when activity settings were used as everyday learning opportunities, the greatest effects in different areas of functioning were recorded. On the contrary, when early interventions were realized in activity settings, not only poorer effects on adaptive functioning were obtained, but also less parental satisfaction was recorded. The authors go so far as to say that in the case of activities useful to increase the abilities necessary to carry out the everyday activities that are realized in significant environments, the values and the personal, family and cultural beliefs of the same family, routines and family habits and, as a consequence, also the expectations of the parents themselves are more likely to be taken into account. On the contrary, realizing learning interventions in activity environments can cause negative reactions, such as stress, uneasiness, perception of loneliness, just because parents' way of thinking and how they conceive educational and rehabilitative activities for their child are not considered.

Moreover, any type of treatment should aim at favouring the development of positive social interactions between parents and their children with disability and between these and the other family members. It must be remembered that children with disability can show interactive behaviours less markedly and/or less effectively than children with typical development and this may contribute to reducing quality of relationships within the family (Barber 2000;

Bornstein 1995; Shonkoff and Phillips 2000). Acting in a way that from the very beginning creates conditions for establishing positive relationships helps to lay the foundations for the development of the child's social competence, which can then be to the advantage of the development of positive relationships with siblings, peers and other members of the community and, therefore, of social inclusion (Guralnick and Alberini 2006). To that aim it is important to favour the development of 'affective reactivity and social signaling, including using facial expressions, gestures, eye-contact, and emotional reactivity to alert the care provider' (Iarocci et al. 2006, p. 13).

The early involvement of parents of children with disability that considers what has been said above makes parents more likely to favour more cohesive relationships, manage difficult situations more effectively, face their educational tasks with stronger self-efficacy beliefs and experience higher levels of quality of life (Soresi et al. 2006). Margalit et al. (2006), involving 80 mothers of children with disability, most of the children having Down Syndrome and being aged three or younger, have shown that, despite recorded variability at pre-test as concerns self-confidence, ability to maintain a positive mood, and levels of stress, early interventions that provided both the necessary therapies for their child and developed a positive child–parent relationship, produced positive results, also in mothers with the greatest difficulties. In general, almost all mothers reported that participation in the programme encouraged them, made them feel supported and also increased their perception of empowerment.

## CONCLUSIONS

In the literature it is increasingly underlined that, in interventions in favour of children with disability, involving parents as early as possible is strongly recommended – even before the birth of the child whenever possible. Action must not only aim at increasing parents' abilities, but also at strengthening those psychological requisites that can favour the development of the child and the quality of life in the family (Soresi et al. 2006; Rondal 2004). The objectives of the services that provide for families of children with disability should pivot, regardless of reference approaches, around four fundamental points: '(1) empowering parents to gain advocacy and partnership skills; (2) enhancing the family's ability to parent their child effectively; (3) helping families build support networks; and (4) enhancing overall family health and wellbeing' (Summers et al. 2005, p. 780). The professional has the responsibility of providing a service that keeps in mind the parents' cognitive and emotional abilities and possibilities, their values and their abilities; he/she has the task of providing interventions and support capable of making parents become active participants in the decisions that must be made to their child's advantage: conscious and dynamic collaborators, but also 'lively' supporters of their own rights and of those of their child.

That requires specific and sophisticated competences that are produced by careful training and continuous updating and by an inclination constantly to verify the effectiveness of one's own work. From the very beginning of their collaboration with parents, professionals should be able to pass on in a clear way all the information they have on the impairments and disabilities of individuals, stating their own limitations and making themselves available to help parents seek other competences and professionalisms. During the activity they should inform the parents, with calm and patience, of the results of the analyses carried out, waiting for them to make sense of them, giving them the possibility of expressing their opinions, and their possible doubts and perplexities, emotions and moods, dreams and hopes, yet without creating false expectations, and while still pointing out what would be better from the professional point of view. In addition, professionals should make their criticisms in a suitable way by concentrating the attention of the recipients on more functional ways of dealing with a difficult situation, and promoting abilities of problem-solving and reinforcing useful efforts and adequate performances. Finally, it may be useful to encourage parents to uphold their rights and those of their children, to be assertive and to encourage contact with bodies, organizations and associations that can supply support and additional assistance (Kerr and McIntosh 2000; Soresi and Nota 2005; Wilgosh and Scorgie 2000).

Besides, it must be remembered that the early involvement of parents to the advantage of the whole family's well-being becomes in the long run an advantageous intervention both for the people involved and for the community and its economic policies. This consideration seems particularly important in the light of the emphasis that in the specialized literature and in the laws of many countries is placed on the need to intervene early in order to minimize the difficulties of children with disability, capitalize upon their strengths, and increase their well-being and that of their families.

In concluding, however, we cannot but show our concern for what is going on, in the midst of the current economic crisis, in a number of countries that are actually reducing public health financing and endangering the possible implementation of adequate and effective prevention and early intervention programmes. That seems also to reduce even further the likelihood that poorer families will get access to the services they need, thus increasing the situation of discomfort and risk in which they are already living. Besides the need to seek alternative ways of financing the services, it should not be forgotten that in terms of cost-effectiveness early interventions have long been shown to be good investments, even in terms of simply holding down expenses (Grant 2005). It has recently been underlined that at-risk children that had attended the High/Scope Perry Preschool Program had as adults shown higher levels of education and had higher incomes and fewer problems with the law. From an economic point of view these results saved the state a remarkable amount of money, quantifiable as a 'profit' of as much as US $5.67 for every dollar spent (Milagros *et al.* 2005). As Grant (2005) maintains, in the long run the initial costs of early interventions are offset by the reduction of 'long term government expenditures for special education, rehabilitation services, and expensive institutional [care]' (p. 248) and all that, besides giving people undeniable advantages, also seems to have positive effects on the community.

## REFERENCES

Andrich, D. (1988). *Rash models for measurement.* Thousand Oaks, CA: Sage Publications.
Antonovsky, A. (1987). *Unraveling the mystery of health.* San Francisco, CA: Jossey-Bass.
Bandura, A. (1977). Self-efficacy: Toward a unifying theory of behavioral change. *Psychological Review.* 84:191–215.
Barber, N. (2000). *Why parents matter: Parental investment and child outcomes.* Westport, CT: Bergin & Garvey.
Bennett, T.L. (2001). Neuropsychological evaluation in rehabilitation planning and evaluation of functional skills. *Archives of Clinical Neuropsychology.* pp. 237–53.
Bornstein, R.F. (1995). Active dependency. *Journal of Nervous and Mental Disease.* 183:64–77.
Brown, I. and Brown, R. (2004). Concepts for beginning study in family quality of life. In A.P. Turnbull, I. Brown and H.R. Turnbull (eds), *Families and people with mental retardation and quality of life: International perspectives.* pp. 25–47. Washington, DC: American Association on Mental Retardation.
Bruscaglioni, M. (1994). *La società liberata.* Milan: Franco Angeli.
Chang, E.C. (2002). Optimism–pessimism and stress appraisal: Testing a cognitive interactive model of psychological adjustment in adults. *Cognitive Therapy and Research.* 26:675–90.
Cohen, M.S. (1999). Families coping with childhood chronic illness: a research review. *Family System & Health.* 17:149–64.
Coleman, P. and Karraker, K. (1997). Self-efficacy and parenting quality: Findings and future applications. *Developmental Review.* 18:47–85.
Coleman, P. and Karraker, K. (2003). Maternal self-efficacy beliefs, competence in parenting, and toddlers' behavior and developmental status. *Infant Mental Health Journal.* 24:126–48.
Cummins, R.A. (2003). Normative life satisfaction: Measurement issues and a homeostatic model. *Social Indicators Research.* 64:225–56.
Dellve, L., Reichenberg, K. and Hallenberg, L.R.M. (2000). Parents coping with caring for their asthmatic child. A grounded theory study. *Scandinavian Journal of Disability Research.* 2:100–13.
Dunst, C.J., Hamby, D., Trivette C.M., Raab, M. and Bruder, M.B. (2000). Everyday family and community life and children's naturally occurring learning opportunities. *Journal of Early Intervention.* 23:151–64.

Dunst, C.J., Bruder, M.B., Trivette, C.M. and Hamby, D.W. (2006). Everyday activity settings, natural learning environments and early intervention practices. *Journal of Policy and Practice in Intellectual Disabilities.* 3:3–10.

Felce, D. (1997). Defining and applying the concept of quality of life. *Journal of Intellectual Disability Research.* 41:126–35.

Fox, L., Vaughn, B.J., Llanes, Wystte, M. and Dunlap, G. (2002). 'We can't expect other people to understand': Family perspectives on problem behavior. *Exceptional Children.* 68(4):437–50.

Grant, R. (2005). State strategies to contain costs in the early intervention program: Policy and evidence. *Topics in Early Childhood Special Education.* 25:243–50.

Guralnick, M.J. (2000). Early childhood intervention: Evolution of a system. In M. Wehmeyer and J.R. Patton (eds), *Mental retardation in the 21st century.* pp. 37–58. Austin, TX: PRO-ED.

Guralnick, M.J. and Albertini, G. (2006). Early intervention in an international perspective. *Journal of Policy and Practice in Intellectual Disabilities.* 3:1–2.

Iarocci, G., Virji-Babul, N. and Reebye, P. (2006). The Learn at Play Program (LAPP): merging family developmental research, early intervention, and policy goals for children with Down syndrome. *Journal of Policy and Practice in Intellectual Disabilities.* 3:11–21.

Jokinen, N.S. and Brown, R.I. (2005). Family quality of life from the perspective of older parents. *Journal of Intellectual Disability Research.* 49:789–93.

Kasari, C. and Hodapp, R.M. (1996). Is Down syndrome different? Evidence from social and family studies. *Down Syndrome Quarterly.* 1:1–8.

Kerr, S.M. and McIntosh, J.B. (2000). Coping when a child has a disability: Exploring the impact of parent-to-parent support. *Child: Care, Health and Development.* 26:309–21.

Kibby, M.Y., Schmitter-Edgecombe, M. and Long, C.J. (1998). Ecological validity of neuro-psychological tests: Focus on the California Verbal Learning Test and the Wisconsin Card Sorting Test. *Archives of Clinical Neuropsychology.* 13:523–34.

King, G.A., Zwaigenbaum, L., King, S., Baxter, D., Rosenbaum, P. and Bates, A. (2006). A qualitative investigation of changes in the belief system of families of children with autism or Down syndrome. *Child: Care, Health & Development.* 32:353–69.

Luckasson, R., Borthwick-Duffy, S., Buntinx, W.H., Coulter, D.L., Craig, E.M. and Reeve, A. (2002). *Mental retardation: Definition, classification, and systems of supports.* Washington, DC: American Association on Mental Retardation.

Mailick, Seltzer, M., Greenberg, J.S., Floyd, F.J., Petee, Y. and Hong, J. (2001). Life course impact of parenting a child with disabilities. *American Journal on Mental Retardation.* 106(3):265–86.

Margalit, M., Al-Yagon, M. and Kleitman, T. (2006). Family subtyping and early intervention. *Journal of Policy and Practice in Intellectual Disabilities.* 3:33–41.

Milagros, N., Belfield, C.R., Barnett, W.S. and Schweinhart, L. (2005). Updating the economic impacts of the high/scope Perry preschool program. *Educational Evaluation and Policy Analysis.* 27:245–61.

Minnes, P. (1998). Mental retardation: The impact upon the family. In J.A. Burack and R.M. Hodapp (eds), *Handbook of mental retardation and development.* pp. 693–712. Cambridge: Cambridge University Press.

Nelson, G. (1984). The relationship between dimensions of classroom and family environments and self-concept, satisfaction, and achievement of grade 7 and 8 students. *Journal of Community Psychology*. 12:276–87.

Nota, L. (2004). Family involvement in the treatment of individuals with intellectual disability. In J.A., Rondal, A., Rasore-Quartino and S., Soresi (eds), *The adult with Down Syndrome. A new challenge for society*. pp. 205–11. London: Whurr Publishers.

Nota, L. and Soresi, S. (2004). Social and community inclusion. In J. Rondal, R. Hodapp, S. Soresi, E. Dykens and L. Nota (eds), *Intellectual disabilities. Genetics, behaviour, and inclusion*. pp. 157–92. London: Whurr Publishers.

Nota, L., Soresi, S., Ferrari, L., Wilgosh, L. and Scorgie, K. (2003). Life management and quality of life of parents of children with diverse disabilities. *Developmental Disabilities Bulletin*. 31:155–81.

Nota, L., Soresi, S. and Perry, J. (2006). Quality of life in adults with intellectual disability. *Journal of Intellectual Disability Research*. 50:371–85.

Olson, D.H. (1986). Circumplex model VII: Validation studies and FACES III. *Family Process*. 26:337–51.

Patterson, J.M. (2002). Learning from the pioneers of collaborative care. *Families, Systems and Health*. 20:375–8.

Prage, M.E., Greenbaum, P.E., Silver, S.E., Friedman, R.M., Kutash, K. and Duchnowski, A.J. (1992). Family functioning and psychopathology among adolescents with severe emotional disturbance. *Journal of Abnormal Child Psychology*. 20:83–102.

Price, F. (1993). Educated power. *Total Quality Magazine*. June.

Putallaz, M. and Hope-Heflin, A. (1990). Parent–child interaction. In S.R. Asher and J.D. Coie (eds), *Peer rejection in childhood*. pp. 189–216. Cambridge: Cambridge University Press.

Rasch, G. (1960/1980). *Probabilistic models for some intelligence and attainment test*. Chicago: University of Chicago Press.

Ready, R.E., Stierman, L. and Paulsen, J.S. (2001). Ecological validity of neuropsychological and personality measures of executive functions. *The Clinical Neuropsychologist*. 15:314–23.

Rondal, J. (2004). L'intervento precoce nelle disabilità intellettive [early intervention with persons with intellectual disabilities]. *Giornale Italiano delle Disabilità*. 4:3–13.

Schalock, R.L. (1999). A quest for quality: Achieving organisational outputs and personal outcomes. In J. Gardner and S. Nudler (eds), *Quality performance in human services*. pp. 55–80. Baltimore, MD: Paul, H. Brookes.

Schalock, R.L. (2004). The concept of quality of life: What we know and do not know. *Journal of Intellectual Disability Research*. 48:203–16.

Schalock, R.L., Brown, I., Brown, R.I., Cummins, R., Felce, D. and Matikka, L. (2002). Conceptualization, measurement, and application of quality of life for persons with intellectual disabilities: Report of an international panel of experts. *Mental Retardation*. 40:457–70.

Scorgie, K., Wilgosh, L. and McDonald, L. (1998). Stress and coping in families of children with disabilities: An examination of recent literature. *Developmental Disabilities Bulletin*. 26:22–42.

Shonkoff, J.P. and Phillips, D.A. (2000). *From neurons to neighbourhoods: The science of early childhood development.* Washington, DC: National Academy Press.

Soresi, S. (2004). Evaluating treatment outcomes. In J.A. Rondal, A. Rasore-Quartino and S. Soresi (eds), *The adult with Down Syndrome. A new challenge for society.* pp. 235–50. London: Whurr Publishers.

Soresi, S. and Nota, L. (2004). School inclusion. In J. Rondal, R. Hodapp, S. Soresi, E. Dykens and L. Nota (eds), *Intellectual disabilities. Genetics, behaviour, and inclusion.* pp. 114–56. London: Whurr Publishers.

Soresi, S. and Nota, L. (2005). Parent training per genitori con figli disabili. In M. Cusinato and M. Panzeri (eds), *Le sfide della genitorialità.* pp. 81–112. Milan: Guerini Scientifica.

Soresi, S., Nota, L. and Sgaramella, T.M. (2003). *La valutazione delle disabilità. Secondo volume.* Pordenone, Italy: Erip.

Soresi, S., Nota, L. and Ferrari, L. (2006). Family setting in Down syndrome. In J.A. Rondal and J. Perera (eds), *Down syndrome: Neurobehavioural specificity.* (pp. 191–211). London: John Wiley & Sons.

Soresi, S., Nota, L. and Ferrari, L, (in press). Qualità della vita e autoefficacia. In S. Soresi and L. Nota (eds), *Portfolio per l'assessment delle disability.* Florence: Organizzazioni Speciali.

Summers, J.A., Poston, D.J., Turnbull, A.P., Marquis, J., Hoffman, L., Mannan, H. and Wang, M. (2005). Conceptualizing and measuring family quality of life. *Journal of Intellectual Disability Research.* 49:777–83.

Thompson, R. and Gustafson, K. (1996). *Adaptation to chronic childhood illness.* Washington, DC: American Psychological Association.

Virji-Babul, N., Eichman, A. and Duffield, D. (2004). Development of Canadian voluntary population based registry on Down syndrome: Preliminary results. (2000–2002). *Journal of Developmental Disabilities.* 10:113–22.

Wallander, J., Varni, J., Babani, L., Banis, H. and Wilcox, K. (1989). Family resources as resistant factors for psychological development in chronically ill and handicapped children. *Journal of Pediatric Psychology.* 14:157–73.

WHO. (2001). *International Classification of Functioning, Disability and Health.* (ICF). Geneva: World Health Organization.

Wilgosh, L., Scorgie, K. (2000). Family life management when a child has severe develop-mental disabilities: A subgroup examination. *Developmental Disabilities Bulletin.* 28:15–18.

Wilgosh, L., Scorgie, K. and Fleming, D. (2000). Effective life management in parents of children with disabilities: A survey replication and extension. *Developmental Disabilities Bulletin.* 28:1–14.

Wilgosh, L., Nota, L., Scorgie, K. and Soresi, S. (2004). Effective life management in parents of children with disabilities: A cross-national extension. *International Journal for the Advancement of Counseling.* 26:301–12.

# 9 School Inclusion: The Italian Model

**LUCIO COTTINI AND LAURA NOTA**

## SUMMARY

School inclusion plays a meaningful role in the development and growth of individuals with disability. In consideration of the fact that to realize inclusive schooling, time and specific professional abilities are necessary, the present work aimed, in the first place, at analysing the current situation after thirty years of school inclusion of students with disability, by underlining its main strengths and weaknesses. Secondly, attention was paid to a variable that shapes successful inclusion experiences, but that is not always taken into account: how to motivate the classmates of students with disability adequately with a view to improving schooling and the social inclusion process.

## INTRODUCTION

In the light of the recent perspectives on disability (*International Classification of Functioning, Disability, and Health (ICF)*: WHO 2001; *Definition, Classification, and Systems of Supports Manual*: Luckasson *et al.* 2002), school inclusion seems to be the only possible way to foster the participation of individuals with disability in social life and to strengthen their levels of self-determination (Nota *et al.* 2002; Wehmeyer 2006; Wehmeyer and Patton 2000). Indeed, school inclusion can also affect the professional development of individuals with disability and guarantee greater opportunities to think positively and effectively about the future (Soresi *et al.*, in press).

Moreover, it has a beneficial effect, since it implies overcoming sociocultural prejudices and marginalizing social barriers by strengthening active participation and the presence of technical, social and organizational solutions; however, it also involves rehabilitative and training actions able to confront the different educational needs that characterize a heterogeneous group of students (Groppo 1983; Soresi and Nota 2001).

*Therapies and Rehabilitation in Down Syndrome.* Edited by Rondal
© 2007 John Wiley & Sons Ltd

Inclusion testifies to consideration for diversity and recognition that students with disability have the same rights as their peers. However, although this has sometimes superficially occurred, this does not mean that these students have to be treated in the same way as their peers from a methodological and didactic point of view. In actual fact, having the same rights does not necessarily mean having to benefit from the same interventions, as they might turn out to be totally inappropriate (Minnow 1990).

Following on from that, the agents of school programmes that aim at facilitating inclusion should be not only disability specialists, but also school officials, non-teaching school staff and curricular teachers, parents and classmates. Their involvement is important because the point is to plan changes to the traditional educational praxis in order to guarantee everyone, be they students, adults or teachers, a significant and satisfying experience. In other words, what we are thinking of is an educational setting that not only pays attention to the needs associated with impairment, but also considers the specificities of each student (Nota *et al.* in press).

## THE ITALIAN MODEL OF SCHOOL INCLUSION: HIGHLIGHTS AND SHADOWS

Even if initially activated without a real educational and organizational projectuality (Cottini *et al.* 2003), the choice Italy made in the 1970s in favour of the generalized presence of pupils with disability in state schools has paid off and yielded significant results. Through a series of laws and bills, culminating in law 104/92 and the dispositions that followed it, attempts have been made to regulate and guide the process of real inclusion of all students in regular classes, even if the application has not always been made in accordance with normative indications.

The debate and reflections currently under way at educational level concern the modalities through which more and more meaning can be given to the inclusion of students with disability in a school undergoing changes, while at the same time defending acquired achievements from some more or less covert attempts to go back to separate institutions (the reference is to the ongoing discussion on the situation of students with autism and with serious deficits).

With the aim of structuring a real-life project for the person with disability, the school experience surely represents a fundamentally important moment in which to create the conditions for real social inclusion.

In order to introduce the state of the art as regards school inclusion comprehensively, we will consider the organizational models that characterize it, thus trying to underline strengths and weaknesses and highlighting future perspectives.

# THE ORGANIZATIONAL MODELS OF INCLUSION

The process of school insertion-inclusion of pupils with disability has been realized in different ways, each of which testifies to the degree of organization, the level of professionalism, and the historical-cultural reality and philosophy of school institutions themselves. A strategic role has surely been played by special education teachers, who, however, have not always succeeded in facilitating changes in school organization and didactics and in involving their colleagues in this process. They have often found themselves 'stuck' in an institution that refuses to accept change and that simply requires the adoption of actions that can enable the class to complete the programme smoothly without any trouble.

The much advocated integrated management of this problem does not find concrete realization in all contexts, at least not at secondary-school level. In short, the situation has certainly improved over recent years, but not enough to do away with the reprehensible habit of 'delegating' to special education teachers the burden and responsibility of planning the school courses for and of students with disability.

To clarify further this fundamental aspect, on which successful inclusion depends for a great part, we are going to illustrate the main organizational models that still today regulate the presence of children with disability in regular classes.

## EMERGENCY MODEL

This model can be easily found in those realities in which the 'support' action is centred on the teacher's particular role (loneliness). The task of 'didactic recovery' – delegated by the institution – is carried out by only one teacher who, in the most favourable situations, has been suitably trained (Fig. 9.1).

The institution does not want to be involved in inclusion. The special education teacher is perceived as a psychological 'crutch' by his/her colleagues. There is no collective planning at the general educational level, there is no shared participation in defining educational objectives (Individualized Educational Plan), and, if there is, it is only formal; relationship and contact with the family is kept by the special education teacher, who often works

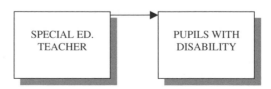

**Figure 9.1.** Emergency model.

without any help from specialized professional figures (multidisciplinary team, etc.).

To be clear, it must be said that the emergency model and the condition of isolation are those most easily found.

## PROGRESSIVE INVOLVEMENT MODEL

In other situations, because of awareness, of increased professionalism and sensitivity, or of social advocacy, the other teachers feel gradually involved without actually meaning to become so (Fig. 9.2). The novelty effect is that the special education activity involves and tends to change the whole school organization: the first elements or factors of the 'support function' (Cottini *et al.* 2003) can be perceived. Such reality can be found more easily in the organization of elementary school (cf. modules) rather than in other types of school. Nevertheless the effect is positive and can determine important consequences as regards advantages for students. All that, however, can be ascribed only to a partial and often confused concept of the teacher's function or, worse still, to an emotional response.

## MODEL OF DISTRIBUTED RESPONSIBILITY

This model corresponds to a completely different philosophy, in which the whole school institution takes on the task of realizing the full inclusion and integration of pupils with disability (Fig. 9.3).

In opposition to the use of only one resource (a special education teacher), a central place is being taken by the 'support function'. Such a model is not easy to implement, since it involves radical methodological and didactic innovations. It has to go through a thoroughgoing revision of the modes of acting and of operating in tune with fellow teachers, with the family, and with other specialized figures (the team). It involves the collective, but not the formal, practice and application of the basics of educational planning, the implementation of efficient calibrated educational technologies, etc.

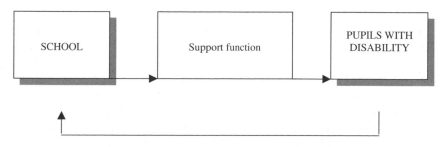

**Figure 9.2.** Progressive involvement model.

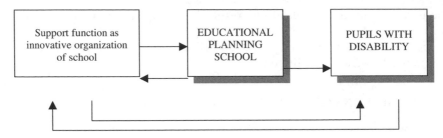

**Figure 9.3.** Model of distributed responsibility.

In this model, '*collectivity*' does not mean the opposite of '*individuality*' or '*specialization*'. It is rather the functional context in which some educational facts that represent the innovative element are expounded.

## TOWARD REAL INCLUSION: FROM EXCEPTIONALITY TO NORMALITY

Let us now examine a series of still unresolved problems by putting forward some lines of action that can allow the actual realization of the *model of distributed responsibility* described above. Practically speaking, this means adopting a series of organizational and methodological procedures that can facilitate the implementation of *special didactics of inclusion*, with the purpose of supplying effective answers, in the regular class, to the very special needs of students with disability (Cottini 2004).

For obvious reasons of space, very brief descriptions will be supplied.

### 1. ORGANIZATIONAL ADJUSTMENTS

#### (a) **Organization of the teacher resource**

To say that the effective school inclusion process of pupils with disability depends largely on the suitable presence and competence of the teaching staff is such an obvious statement as to appear self-evident. Going into more depth, however, some reflections that are relevant to the quality of the inclusion process can be made. If only quantitative aspects are considered, the risk is that of focusing on what does not represent the main problem. In Italy there are around 60000 special education teachers for fewer than 120000 students with disability and, in addition, local bodies appoint several assistants, who very often perform tasks well beyond mere physical care. In general, therefore, the ratio cannot be viewed in a negative light. What does appear worrisome is, instead, the recurrent and almost universal request that the school schedule of students with disability be 'covered' by specialized teachers.

It is not absolutely certain that increasing the number of special education teachers will bring real progress to the quality of inclusion; paradoxically, the opposite may well be true with the possible activation of separation rather than inclusion processes. The problem, therefore, is always the organization of the already mentioned support resources, the integration between these teachers and the curricular ones, and the training of the whole teaching staff.

Improving the *ability to plan and to run together* the educational work of special education teachers and of curricular teachers is an essential condition for the quality of school inclusion. Unfortunately, it must be recognized that such integrated management is not always implemented, especially in secondary school.

### (b) Organizational flexibility

It is important to guarantee greater curriculum flexibility, as well as to experiment with new forms of organization of school schedules and spaces and also to plan extramural activities. The acquisition of autonomy for school institutions allows the flexible articulation of the organization of educational activities according to everyone's specific needs. Such flexibility should lead to rethinking various organizational parameters, on which success and quality of inclusion can depend:

- the modular articulation of the amount of yearly time available for every discipline and activity;
- the modular articulation of groups of pupils (same class, different class, different school grades);
- the aggregation of disciplines in disciplinary areas and ambits; and
- the activation of individualized educational pathways, in consideration of the class and group inclusion of pupils, pupils with disability among them.

### (c) Partnership with the families

For a long time, the family of a child with disability was only seen in a pathologically framed perspective: in other words, only the negative emotions and the stress linked to the management of a child with disability were underlined (sometimes, combined with offering the family therapeutic courses; cf. Ferguson and Asch 1989).

By contrast, in recent years, awareness of the family as having some important potentialities that must be strengthened and exploited has begun to come across. By being handed specific abilities (parent training), families become protagonists (and not merely spectators) of their child's inclusion process, in a close collaborative relationship with the school (Soresi and Nota 2001).

**(d) Collaboration with healthcare and social services and local bodies**

Once again, it is a matter of establishing partnership relationships with the bodies responsible for inclusion and especially with Health and Social Services and local bodies. Such collaboration should lead to a shared life project, with measures that, first of all, support the quality of school attendance of students with difficulty, their school-career counselling and educational continuity; allow the best possible use of the available resources, understood both as technologically advanced equipment and as specific professional competences; and favour operational co-ordination to allow optimization of the cost–benefit ratio in relation to resources employed. In reality, this collaboration between schools and other bodies is hardly ever realized, above all as a result of a lack of funds and a paucity of health-care workers available or through the lack of a body capable of effective co-ordination, and able to bring together the different actors in the integrated project for the person with disability.

## 2. METHODOLOGICAL–DIDACTIC ADJUSTMENTS

**(a) Individualized objectives and class objectives**

To foster the possibility of high-quality class attendance by students with disability, it is fundamental to work carefully on the adjustment of the objectives planned for the class and those of the individualized educational plan.

To be able to make such integration work, first of all, individualized plans must be drafted by all the curricular teachers, and not by the special education teacher alone. In this way it is easier to see whether among the planned class objectives there are some that may also be suitable for the student with disability. A number of such experiences have clearly shown that inclusion is possible and beneficial for all the students of the class (Celi 1999; Cottini 2004).

But objective adjustment does not have to be one-way, that is the mere adjustment of individualized planning in order to make it similar to class planning. In some situations there are activities thought to be for the advantage of the pupil with difficulty in which classmates with typical development can also participate. And this is not a simple slowing down, since the classmates can derive important cognitive advantages (for instance, going over some parts of the programme, with the breaking down of complexes of tasks into sequences, etc.) and social advantages.

Besides the attempt to draw the individualized objectives planned for the child with disability near to those for the class, other methodologies exist which are able to reconcile the demands of individualized teaching and those of real inclusion. One of the most important refers to the full use of the so-called 'classmate resource', which is currently little used to the advantage of inclusion (see below).

The need to keep students with disability in class as much as possible, allowing them to participate in the same learning situations as their classmates, has been addressed by some authors (for example, Cottini 2005), who have distinguished between 'learning a task' and *'participation in the culture of a task'*. In other words, even when adjustments of objectives and methodologies that permit the meaningful learning of tasks of the same type as those of the classmates are not possible, it is in any case beneficial to let students with disability participate in the activities of their class, enabling them to grasp at least some of the elements needed to understand the topic dealt with. In this way, pupils perceive that the assignments directed to the whole class are not totally foreign to them, and this surely must encourage them to feel an integral part of the class, and also motivates their more active commitment to the tasks in which they do participate.

In sum, there are indeed a number of possibilities for reconciling the need to personalize teaching and safeguarding the inclusion perspective. Nonetheless, we also underline the possibility and the utility of planning for times, which can be shorter or longer according to circumstances, in which also to privilege a *one-to-one* teaching situation outside the class. The utility of basic learning to facilitate inclusion is so important that, in some conditions, it can justify students with disability leaving the class. The main point is that such times must be limited experiences and that they have to be planned in the interest of students with disability and their inclusion. In other words, they are justified only if the pursued objective is of extreme importance and if conditions do not exist to organize class teaching in the ways mentioned above or to envisage shared attendance.

### (b) Individualization of teaching

To individualize teaching does not mean simply taking into consideration the specific educational needs of students with disability, but also becoming increasingly aware of the deep individual differences both in cognitive learning styles and in teaching styles. Students' school failures are very often due to a lack of correspondence between the student's specific cognitive style and the style of the teacher giving the lesson. Obviously, then, completely ignoring these aspects may penalize above all students who have cognitive deficits (and are therefore less ready to adapt to the style imposed by the teacher).

It must be underlined, however, that, behind the expression 'individualized teaching', pathways not beneficial to inclusion are often concealed. In many cases individualization is synonymous with separation, with individual work done by students with disability with the special education teacher in contexts other than the class. As we have mentioned above, this condition can certainly be part of personalized planning. When, however, going away from the classroom becomes systematic, two serious risks are run: decreased responsibility of curricular teachers and increased marginalization of students with disability.

### (c) Collaboration

As has already been underlined, this is one of the aspects most lacking in the inclusion of students with disability: unfortunately, delegating to the special education teacher is still frequent, with consequent decreased whole-school responsibility. Future developments will have to stimulate forms of collaboration between all teachers; this will be possible inasmuch as the inclusion of the child with disability is not left to improvisation, but based on reliable and effective methodologies. All this, however, has already been discussed above.

### (d) Studying disability in class

An extremely interesting methodological indication is related to the study of disability in class. This topic is linked to those that will be described below in terms of activating the 'classmate resource'. When disability becomes an object of scientific study, stimulating classmates' discussion and in-depth investigation of it, fears and uncertainties decrease and diversity increasingly assumes the value of an everyday condition that does not challenge the dignity and the uniqueness of the person, but rather emphasizes it. Knowledge also facilitates an understanding of which may be the best and most natural answers to the specific needs of individual students with disability. Information on disability can be inserted into the curriculum in a number of different ways (Ianes 2001), such as:

- inviting to the class older students with disability, parents of students with disability, physicians, therapists, and teachers;
- presenting and discussing in class videos, television programmes, books, magazines and articles on disability;
- doing research on famous people with disability;
- getting information on aids and technologies available for the reduction of difficulties; and
- proposing activities that, through simulation, allow students to understand how life can feel with a physical, sensory or cognitive deficit.

### (e) New technologies

Today the rapid progress in the world of technology offers important hardware aids that can deal with sensory and/or motor problems connected to disability (for instance, adjusted keyboards, touch screens, etc.). Moreover, it is also possible to resort to diagnostic, didactic and rehabilitative software.

Unfortunately, the diffusion of this in schools is fairly limited, since inclusion of students with disability is still handled according to the logic of emergency (*'when the problem emerges, we will think about what software to buy...'*), rather than through planning to employ aids and technologies useful to a type of teaching sensitive to varying educational needs and cognitive styles (Cottini 2004).

### (f) Inclusive school-vocational training pathways

So that the school course can fully develop its inclusive potentiality, it is of fundamental importance to relate school to vocational training. In this way some interesting working perspectives can be accessed by some youths or young women with cognitive impairment, who, on some occasions, do not seem to draw particular benefits from attending secondary school.

## CLASSMATES' RELATIONSHIPS WITH CHILDREN WITH DISABILITY

Classmates are an important factor for school inclusion. Over twenty years of research has clearly highlighted that the physical placement of children with disability in a general classroom cannot, by itself, create satisfying relationships with peers and does not ensure that the former are automatically accepted by the latter. This may be due to a number of factors, the first of which concerns attitudes toward individuals with disability.

The attitudes of children with typical development toward their peers with disability are often negatively biased if compared with their attitudes toward children with typical development (Nowicki 2002).

Behavioural intentions to interact with these children seem to change with type of disability and type of 'relationship' requested. Weiserbs and Gottlieb (2000), for instance, have shown that a group of elementary school children was more inclined to help and establish relationships with peers with temporary rather than permanent disability. In line with these results Nota *et al.* (2005) noted that there was more willingness to help and establish friendly relationships with peers with physical rather than intellectual (Down Syndrome) disability; in addition, they found that there was greater propensity to establish relationships based on help rather than on friendship.

It should be recalled that friendship is the outcome of a personal decision based on the recognition of common interests and of being able to share experiences and activities, emotions and feelings (Berndt and Perry 1986; Nota and Soresi 1997; Weiserbs and Gottlieb 1995). On the contrary, helping relationships involve specific behaviours that are carried out in specific situations and that do not necessarily require intense and lasting emotional investments. Secondly, perception of the social consequences associable to helping and to friendship could be different: if on the one hand helping and solidarity behaviours could trigger positive evaluations in the peer group and in adults, on the other, 'friendly' behaviours might stimulate perplexities and worries, such as the fear of no longer being able to see one's 'old friends'.

Classmates' social ability levels also seem to be related to attitudes shown toward peers with disability. Ferrari *et al.* (in press) have recently compared propensity to help and establish friendly relationships with children with motor disability vs. those with Down Syndrome in three groups of children with high, average and low social abilities. The children of the first group reported greater propensity to help and establish friendly relationships with individuals with both motor difficulties and intellectual disabilities. These results may be due to the more socially able children being more capable of grasping context expectations, in the case in point adults' expectations about involving persons with difficulties (Chadsey-Rusch 1992; Nota and Soresi 1997). On the other hand, these children may perceive the helping and friendly behaviours that should be implemented in particular situations as easier to carry out, since they already form part of their relational repertoire. On the contrary, children with low social abilities may perceive such behaviours as difficult to carry out, and lower perceived behavioural control could in fact encourage the expression of less positive attitudes (Roberts and Lindsell 1997; Roberts and Smith 1999).

Another factor that can affect scarce interactions between children with and without disability seems to involve prior knowledge. Children differ in the way they know about the various typologies of disability and, especially the younger ones, know even less about cognitive disabilities. Physical disabilities that require the use of clearly identifiable supports like a wheelchair are better understood by small children, who, on the contrary, seem to be less aware of the characteristics of Down Syndrome (Diamond 1996; Woodwart 1995). The lack of specific knowledge, especially about mental retardation, makes this condition less clear and understandable, so much so that children may have some 'naïve' reactions, such as the fear of 'being infected' (Nikolaraizi *et al.* 2005; Nota *et al.* 2005).

As regards the factor *knowledge*, some studies have examined the information that children are given about individuals with disability. For example, Weiserbs and Gottlieb (1995) found that elementary school children that had been given further information on the difficulties of a possible future classmate and on the kind of help that might be required of them tended to show more negative attitudes than children that had not been given such information. In line with that, Nota *et al.* (2005) found that the extra information given to those children that wanted to become friends with a classmate with disability on what would be required of them in terms of help and support (sitting near him/her, giving further examples, etc.) caused lower propensity to supply help and friendship in the older subjects (9–11-year-olds vs. 6–8-year-olds), regardless of whether the classmate had either motor disability or Down Syndrome. In contrast, Laws and Kelly (2005), in giving information on hypothetical classmates, described not only their disabilities (cerebral palsy and having to use a wheelchair vs Down Syndrome), but also the activities that they liked doing. The authors noted increased positive behaviours toward future classmates with intellectual disability in the little girls of their sample and increased negative feelings toward physical disability both in the little boys and the little girls.

It seems therefore that the information given to children about future classmates with disability is important and can strongly affect their attitudes. In the case of Nota, Ferrari and Soresi's (2005) work it seems clear that children are likely to perceive in the additional information the risk of a higher involvement of theirs with the classmate with disability. In Laws' and Kelly's (2005) work the description of the interest of the child with disability in activities that might also be 'attractive' to the classmates played an essential role both in improving and in worsening their attitudes. The authors themselves say that 'the more negative attitudes towards physical disability among the boys could be because many boys are interested in physical activity and may see children with physical disabilities to offer limited potential in this respect' (p. 96).

A third factor capable of affecting classmates' actions is prejudice toward and stereotypes of individuals with disability. By considering groups of people (for instance, the deaf, the blind, etc.) rather than single individuals, the tendency is to go by simplifications and generalizations and produce those stereotypes that, overlooking individuality, lead to global representations that are often responsible for evaluation errors (Soresi 1998). Abrams, Jackson and St Claire (1990) have clearly shown that even elementary school children tend to consider individuals with disability in a stereotyped way, as if they belonged to a single group of people regardless of their individual impairments and disabilities, and often believe that they have behaviours that are far distant from the expected 'normal' ones. Terms like 'handicapped' or 'retarded' seem to evoke such strong stereotypes that sub-categorizations and differentiations of various types of disability as well as the multifaceted problems that can be associated with them are not even contemplated (Gottlieb and Gottlieb 1977).

Attitudes, behavioural intentions and knowledge are particularly significant aspects, as they are factors that can affect behaviour (Ajzen and Fishbein 1980). It actually seems that in classes where there is a pupil with disability, children with typical development often do not interact 'spontaneously' with him/her and avoid choosing him/her as a playmate or study mate (Diamond *et al.* 1992; Guralnick 1999; Roberts and Zubrick 1993; Sale and Carey 1995; Vandell 1982).

Friendly relationships in school also seem to be absent. Carr (1995) observed that about half the 11-year-olds with Down Syndrome involved in the research thought they had a friend, but in most cases it was either a relation or a family friend. Freeman and Kasari (2002) involved 54 children, 27 with Down Syndrome and 27 friends of theirs. Most playmates of the children with intellectual disability were children with typical development, but they were at least one year older and did not attend the same class. The latter considerations raised doubts on the authenticity of the friendships and on their likely duration.

## CLASSMATES' INVOLVEMENT IN FAVOUR OF INCLUSION

The data that can be found in the literature suggest the necessity of planning for some specific forms of classmates' involvement to the advantage of inclusion. The fundamental premise is that, to be more effective, child involvement must take place in an inclusive context, where the individual in difficulty is considered to all intents and purposes as a member of the group, and where roles and perspectives essentially held in common with the others are recognized in him/her.

In this connection, we also know that children's attitudes derive from learning and that significant influence is exercised by parents' and teachers' beliefs and attitudes (Gollnick and Chinn 2002), by the knowledge supplied in the school context (Stoneman 2001), and the type of rules and values that exist in their life setting (Gollnick and Chinn 2002; Otis-Wilborn 1995).

Classmates' involvement giving advantage to inclusion seems to require three things:

(1) first of all, teachers' and parents' involvement, so that these important figures are 'carriers' of positive beliefs and attitudes toward disability and diversity in general (Nota and Soresi 2004; Stoneman 2001);
(2) the use of strategies that actually stimulate interaction in school contexts between children with typical development and those with disability; and
(3) the realization of programmes that aim at teaching how to help and interact with those classmates that have the greatest difficulties.

Since what is underlined in point (1) has already been the object of previous publications (Nota and Soresi 2004; Soresi 1998; Soresi and Nota 2001; Soresi and Nota 2004), here only points (2) and (3) will be discussed in depth.

In connection with the importance of using strategies that stimulate effective interactions between children with disability and those without, Hamilton (2005) has shown that in school contexts individuals with Down Syndrome show social behaviours that bear little relation to the activities carried out compared with those of their classmates with typical development, and that the latter are much more keen on seeking interaction with their classmates during the same activities. The author emphasizes that the quality of school experience must be improved: it is not enough to make reference to indirect strategies to promote activities and interactive engagement, that is to say devising developmentally appropriate materials within designated activity and play areas. The idea that producing such conditions and putting children together can create social interactions – that is, adhering to the proximity model of integration (Jenkins *et al.* 1985) – has not turned out to be very fruitful.

The planning of educational activities should include the involvement of the classmates as 'intervention agents' and the reinforcement of target behaviours (Odom and Wolery 2003). To this aim, the use is recommended of 'relatively intrusive strategies such as positioning children, prompting and reinforcing peer interaction, appropriate modelling interactive behaviour, and interpreting for the typical children the meaning of the social behaviour of the children with disabilities' (Hamilton 2005, p. 133). So help and support must be stimulated in an explicit way, initially for brief and well-defined assignments, and giving clear indications on what children without disability have to do. This can favour greater understanding of the conditions of individuals with disability and stimulate some sort of social proximity, a prerequisite for the development of friendly relationships (Weiserbs and Gottlieb 1995).

As regards the setting up of specific interventions, Weiserbs and Gottlieb (1995, 2000) suggest care in the way classmates with disability are 'introduced' to the rest of the class, as the information on their difficulties and on the help that must be supplied to them, can stimulate negative attitudes. In other words, such information seems to focus attention especially on the difficulties, on the extra workload that would be required following inclusion and on the disadvantages that would be associated with it. It would be better to give information that stimulates a positive image of the individuals in difficulty, centred on the interests and abilities that these children have in common with their classmates and that can help them think of activities that can be done together.

Specific educational activities should also aim at increasing the knowledge that children have of disabilities in general and of the classmates in difficulty they come into contact with, and at enabling them to recognize when and how it is useful and positive to give them help (Brunati and Soresi 1990; Soresi 1998; Soresi and Nota 2001). Knowledge should be supplied not only about the difficulties these children may have but especially about their abilities and the ways in which these children can participate in and contribute to school activities (Diamond and Innes 2001). These interventions should also aim at the reduction of stereotyped views of disability, of miscomprehensions and undue generalizations. The increase of articulated and precise knowledge, also accompanied by guided experiences and supervised by the educator, should favour a conceptual change that could also support more positive attitudes (Au and Romo 1996; Magiati *et al.* 2002).

In such intervention activities children could also be encouraged to revisit the idea of friendship and mutual support and helped to see the advantages they could have from friendships with children with disability. The same children could then be stimulated to sustain and strengthen actions of help and solidarity that others manifest toward classmates in difficulty. This would mean acting on peer-related social competence in a way that would extend the range of positive social behaviours so that the children would become able to interact effectively in markedly heterogeneous social contexts (Guralnick 2001). Thus a more supportive class environment would be created, a contrived situation in which classmates support one another in positive interaction, favouring a greater propensity to anticipate the positive consequences of an action done to the advantage of a person with disability (Soresi 1998; Soresi and Nota 2001).

## CONCLUSION

As we have underlined, the long course taken in Italy toward a real process of school inclusion of individuals with disability can be considered as the progressive overcoming of an approach based on the exceptionality of the phenomenon. It is absolutely necessary to continue along this path, not asking for laws and implementing simple interventions devised exclusively for students with disability. Rather, the need – still little felt today – should be that of planning new didactic organizations, able to facilitate the growth of all students, whatever their problems, deficits or educational needs. The issue of the inclusion of students with disability must become a *variable inside* the system, really able to stimulate increasingly rapid innovation. Between quality of inclusion processes and quality of school a relationship of mutual influence exists: only a high-level school can be the substratum on which to implement really inclusive experiences for students with special educational needs. Such experiences will reflect on the organization of the whole educational system, determining positive effects (at methodological level, on organizational flexibility, on the 'climate' of the class, on respect for differences, etc.) that in the end will benefit everyone.

Moreover, a school service aiming at effective inclusion cannot but consider the need to programme interventions that spread the knowledge necessary to reduce the stereotypes and prejudices that still exist about disability and about situations needing many types of support (learning difficulties, sociocultural disadvantages, etc.) and to increase the abilities necessary to the activation of suitable interaction networks.

Quality of interaction, once again, requires specific interventions and constant professional attention on the part of teachers: if this can be successfully realized, the opportunity will also be created to experience membership of a heterogeneous community and to increase the likelihood of improving understanding of others, mutual acceptance and tolerance (Helmstetter *et al.* 1994; Peck *et al.* 1990; Soresi and Nota 2001).

# REFERENCES

Abrams, D., Jackson, D. and St Claire, L. (1990). Social identity and the handicapping functions of stereotypes: children's understanding of mental and physical handicap. *Human Relations.* 43:1085–98.

Ajzen, I. and Fishbein, M. (1980). *Understanding attitudes and predicting social behaviour.* Englewood Cliffs, NJ: Prentice-Hall.

Au, T.K.F. and Romo, L.F. (1996). Building a coherent conception of HIV transmission – a new approach to AIDS education. *Psychology of Learning and Motivation–Advances in Research and Theory.* 35:193–241.

Berndt, T. and Perry, T. (1986). Children's perceptions of friendships as supportive relationships. *Developmental Psychology.* 22:640–8.

Brunati, L. and Soresi, S. (1990). Un programma di coinvolgimento precoce per facilitare l'integrazione di soggetti handicappati. In S. Soresi (ed.), *Difficoltà di apprendimento e ritardo mentale.* pp. 311–32). Pordenone: Erip.

Carr, J. (1995). *Down's syndrome: children growing up.* Cambridge: Cambridge University Press.

Celi, F. (1999). Programmazione individualizzata e obiettivi della classe: come collegarli? In D. Ianes and M. Tortello (eds), *La qualità dell'integrazione scolastica.* pp. 125–30. Trent: Erickson.

Chadsey-Rusch, J. (1992). Toward defining and measuring social skills in employment settings. *American Journal on Mental Retardation.* 96:405–18.

Cottini, L. (2004). *Didattica speciale e integrazione scolastica.* Rome: Carocci.

Cottini, L. (2005). Il dentro e il fuori dell'integrazione. *Autismo e Disturbi dello Sviluppo.* 3(2):151–70.

Cottini L., Gardin, A. and Fedeli, D. (2003). L'integrazione scolastica. In L. Cottini (ed.), *Bambini, adulti, anziani e ritardo mentale.* pp. 115–33. Brescia: Tannini.

Diamond, K. (1996). Preschool children's conceptions of disabilities: the salience of disability in children's ideas about others. *Topics in Early Childhood Special Education.* 16:458–75.

Diamond, K.E. and Innes, F.K. (2001). The origins of young children's attitudes toward peers with disabilities In M.J. Guralnick (ed.), *Early childhood inclusion: focus on change.* pp. 159–77. Baltimore, MD: Brookes.

Diamond, K., Le Furgy, W. and Blass, S. (1992). Attitudes of preschool children toward their peers with disabilities: a year long investigation in integrated classrooms. *The Journal of Genetic Psychology.* 154:215–21.

Ferguson, P. and Asch, A. (1989). Lessons from life: personal and parental perspective on school, childhood and disability. In D., Biklen (ed.), *Disability and society.* pp. 322–41. Chicago: NSSE.

Ferrari, L., Nota, L. and Soresi, S. (in press). Abilità sociali e atteggiamenti verso i compagni con disabilità. *Giornale Italiano delle Disabilità.*

Freeman, S.F.N. and Kasari, C. (2002). Characteristics and qualities of the play dates of children with Down syndrome: emerging or true friendships? *American Journal on Mental Retardation.* 107(1):16–31.

Gollnick, D. and Chinn, P. (2002). *Multicultural education in a pluralistic society.* Columbus, OH: Merrill Prentice Hall.

Gottlieb, J. and Gottlieb, B.W. (1977). Stereotypic attitudes and behavioral intentions toward handicapped children. *American Journal of Mental Deficiency.* 82(1): 65–71.

Groppo, M. (1983). Analisi critica dell'integrazione scolastica degli handicappati. In L. Silvestrelli (ed.), *Psicologia ed Handicap.* Rome: Bulzoni.

Guralnick, M.J. (1999). The nature and meaning of social integration for young children with mild developmental delays in inclusive settings. *Journal of Early Intervention.* 22:70–86.

Guralnick, M.J. (2001). Social competence with peers and early childhood inclusion: need for alternative approach. In M.J. Guralnick (ed.), *Early childhood inclusion. Focus on change.* pp. 481–502. Baltimore, MD: Brookes.

Hamilton, D. (2005). An ecobehavioural analysis of interactive engagement of children with developmental disabilities with their peers in inclusive preschools. *International Journal of Disability, Development and Education.* 52:121–37.

Helmstetter, E., Peck, C.A. and Giangreco, M.F. (1994). Outcomes of interactions with peers with moderate or severe disabilities: a state-wide survey of high school students. *Journal of the Association for Persons with Severe Handicaps.* 19:263–76.

Ianes, D. (2001). *Didattica speciale per l'integrazione.* Trent: Erickson.

Jenkins, J.R., Spletz, M.L. and Odom, S. (1985). Integrating normal and handicapped preschoolers: effects on child development and social interaction. *Exceptional Children.* 52:7–17.

Laws, G. and Kelly, E. (2005). The attitudes and friendship intentions of children in United Kingdom mainstream schools towards peers with physical or intellectual disabilities. *International Journal of Disability, Development and Education.* 52:79–99.

Luckasson, R., Borthwick-Duffy, S., Buntinx, W.H., Coulter, D.L., Craig, E.M. and Reeve, A. (2002). *Mental retardation: definition, classification, and systems of supports.* Washington, DC: American Association on Mental Retardation.

Magiati, I., Dockrell, J.E. and Logotheti, A.E. (2002). Young children's understanding of disabilities: the influence of development, context and cognition. *Applied Developmental Psychology.* 23:409–30.

Minnow, M. (1990). *Making all the difference: inclusion, exclusion and American law.* Ithaca, NY: Cornell University Press.

Nikolaraizi, M., Poonam, K., Favazza, P., Sideridis, G., Koulousiou, D. and Riall, A. (2005). A cross-cultural examination of typically developing children's attitudes toward individuals with special needs. *International Journal of Disability, Development and Education.* 52:101–19.

Nota, L. and Soresi, S. (1997). *I comportamenti sociali: dall'analisi all'intervento.* Pordenone: Erip.

Nota, L. and Soresi, S. (2004). Social and community inclusion. In J. Rondal, R. Hodapp, S. Soresi, E. Dykens and L. Nota (eds), *Intellectual disabilities: genetics, behavior, and inclusion.* pp. 157–92. London: Whurr Publishers Limited.

Nota, L., Rondal, J. and Soresi, S. (2002). *La valutazione delle disabiltità (Vol. 1).* Pordenone: Erip.

Nota, L., Ferrari, L. and Soresi, S. (in press). Facilitating school inclusion. *International Journal on Disability and Human Development.*

Nota, L., Ferrari, L. and Soresi, S. (2005). Elementary school children's willingness to help and be friends with disabled peers. *International Journal on Disability and Human Development*. 4:131–8.

Nowicki, E. (2002). A meta-analysis of school-age children's attitudes towards persons with physical or intellectual disabilities. *International Journal of Disability, Development and Education*. 49:243–65.

Odom, S.L. and Wolery, M. (2003). A unified theory of practice in early intervention/ early childhood special education: evidence-based practices. *Journal of Special Education*. 37:164–73.

Otis-Wilborn, A. (1995). Conceptualizing and reconceptualizing curriculum. *The Volta Review*. 97:19–32.

Peck, C.A., Donaldson, J. and Pezzoli, M. (1990). Some benefits nonhandicapped adolescents perceive for themselves from their social relationship with peers who have severe handicaps. *Journal of the Association for Persons with Severe Handicaps*. 15:241–9.

Roberts, C.M. and Lindsell, J.S. (1997). Children's attitudes and behavioural intentions toward peers with disabilities. *International Journal of Disability, Development and Education*. 44:133–45.

Roberts, C.M. and Smith, P.R. (1999). Attitudes and behaviour of children towards peers with disabilities. *International Journal of Disability, Development and Education*. 46:35–50.

Roberts, C.M. and Zubrick, S. (1993). Factors influencing the social status of children with mild academic disabilities in regular classrooms. *Exceptional Children*. 59(3):192–202.

Sale, P. and Carey, D.M. (1995). The sociometric status of students with disabilities in a full-inclusion school. *Exceptional Children*. 62(1):6–19.

Soresi, S. (1998). *Psicologia dell'handicap e della riabilitazione*. Bologna: Il Mulino.

Soresi, S. and Nota, L. (2001). *La facilitazione dell'integrazione scolastica*. Pordenone: Erip.

Soresi, S. and Nota, L. (2004). School inclusion. In J. Rondal, R. Hodapp, S. Soresi, E. Dykens and L. Nota (eds), *Intellectual disabilities: genetics, behavior, and inclusion*. pp. 114–56). London: Whurr Publishers Limited.

Soresi, S., Nota, L., Ferrari, L. and Solberg, S. (in press). Career Guidance for Persons with Disabilities. In J.A. Athanasiou and R. Van Esbroeck (eds), *International Handbook of Career Guidance*. Berlin: Springer.

Stoneman, Z. (2001). Attitudes and beliefs of parents of typically developing children: effects on early childhood inclusion. In M.J. Guralnick (ed.), *Early childhood inclusion. Focus on change*. pp. 101–26). Baltimore, MD: Brookes.

Vandell, D.L. (1982). Are fathers like mothers? *Contemporary Psychology*. 27:281–2.

Wehmeyer, M.L. (2006). L'autodeterminazione: il nuovo paradigma per la disabilità. *Giornale Italiano delle Disabilità*. 6:3–13.

Wehmeyer, M.L and Patton, J.R. (2000). *Mental retardation in the 21$^{st}$ century*. Austin. TX: Pro-Ed.

Weiserbs, B. and Gottlieb, J. (1995). The perception of risk over time as a factor influencing attitudes toward children with physical disabilities. *The Journal of Psychology*. 129:689–99.

Weiserbs, B. and Gottlieb, J. (2000). The effect of perceived duration of physical disability on attitudes of school children toward friendship and helping. *Journal of Psychology: Interdisciplinary and Applied*. 134:343–5.

WHO (2001). *International Classification of Functioning, Disability and Health (ICF)*. Geneva: World Health Organization.

Woodwart, R. (1995). The effects of gender and type of disability on the attitudes of children toward their peers with physical disabilities. *Therapeutic Recreation Journal*. 29:218–27.

# 10 Mainstream or Special Education for Teenagers with Down Syndrome

**SUE BUCKLEY, GILLIAN BIRD, BEN SACKS AND TAMSIN ARCHER**

## SUMMARY

This chapter presents findings from a study designed to compare the achievements of Down syndrome teenagers educated in mainstream classrooms with those educated in special education classrooms throughout their full-time education. Progress is reported for speech and language, literacy, socialization, daily living skills and behaviour. For all the teenagers, there is evidence of progress with age on all the measures except for communication. Communication continued to improve through teenage years for the included children but not for those in special education classrooms. There were no significant differences in overall outcomes for daily living skills or socialisation. However, there were large significant gains in expressive language and literacy skills for those educated in mainstream classrooms. Teenagers educated in mainstream classrooms showed fewer behavioural difficulties. Further, comparison with data published by these authors in an earlier study, showed no improvements in school achievements in special education over a 13-year period in the UK (1986–1999).

## INTRODUCTION

In 1987, two of the authors of this article published information on the development and lives of a large and representative group of 90 teenagers with Down syndrome (Buckley and Sacks 1987). In some ways, the progress of the teenagers was disappointing – very few had made any useful progress at all with reading, writing, number and money, and social independence skills such as crossing roads and travelling alone were very limited. Most led rather isolated social lives and only 42% had speech that was intelligible to those meeting them for the first time (for example in a shop or café). The authors

*Therapies and Rehabilitation in Down Syndrome.* Edited by Rondal
© 2007 John Wiley & Sons Ltd

commented that their findings should not be taken as indicating what teenagers with Down syndrome could achieve, but rather, that the findings may be due to the nature of the curriculum in special schools, low academic expectations, being bussed out of their own communities every day to school and social attitudes which did not allow children with Down syndrome into clubs and activities in their communities. In 1987 94% of the teenagers were in schools for children with severe learning difficulties (SLD), 6% in schools for children with moderate learning difficulties (MLD).

In 1988, as a result of this study and in line with legislative change towards inclusion in education in the UK, the Portsmouth team began to develop inclusive education in local mainstream schools for the children with Down syndrome starting school in the southeast part of the county of Hampshire. In the rest of the county most children with Down syndrome continued to be placed in special schools. The Down Syndrome Educational Trust funded a psychologist to work with the schools, parents and the Education Authority to develop successful inclusion. This work has provided a unique opportunity to compare the outcomes of special versus mainstream education for two groups of children with Down syndrome of similar backgrounds and ability. It enables us to test out our view that the teenagers in 1987 were underachieving and socially isolated as a result of segregated special education. Are the teenagers who have been included in mainstream education showing the predicted benefits of going to school with their typically developing local children? Specifically, we hoped that included children would be more likely to have friends in the neighbourhood and better social lives as teenagers, with better social independence skills for getting around their communities, more friends and more involvement in clubs and activities, that their speech, language, behaviour and social development would benefit from being with typically developing peers and that their academic achievements would improve. Does the evidence demonstrate these benefits?

In 1999 we repeated the survey (Buckley *et al.* 2006) that we had carried out in 1987 with the current group of teenagers, including some additional measures. This enables us to compare the benefits of mainstream and special education for the 1999 teenagers and also to ask if, as a group, they are benefiting from changes in social attitudes and better education when compared to the 1987 teenagers.

Many of the results of the study were not as the researchers might have predicted, and the findings raise some important issues for parents and educators of teenagers with Down syndrome to consider.

## THE 1999 STUDY

In 1999, information was collected for 46 teenagers, 28 in special schools (24 in SLD and 4 in MLD schools) and 18 in inclusive schools. The young people in the two groups were placed in mainstream or special schools on the basis of where they lived; they were from similar social and family backgrounds and were likely to be of similar potential abilities when they started school. The results we report are unlikely to exaggerate any advantages of inclusive education for the following reasons:

1. When we compared the progress of the two groups, to ensure that we were comparing young people of potentially similar abilities, the five 'least able' teenagers from the special schools were taken out of the comparison group, before the two groups were compared. These five 'least able' teenagers are those with significantly more developmental delay and health problems than the rest of the group. Two of them have autism in addition to Down syndrome and three of the five have significantly difficult behaviours. These young people have had multiple difficulties since childhood, and children with this level of difficulty would not have been placed in mainstream classes in any part of the county at the time of the study.

2. The average age of the mainstream group is two years younger than the average age of the special school group. This would reduce the likelihood of finding higher scores on any measures for the total mainstream group, as we know from our 1987 study that the teenagers in all groups are likely to be progressing with age on the measures we used.

It is also important to note that the teenagers in the mainstream schools have been fully included in age-appropriate classes in their local schools, supported by a Learning Support Assistant for the majority of the day. They have not been in special classes or resource rooms in mainstream schools and, usually, they have been the only child with Down syndrome or a similar level of learning difficulty in school until they reached secondary schools. In secondary school, some have continued to be the only teenager with Down syndrome, but some have been with one or two others with Down syndrome.

In both 1987 and 1999, the information was collected by surveys. In both studies, parents completed a questionnaire designed by the authors, the Sacks & Buckley Questionnaire (SBQ). In the second study, additional standardized questionnaires were also used, the Vineland Adaptive Behaviour Scale (VABS; Sparrow *et al.* 1984) and the Conners Rating Scales (CRS; Conners 1997). The two main questionnaires (the SBQ and VABS) both contain measures of personal independence skills – *Daily Living Skills* – which include measures of skills in dressing, toileting, bathing, cleaning, laundry and meal preparation, also time, money, telephone use and road safety. They also both contain measures of speech, language and literacy skills – *Communication Skills* – and measures of friendship, leisure and social skills – *Socialization Skills*. The Vineland Adaptive Behaviour Scale provides normative data which allows scores achieved on the scales to be translated into age equivalent scores. This is useful because it allows us to compare the progress of the teenagers across different aspects of their development. We would expect progress to be even for typically developing teenagers, that is, all skills will be at approximately the same age-level. Previous research suggests that we will find an uneven profile for teenagers with Down syndrome, with Communication skills lagging significantly behind Daily Living and Socialization Skills. The age-equivalent scores also allow us to identify the extent of progress with age during the teenage years and this is illustrated in the first set of histograms in Figure 10.1.

## PROGRESS WITH AGE

The first two histograms in Figure 10.1 indicate that Daily Living Skills and Socialization Skills can be expected to improve significantly as young people with Down syndrome progress through their teens (though with the caution that these figures are for different teenagers in each age group, not the same teenagers as they get older). When we look at the third histogram in Figure 10.1, for Communication Skills, we see significant progress for the oldest group of mainstreamed teenagers but no significant progress with age for the teenagers in special education. These differences in progress in speech, language and literacy will be explored in more detail in the next section.

The first important conclusion we can draw from this piece of research is that we can expect significant progress in all areas of development during the teenage years. There is no evidence for a 'plateau' being reached, or even a slowing of progress.

The reader will also have observed that there are no significant overall differences in the Daily Living Skills or Socialization Skills of the teenagers educated in special or mainstream schools, though there is a difference on one measure which contributes to the Socialization Skills score – the Interpersonal Relationships Scale. This difference may be important and is discussed in more detail in the next section.

## A MORE DETAILED LOOK

For each main scale on the VABS there are three subscales which contribute to that score and the information for these subscales is illustrated in Figure 10.2.

### DAILY LIVING

The first histogram illustrates that for Daily Living Skills the teenagers were performing at a similar level in personal and practical skills in the Domestic (e.g. preparing meals, cleaning, taking care of laundry), Personal (e.g. independence in toileting, bathing, dressing) and Community (e.g. staying at home

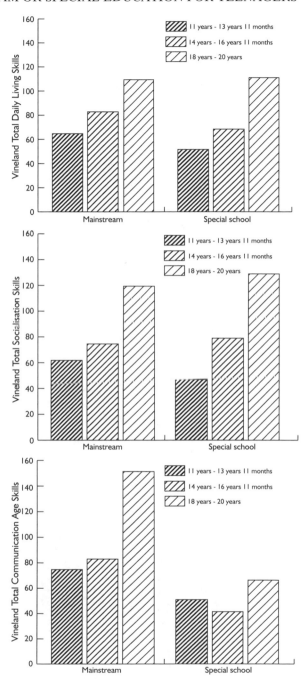

**Figure 10.1.** Extent of progress with age.

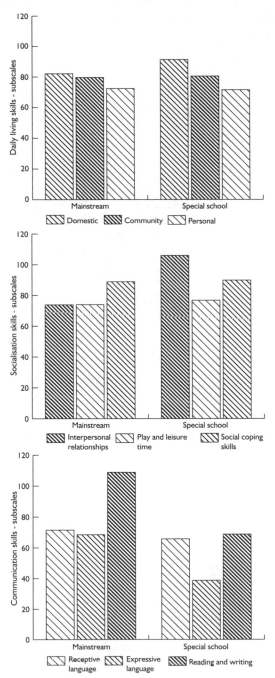

**Figure 10.2.** Scores on the three Subscales of the Vineland Adaptive Behaviour Scale.

alone, time, money, telephone and road skills) areas. It also illustrates that there were no significant differences in skills between the teenagers in the mainstream or the special school groups.

## SOCIALIZATION

The second histogram, however, illustrates that for the Socialization Skills measure there is a difference for the Interpersonal Relationships subscale, which covers social interaction, dating and friendship skills. There were no differences on the Play and Leisure (going to clubs, games, hobbies, leisure activities) or on the Coping Skills (awareness of manners, social sensitivity and social rules) subscales.

On the Interpersonal Relationships subscale, the teenagers educated in the special schools scored significantly higher, largely due to differences in scores for the oldest age groups. The older teenagers in special education were more likely to have a boyfriend or girlfriend, a special friend and to belong to clubs than those from mainstream education.

This was the only measure of the many measures used in this research which showed a significantly better outcome for teenagers in special education.

The numbers of teenagers in the study are quite small – 18 in mainstream education and 23 in special education – so that further research is needed to explore the significance of this finding. However, one possibility is that the teenagers in special education have had more opportunity to develop mutually supportive, reciprocal friendships with peers of similar abilities and interests than those included in mainstream schools.

## COMMUNICATION

The third histogram in Figure 10.2 illustrates the results for the three subscales in the Communication Skills score. For the teenagers in mainstream schools, the results indicate that their receptive and expressive language is progressing at the same rate and that reading and writing is a specific strength and better than might have been predicted from their other language abilities. Their expressive language is 2 years and 6 months ahead of the special school group. Some 78% of the mainstream teenagers are rated as being intelligible to strangers compared with 56% in special schools in 1999 and 42% in 1987. For the teenagers in special education, their receptive language is at a similar level to those in mainstream school but their expressive language is more than 2 years behind their receptive language. Their reading and writing abilities are at the same level as their receptive language but significantly behind the reading and writing skills of the mainstreamed teenagers, the difference being more than 3 years.

It is possible that the improved expressive language of the teenagers in mainstream schools is linked to their reading and writing progress. Researchers suggest that expressive skills are delayed by hearing, speech-motor difficulties, auditory memory and auditory processing difficulties (Chapman 1977; Gunn and Crombie 1996; Fowler 1999; Chapman 2001). Therefore, it may be easier for young people with Down syndrome to learn vocabulary and grammar from written language, than from spoken language. In addition, phonics work plus reading practice may improve speech-motor production skills and speech intelligibility.

The teenagers being educated in mainstream classrooms, with the individual help of a Learning Support Assistant, will have received daily literacy teaching with their typically developing peers. They will also have recorded their learning in all lessons by writing it down and reading it – with whatever level of support was needed to achieve this. Therefore the level of engagement in literacy activities for all the teenagers in the mainstream classrooms will have been much greater than that experienced by teenagers in the special school classrooms.

## OVERALL PROFILES

In Figure 10.3 the histograms show the overall results for the main developmental areas – *Daily Living, Socialization* and *Communication Skills*. For the teenagers in the mainstream schools there are no significant differences in the progress being made in each of these areas of development. Communication Skills are good, largely due to their progress with expressive language and literacy. For the teenagers in the special schools, their Communication Skills are significantly delayed relative to their Daily Living and Socialization Skills.

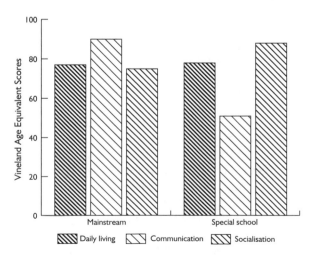

**Figure 10.3.** Overall results for the main developmental areas.

As already noted, this special school profile is, in fact, the one that researchers would expect to see for teenagers with Down syndrome. A number of studies have found that speech and language skills, particularly expressive skills, are specifically delayed relative to both nonverbal cognitive abilities and to social and independence skills.[7,8]

The results of our study suggest that it is possible to bring communication abilities in line with social and practical abilities for teenagers with Down syndrome, by including them in mainstream classrooms. The results indicate that a major factor may be the development of reading and writing and the use of literacy activities to teach and to support spoken language development.

Another major factor may be that the mainstreamed teenagers have been surrounded by typically developing competent spoken language users since they entered preschools at 3 years of age, and this spoken language and communication environment will have been very different to that experienced by the teenagers in the special schools. Almost all of the special school group have been in special schools for children with severe learning difficulties for their entire school career and this means that they have been with children the majority of whom have very significantly impaired language.

## COMPARISON WITH OUTCOMES IN 1987

Perhaps the most surprising and important finding of this study was the lack of progress in special school education between 1987 and 1999. We confidently predicted that all teenagers would be doing better in the 1999 group as we know that the special schools have had higher expectations and more academic programmes in the past ten years than they did 15–20 years ago. However, we found no improvements in 1999, when compared with 1987, for spoken language skills, reading, general knowledge and overall school achievement – achievements were the same as in 1987. There were small gains in writing and number.

It is important to remind the reader that the children in the special schools were not less able than the earlier cohort. At the time that these children entered school there was very little mainstreaming where they lived and our data confirms this point, as in many areas of development their skills are the same as both the 1987 group and the 1999 mainstream group.

Our findings suggest that it is not possible to provide optimal learning environments in special schools and classrooms, however hard the teachers work. It suggests that learning within a typically developing peer group may be essential for optimal progress for two main reasons:

1. the typical spoken language of the peer group because this provides a stimulating language learning environment

2. the classroom learning environment and curriculum – the pace of learning has been much greater for those in mainstream because they have been in all academic lessons with individual support for their learning.

We can use the example of literacy to explore this further. The included teenager has had daily literacy lessons with his or her typically developing peers. The classroom curriculum is set for the mainstream children and their learning provides role models for literacy for the student with Down syndrome. He or she will be working with support within the class on individually set targets for literacy. A literacy lesson in a special school classroom will, of necessity, be very different. In the special school, the teacher will have perhaps six pupils, all with significant learning difficulties, and will design a literacy activity for this group – two of whom may be autistic, two with severe behaviour difficulties and two with Down syndrome – all have significantly delayed speech and language and only three are able to write their names. Sharing a story together may be an appropriate literacy activity for this group of children, rather than formal literacy instruction. The aim of this example is not to criticise special schools – it is to try and give a real picture of the different demands and resources of the two situations and to try to explain our findings. The same comparison would apply to numeracy lessons in mainstream and special classrooms.

There were no gains between 1987 and 1999 in Daily Living Skills for teenagers in mainstream or special education and significant gains in Social Contacts and Leisure activities for both groups. We suggest that Daily Living Skills are mostly learned at home and therefore not influenced by school placement and, similarly, that the improvement in social inclusion reflects a general change in social attitudes and social acceptance in the community rather than school placement effects. Social lives out of school are also more likely to be influenced by families than schools.

## PERSONALITY AND BEHAVIOUR

Another major area of developmental importance that was looked at in these Hampshire teenage studies was the extent of behaviour difficulties, including the questions of whether any behaviour difficulties change with age and if school placement has any influence on behaviour.

We were aware from our inclusion support work that difficult or disruptive behaviour is a major cause for the breakdown of mainstream school placements. We were also concerned to find out if the demands of coping in a mainstream classroom actually increased behaviour difficulties.

Significantly difficult behaviour affects the learning and social opportunities of a teenager with Down syndrome and can create considerable stress for teachers and for families. Conversely, teenagers who can behave in a socially acceptable and competent manner will be more likely to have friends, to have active social lives and to be successful in work as adults, than those who do not.

Difficult behaviours need to be considered in relation to the helpful and socially sensitive behaviour and the positive personalities that are characteristic of most teenagers with Down syndrome. Many references to the positive aspects of teenagers personalities were made by parents during the recent Hampshire survey, for example:

> '*J. is a happy and content girl, very understanding, helpful and has a great personality – she brings out the best in everyone.*'
> '*He is happy and outgoing and lots of people know him so we talk to more people because of him.*'
> '*She is a wonderful, happy and most loved member of our family. She is kind, caring, happy and thoughtful.*'
> '*A. has a positive approach to life and brings that to the family. His caring nature and enthusiasm are infectious. I think he has made the family dynamics easier than they would have been, especially the teenage years.*'
> '*She is good company, always happy, funny and content.*'
> '*Good point is, he is a happy lad who is good fun and has taught us a lot.*'
> '*Very loving, trusting and happy boy – enjoys life and is very sociable.*'
> '*Our daughter brings more love, fun and laughter to family life and though she will never be 'academic' there are other qualities she has which cannot be measured.*'
> '*He is popular, friendly and non-judgemental . . . he has added another dimension to our lives.*'
> '*Brings a lot of happiness to our lives. Her disruptiveness – being rude or awkward – can cause parents and sister to get cross and upset.*'

The last quote highlights the fact that difficult behaviours occur only sometimes and do not define the person's character. Someone with a positive personality can be difficult at times and this would characterize most of the teenagers in the survey. However, this does not mean the difficult behaviours are not distressing when they do occur and most parents and teachers are pleased to obtain advice on how to handle them.

Several measures were used to collect information about any behaviour difficulties that the teenagers had. There were behaviour questions on the original Sacks and Buckley Questionnaire (Buckley and Sacks 1987) and a Maladaptive Behaviour Scale on the Vineland Adaptive Behaviour Scales (Sparrow *et al.* 1984). In addition, the Conners Behaviour Rating Scale (Conners 1997) provides measures of several different aspects of behavioural difficulties, hyperactivity, cognitive problems or inattention, oppositional behaviour and Attention Deficit/Hyperactivity Disorder (ADHD).

All the measures illustrated that difficult behaviours tend to improve with age for most individuals, with only one teenager over 18 years in the mainstream schools comparison group having even a moderate level of difficulties.

This strongly suggests that many of the behaviours reported for the younger teenagers may be linked to general cognitive delays and immaturity.

Our concerns about the demands of mainstream placements increasing behaviour difficulties were not confirmed. There was only one measure on which the teenagers from the different school systems scored significantly differently – The VABS Maladaptive Behaviour Scale – and these results are illustrated in Figure 10.4. The scores can be classified in terms of the severity of the behaviour difficulties. As the data below show, significant behaviour difficulties only affect a minority. The teenagers in the mainstream schools were less likely to have difficulties, with 63% having no significant difficulties compared with 41% in the special schools, 25% having a moderate level of difficulties compared with 27% in the special schools and 12% (one in eight) having significant behaviour difficulties compared with 32% (one in three) in special schools.

The reader is reminded that the five 'least able' teenagers in the special schools are not included in this comparison. Three of these five had very high scores for difficult behaviours and the remaining two had low scores.

This means that in the whole sample of teenagers, and the whole sample is representative of the full range of teenagers with Down syndrome, 26% (one in four) have some significant behaviour difficulties which will probably be causing problems at home and at school on a daily basis.

The Vineland Maladaptive Behaviour Scale predominantly includes questions about two main types of behaviour, those that may reflect anxiety and nervousness and those that reflect conduct disorder and poor attention.

On the Conners Behaviour measures, which focus on conduct disorders and attention difficulties, there were no significant differences between the levels

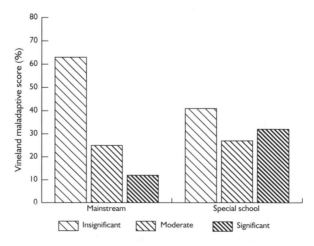

**Figure 10.4.** Vineland maladaptive scores.

of difficulties for the teenagers in mainstream or special schools. Scores of the teenagers with Down syndrome are compared with norms for typically developing teenagers. The proportion of the total Down syndrome group who had serious difficulties was 16% on each of the Oppositional Behaviour, the Cognitive problems/inattention and the ADHD measure and 37% on the Hyperactivity measure. The reader should note that some 5% of the typically developing population of teenagers of the same age will score in the serious difficulties range as defined by the Conners Scales.

The hyperactivity measures include, being always 'on the go', hard to control while shopping, runs about or climbs excessively in situations where it is inappropriate, restless in the squirmy sense, has difficulty waiting in line or taking turns, has difficulty playing or engaging in leisure activities quietly. The high score here may reflect immaturity and improve with age, as similar findings have been reported by other researchers and interpreted in this way (Cuskelly and Gunn 1997; Stores *et al.* 1998).

## THE LINK BETWEEN BEHAVIOUR AND POOR COMMUNICATION SKILLS

As with other studies, and the authors' 1987 study, there was a significant relationship between expressive communication skills and behaviour difficulties – the more limited a teenager's expressive language ability, the more likely he or she is to have behaviour difficulties. The implication here is that at least some difficult behaviours are the teenager's way of communicating when he/she does not have the language to do so. In addition, some behaviours may be the result of the frustration that arises when an individual is not understood.

## HAS INCLUSION ACHIEVED WHAT WE HOPED FOR?

We stated at the beginning of the article that we hoped that included children would be more likely to have friends in the neighbourhood and better social lives as teenagers, with better social independence skills for getting around their communities, more friends and more involvement in clubs and activities, that their speech, language, behaviour and social development would benefit from being with typically developing peers and that their academic achievements would improve, when compared with the teenagers receiving special education in segregated schools. Does the evidence demonstrate these benefits? The answer is 'yes' for spoken language, behaviour, social development and academic benefits and 'no' for the social inclusion benefits.

The language and academic benefits were greater than we expected. The big gains for the included teenagers were for expressive language, literacy and, to a lesser degree, numeracy and general academic attainments. The average gain for expressive language was 2 years and 6 months and for literacy, 3 years and 4 months. These age-related scores are based on norms for typically developing children who are expected to progress 12 months on the measures in a school year. Children with Down syndrome usually progress about 4–5 months on these measures in a year – they are making progress but at a slower rate than typical children. Therefore, considered in relation to expected gains, the teenagers in mainstream school have gained the equivalent of 5–6 years progress in spoken language and literacy when compared to the teenagers educated in special classrooms.

There were some gains in social development and behaviour. The teenagers in mainstream schools were more socially mature, with more age-appropriate social behaviour and more social confidence. However, the social inclusion gains were not as great as we expected. On the standardized measures there were no gains for the included teenagers and the suggestion of a disadvantage. There were no significant differences in social independence skills, social contacts, leisure activities and community inclusion. Parents were as concerned about the social isolation of their teenagers as they had been in 1987, even though there was evidence of some improvements for everyone since that time.

The benefits of having daily contact with typically developing children and teenagers in the local area during the school day did not result in more inclusion and friendships during the teenage years. In addition, the included teenagers seemed to be less likely to have special friends, boyfriends or girlfriends and a social life of their own in their late teens, perhaps as the result of having less contact with peers with similar intellectual disabilities or peers with Down syndrome in school.

## WHAT ARE THE IMPLICATIONS FOR PARENTS AND FOR TEACHERS?

1. That all children with Down syndrome should be educated within mainstream classrooms to ensure that they are able to develop their speech and language to the level that is optimal for each child.

   The importance of speech and language development for cognitive and social development cannot be overemphasized. Words and sentences are the building blocks for mental development – we think, reason and remember using spoken language, either silently 'in our minds' or aloud to others. Words provide the main source of knowledge about our world.

   Any child with speech and language delay will have mental delay (except for a signing baby in a deaf signing family, when sign will be as good as speech for mental development). In addition, speech and language skills influence all aspects of social and emotional development – the ability to negotiate the social world and to make friends, share worries and experiences and be part of the family and community.

2. That all children with Down syndrome should be educated in mainstream classroom to learn alongside their peers and to access the academic curriculum adapted to their individual rate of progress.

   Full inclusion in the curriculum leads to much better literacy and numeracy skills, and general knowledge. The level of supported literacy experience across the curriculum also provides an important support for spoken language development.

3. Our research indicates that it is not possible to provide a maximally effective learning environment in a special education classroom.

   Children with Down syndrome need to learn with their nondisabled peers with the necessary individual support to make this successful.

4. The social aspects of inclusion need to be addressed.

   Children with Down syndrome in mainstream schools need more opportunities to socialize with a peer group of children with similar levels of intellectual disability. This can be achieved by closing special schools and classes and including all children with learning disabilities in mainstream school communities – at present many children who would provide this peer group in the UK are still in special schools. The children with Down syndrome have had a parent lobby and more of them are fully included than their peers with similar levels of intellectual disability. It can also be achieved out of school, by ensuring that children with Down syndrome have friends with similar disabilities out of school.

5. Friendships with nondisabled peers need more support within school communities.

   Teachers and parents need to do more to ensure that these friendships carry on outside school. We wish to see an improvement in understanding and support for teenagers and adults with Down syndrome in their homes, workplaces, shops and leisure activities as a result of inclusion. This is not yet happening and needs to be addressed within schools.

These are statements supported by the evidence, and the evidence of earlier reviews of the benefits of inclusion (Cunningham *et al.* 1998). No study has provided evidence for any educational advantages of special education, only disadvantages, and the practical daily living and social skills are as good or better in mainstream education. The only benefit seems to be contact with a peer group of similar disability – and, considering the significant disadvantages of special education, that need is better met out of school, and in better planned inclusion.

Our conclusions are uncompromising and if we are to achieve the full benefits of inclusive education for all our children we need to implement effective support and training programmes. We may also need some variety of provision. Most children with Down syndrome will benefit from the full classroom inclusion that we describe, supported by a learning support team. In many schools, a learning resource area which provides for small group work is needed for some children and can provide a place to meet the peer group with similar levels of intellectual disability.

If we include all children with Down syndrome and all children with intellectual disabilities, then some children may benefit from being in a resourced school. For those children with the greatest levels of disabilities, planning and providing for them may be best done within a specifically resourced school. This does not mean being educated in a special class or resource room – it means that we concentrate skills and human resources in some schools to develop the necessary expertise for successful inclusion of those with the greatest needs. It also means that the children have access to a similar ability peer group as well as benefiting from being included in the mainstream community.

There can be no single prescription for successful inclusion as the school systems in different countries and communities vary widely. The way to move towards full inclusion may be different in different communities and, importantly, different models may work equally well if the attitudes of the school community towards inclusion are positive and the aim is to seek the full inclusion of the child into the social and educational world of the school, while also meeting his or her learning and developmental needs.

## POSTSCRIPT

Some critics of our work have suggested that inclusion in Hampshire is 'special' and only successful because the Trust staff support the schools. In fact, from 1988, the teachers and the Trust's psychologists learned together year by year. It was the teachers in the schools who showed us how to make inclusion successful. We did not visit more than once a term on average, unless asked to help with a problem. We did not start workshops on inclusion for teachers until 1993 and they were based on sharing what we were learning from the teachers. The children in the study differ widely in ability, behaviour, social needs and family backgrounds. The children studied have been spread through some 25 primary schools (infant and junior) and some 12 secondary schools, in inner city, urban and rural areas – these schools are likely to be representative of schools across the UK.

For the past 9 years, we have been running training for inclusion throughout the UK and across the world and we see many, many examples of similarly successful inclusion everywhere. Our schools experienced problems at times, like all schools developing inclusion, but the positive staff attitudes towards inclusion and the support of the Education Authority meant that problems were solved – not seen as a reason to move a child to a special school. At transition points from infant to junior to secondary it was assumed that the children would stay in the mainstream system and everyone planned accordingly. On the basis of parental choice two teenagers moved to MLD provision for secondary education and two moved to mainstream from MLD at this point!

It may be important to note that these teenagers were included before the introduction of IEPs (Individual Education Plans) or SENCOs (Special Educational Needs Co-ordinators) into UK schools. Schools are much better resourced to succeed now – though we do need to be sure that too much planning and special needs expertise does not result in lowered expectations.

We asked teachers to fully include the children in the class activities and told them we would help them to adapt once it was necessary. The children tended to surprise us all and fewer adaptations were needed in infant school than we had anticipated. There is the danger that an IEP could reduce expectations, depending on who writes it and their experience of working with children with Down syndrome in education. The children in this study also had no signing in their classrooms and, at first, no speech and language therapy service. They had to cope and make themselves understood in a spoken language environment and we encouraged teachers to use reading activities to develop their spoken language. We have no way of knowing how much this contributed to their significant speech and language gains, but we are very cautious about the current widespread use of symbols and signing in primary school years – for some children it is necessary and appropriate but not for all just because they have Down syndrome.

You might sum up our approach as focusing on children first – seeing children with Down syndrome as full members of the class and community and playing down differences. They do have special needs and teachers need to know how to address these but we still need to change public and professional attitudes so that they really do treat our children as children first. When we achieve this, we will really see the full benefits of inclusion.

# REFERENCES

Buckley, S. and Sacks, B. (1987). *The Adolescent with Down Syndrome: Life for the Teenager and for the Family.* Portsmouth, UK: Portsmouth Polytechnic.

Buckley, S.J., Bird, G., Sacks., B. and Archer, T. (2006). A comparison of mainstream and special school education for teenagers with Down syndrome: effects on social and academic development. *Down Syndrome Research and Practice.* 9(3):51–67.

Chapman, R.S. (1997). Language development. In SM Pueschel, M Sustrova (eds), *Adolescents with Down Syndrome: Towards a More Fulfilling Life.* (pp. 99–110). Baltimore, USA: Paul H. Brookes Publishing.

Chapman, R.S. (2001). Language, cognition, and short-term memory in individuals with Down syndrome. *Down Syndrome Research and Practice.* 7(1):1–7.

Conners, C.K. (1997). *Conners Rating Scales-Revised*. Toronto, Canada: Multi-Health Systems Inc.

Cunningham, C.C., Glenn, S., Lorenz, S., Cuckle, P. and Shepperdson, B. (1998). Trends and outcomes in educational placements for children with Down syndrome. *European Journal of Special Needs Education*. 13(3):225–237.

Cuskelly, M. and Gunn, P. (1997). Behaviour concerns. In S.M. Pueschel and M. Sustrova (eds), *Adolescents with Down Syndrome: Towards a More Fulfilling Life*. (pp. 111–128). Baltimore, USA: Paul H. Brookes Publishing.

Fowler, A. (1999). The challenge of linguistic mastery. In T.J. Hassold and D. Patterson (eds), *Down Syndrome: A Promising Future Ttogether*. (pp. 165–184). New York, USA: Wiley–Liss.

Gunn, P. and Crombie, M. (1996). Language and speech. In B. Stratford and P. Gunn (eds), *New Approaches to Down Syndrome*. (pp. 249–267). London, UK: Cassell.

Sparrow, S.S., Balla, D.A. and Cicchetti, D.V. (1984). *Vineland Adaptive Behaviour Scale*. Minnesota, USA: american Guidance Service.

Stores, R., Stores, G., Fellows, B. and Buckley, S. (1998). Daytime behaviour problems and maternal stress in children with Down syndrome, their siblings, and non-intellectually disabled and other intellectually disabled peers. *Journal of Intellectual Disability Research*. 42(3):228–237.

# 11 Professional Inclusion as Global Therapy for the Individual with Down Syndrome

JUAN PERERA

## SUMMARY

The concepts of therapy and rehabilitation are complementary and acquire their full meaning when applied to the professional inclusion of individuals with Down syndrome.

This chapter focuses on two questions: (a) the limitations presented by individuals with Down syndrome who will respond to rehabilitation by means of professional inclusion; and (b) the results of current studies on professional inclusion as a therapy.

It also analyses the importance of the individual programme of ordinary employment versus protected employment and of supported employment. It concludes that professional inclusion is an excellent global therapy for individuals with Down syndrome.

## INTRODUCTION

The first question we must ask is whether professional inclusion can be considered a form of therapy and consequently whether a chapter titled 'Professional Inclusion as Therapy' should be included in a book such as this one.

Therapy can be defined as an 'activity aimed at curing diseases or, in behavioural disorders, subject to limitations, which a patient may present, improving their general adaptation and the expression of their potential. It requires, upon the client's request, a professional who understands their potential for change and the most effective methods for applying it'. (Vizcarro 1995)

Furthermore, the word rehabilitation (achieving popularity after the Second World War) and relating to medicine, describes 'all multidisciplinary action in favour of the person with physical or mental disability, or rather with difficulties with respect to social adaptation in the dimensions of education, psychology, emotional, or professional'. (Switzer 1986)

*Therapies and Rehabilitation in Down Syndrome.* Edited by Rondal
© 2007 John Wiley & Sons Ltd

Both concepts are complementary when focused on the professional dimension of Down syndrome, as they can explain the process or set of measures that permit or facilitate the start or return to work of a disabled person (Puig de la Bellacasa 1995). They are a part of rehabilitation as an integral process or global action model, in which various areas are distinguished, although each is dependent on the other.

The terms used in the above definitions, 'overcome limitations . . .', '. . . improve the general adaptation and expression of their potential . . .' etc. take on their full meaning when applied to the professional inclusion of people with Down syndrome and justify the title of this chapter.

To focus on the subject, two questions should be examined:

1. What limitations do people with Down syndrome present that are susceptible to rehabilitation through professional inclusion?
2. Which results from current studies on professional inclusion are positive, in other words, therapeutic, in the broadest sense of the word, for people with Down syndrome?

## LIMITATIONS PRESENTED BY PERSONS WITH DOWN SYNDROME SUSCEPTIBLE TO REHABILITATION OR THERAPY BASED ON PROFESSIONAL INCLUSION

Although the current trend of evaluating the cognitive and personality aspects of people with Down syndrome is based on their potential and not their limitations, it is necessary here to define their limitations, as these are what we are trying to compensate for, conceal or improve by means of the therapeutic model of professional inclusion.

After examining the psychological scientific literature on the cognitive aspects of Down syndrome (Berry *et al.* 1984; Carr 1995; Buckley and Sacks 1987; Cicchetti and Beeghly 1990; Cunningham 1995; Hodapp 1996 and Hodapp *et al.* 1999; Nadel 1999 and 2006; Devenny 2006; Rondal 1995, 2006; Perera 1995; Pueschel 1998; Wishart 1992; Wisniewski *et al.* 1996) I shall point to certain especially significant elements that affect the cognitive process of people with Down syndrome:

1. Mental retardation: weak and strong points in cognitive process.
2. Problems with visual and auditory perception.
3. Alterations to the perception of space and time.
4. Specific limitations affecting the various types of memory.
5. Defects in the attention and alertness systems.
6. Impairment of the information reception, processing and integration mechanisms.
7. Lack of consolidation of acquired knowledge.
8. Language and communication problems.

Furthermore, if we examine certain studies published on the personality and behaviour of people with Down syndrome (Caltagirone *et al.* 1990; Pueschel *et al.* 1991; Wootton 1991; Schapiro *et al.* 1992; Cuskelly and Gunn 1993; Seltzer *et al.* 1993; Pueschel *et al.* 1996; Perera 1999a; Beeghly 1999; Cuskelly *et al.* 2003; Fidler 2006; Hodapp 2006), we find additional personality and behavioural traits, which obstruct their social integration, their full development as people and, in particular, their adaptation to work:

1. Less interaction with the environment (difficulty in responding and adapting to change).
2. Limited capacity to analyse and interpret external events.
3. Resistance to effort. Lack of responsibility in maintaining effort.
4. Low level of personal autonomy and a tendency to depend on older adults.
5. Low level of awareness of their limitations. Inability to anticipate dangerous situations.
6. Low expectations of success.
7. Lack of initiative.
8. Lack of motivation.

If we wish to achieve the professional inclusion of a person with Down syndrome, we will have to design their training and incorporation into the workplace using a methodology aimed at overcoming these limitations and evaluating the results (Perera 2002).


## THE INDIVIDUAL PROGRAMME

This therapeutic approach should include professional evaluation and orientation, effort training and psycho-motivational adaptation training, specific training for the job, pre-work practices and activities, adaptation of the individual to the job in question, plus the adaptation of the job itself to the individual (together with ergonomic studies and the rehabilitation mechanism applied to the specific case), selective and normalized placement, psychological and social measures aimed at the individual, their environment and the work group into which they are placed. In addition other actions of a social nature aimed at resolving problems with respect to travelling to work, personal autonomy etc. will be required.

It is especially important that this commence immediately and, where possible, in the later stages of basic education. Pre-work training, education for personal autonomy and survival skills and habits, together with the importance of practical knowledge and activities of an occupational nature, represent the compensatory foundations of the process of orientation, work training, and job placement.

The success of professional inclusion is particularly related to the appropriate creation and application of an 'individual programme', which consists of the harmonized design of an ordered, sequential process of activities and intervention, established by common agreement between the professionals (psychologist, educator, occupational therapist, doctor, social worker etc.) and the patient (and in the event, his/her family), the final objective of which is the active compensation or substitution of limitations by means of the individual's capacities (Switzer 1986). By its very nature, it should be flexible and gradual, and be subject to periodic review. Its success shall be measured by factors similar to those of special education: individual development and total integration into the environment in which they live. This includes the goal of finding a job that is appropriate for the individual, which is the ultimate objective of professional inclusion in the context of the global programme.

## ORDINARY EMPLOYMENT VERSUS PROTECTED EMPLOYMENT

The studies conducted by Erik Samoy (1992) and Samoy and Waterplas (1995) were important points of reference regarding the protected employment situation in the European Union. These studies present an interesting classification of the same: they highlight different types of employment service provision for people with disability, ranging from competitive work in ordinary companies, with infrequent support and highly normalized, to the final level, where the protected work centres with substitutive employment functions in the environment are located. The final reports of the various work groups within the Community Program Helios II (1993–1996) follow the same direction, especially the report corresponding to the group that worked on Transition and Flexible Employment (Helios II 1995–1996).

In the 1990s, transition to the open market was considered from two perspectives (Martínez 2001): for the all-out defenders of protected centres, as a political mandate with the sole objective of reducing or eliminating aid to protected centres. For the others, transition was a principle and procedure, which could bring about the participation of people with disability in productive processes in ordinary companies, forcing the health-care and protected employment systems to make the change to employment in the community.

Furthermore, there is a somewhat eclectic movement that started in the 1990s and consolidated at the beginning of the twenty-first century, and which has gained ground in Spain and other countries, that considers protected employment and ordinary employment not as opposing elements but as complementary to one another: they are rungs on the same ladder. They all involve work, but at different levels: occupational centres, special employment centres, supported employment in ordinary companies, work enclaves, self-employment or full employment are permeable phases of a single process – professional inclusion.

What is important is that the disabled worker is always situated at the highest level in accordance with his/her ability, preparation and performance.

Here, the word permeable means the possibility of descending or ascending the ladder according to the individual's situation and the employment available (Perera 1999b).

The philosophy of this system is clear and the procedure is simple but difficult to put into practice in many European countries, due to the fact that the centres, for structural and/or economic reasons, are resistant to change, on many occasions depending on family support (Martínez 2001).

## THE ROLE OF INCLUSION CENTRES AND SERVICES

Family support is one of the most relevant elements for the promotion of the disabled person. It is a complex and individualized interaction, which adopts forms and relationships in each family. These usually vary over time depending on the progress of the child with disability. However, it is also a fact that a large number of people with disability do not channel their needs through current centres and services, neither those related to employment nor those related to health care. This may be due, among other causes, to:

1. The fact that their aspirations are different, or higher, than such services can offer; these are usually people who have been educated in ordinary classrooms, or are in the last stages of training.
2. The passive systems of protection.
3. The dissuasive factor of the economic contribution, as cofinancing by the family or the disabled person in question, to maintain services.

Although there are no general formulas, we can affirm that the more family members involved, all holding values that include positive promotion, the better the access to opportunities and the greater the sharing of the daily problems and support needs of the family member with the disability will be.

One of the most positive characteristics of the family nucleus is its capacity to anticipate the future, which makes everyday life with respect to future needs more accessible and practicable.

There is a set of variables, which we consider as important when making decisions in favour of the professional inclusion of a disabled person. It is important to understand what position the disabled person occupies in the family with respect to points such as the following (these examples are not exhaustive): type of family; involvement; positive recognition of disability; values that include productiveness, independence and participation; class and level of disability; pensions recognised or recognisable; itinerary relating to health care, attention or promotion; concept of professionals, specialization and global health care; system of services for people with disability at working age; concept of education and training; confluence between person, family and mediator with respect to the immediate future; and the starting point for inclusion. This last point is especially relevant, given that the path becomes more practicable (1) if all those involved believe that they can and should make the transition to employment at that time, (2) if the person who proposed the transition or promotion itinerary is not a fourth element, apart from the person, family and centre, and (3) if transition commences at the centre or service itself in conjunction with the other relevant actors.

The aim is to achieve good family support, guided by positive values, and with the motivation and support of the mediators. In such cases, we suppose an inversely proportionate relationship between family support and segregation. However, professionals and institutions have an added challenge: preventing lack of family support from becoming another element in the selection of risks. Both groups are important: those who have family support, and those who do not/those who have lost it.

The first group – those who have family support – define the path down which we must direct the efforts of the institutions, in order to satisfy the desires and aspirations of these people and their families.

The second group – those with no family support/those who have lost it – remind professionals for which values they are working. It spells out what the starting point is for both health care and promotion.

In both cases, the institutions, centres, services, and human resources, including managers, technicians or active care-givers, must decide what their role is in transition into the community. They should guide the resources they possess, centres and services, their professionals and personnel, to implement initiatives in the community that can only be developed with guaranteed success with the resources they have at their disposal. The initiatives must be in line with the reference values, aspiring to the gradual change of the segregated centres, transforming them into centres of transition, and pursuing the search for quality by means of promotion through employment.

To the question of what impedes centres and services, along with their affected personnel, from making the transition, responses will follow to overcome internal barriers (reference values, organization, flexibility, human resources, family attitude and collaboration, user expectations, companies, types of job, development of mixed systems etc.) as well as external barriers (pensions, travel to work, financing etc.). Overcoming these obstacles is, paradoxically, the most specialized and technical of all; the responsibility to initiate transition is in the hands of professionals and the institutions in which they work.

## SUPPORTED EMPLOYMENT

Supported employment is without doubt one of the most widely used work inclusion models around the world for disabled individuals, and the most studied and documented in Spain (Bellver *et al.* 1993; Canals and Doménech

1991; Jordán de Urries *et al.* 2005; Luckasson *et al.* 1992, 2002; Programa ECA Caja Madrid 2005; Verdugo and Jordán de Urríes 2001; Verdugo *et al.* 1998a; Verdugo *et al.* 1998b; Pascual 2003).

It is good because it is flexible. On the one hand it considers the individual with the cognitive and behavioural limitations described above, and determines the support that each worker requires. On the other hand, it analyses the job in depth and the environment in which each worker will be located in the company.

The supported employment programme is based on the idea that there can and should be correspondence between company requirements and the individual's capacity, a capacity which, in principle, may appear limited, due to the individual being disabled, but which, given the right conditions, may fully develop so that the task is undertaken perfectly and the worker is paid in proportion to his/her work.

The process is complex, as the worker must be supported by an institution that:

1. has precise knowledge of the potential and conditions of the person;
2. can analyse the job of work in all its scope (e.g. tasks, superiors and colleagues, times, travel to work);
3. possesses an employment trainer, a professional with therapeutic abilities to prepare the worker according to the specific tasks the person is to carry out; he/she shall accompany the worker in the early stages on the job, make an on-site analysis of any problems that may arise and create appropriate solutions;
4. act as permanent intermediary between worker and company.

Secondly, the company's management must understand that the project is worthy. It should not act as an instrument of charity but should offer a job of work considered necessary for the company's operation and covering a need; and importantly, they must be aware of what is being offered to a citizen who needs a job to achieve their personal fulfilment, in conditions which, not being costly for the company, meet the specific needs of the person.

Obviously, an atmosphere of trust and complicity must be established between the institution promoting the worker, responsible for providing support at all times, and the company that employs the worker. As is common with new projects, its mere presentation provokes a cloud of doubts and even rejection. We are so used to admitting that the natural place for a worker with Down syndrome is the protected workshop or special employment centre, that is seems an unrealistic aim to try to implant and extend the scope of supported employment. Nevertheless, the same occurred some years ago when we decided to go beyond the special school stage, which was considered the natural and logical place for the intellectually disabled student to receive his/her education. We can remember the resistance to change, and even scandal in some cases, which gave rise to the introduction, by law, of integration at school (Flórez 2003).

In the USA in 1985, the year in which the federal government introduced supported employment for disabled people, there were 10 000 workers in this system. Ten years later, there were more than 140 000 workers, and the number has continued to increase. Moreover, even when one accepts the complexity of the system, the reality is much more promising. There is no one better than those who have decidedly chosen to seek jobs of work in ordinary companies to convince companies of the humanity and profitability of the system, and to train and support disabled workers, including those whose mental deficiency is more serious.

The project is convincing and practicable to such an extent that some companies decide to take on the responsibility of training the disabled worker in the workplace, thus releasing the employment trainer from this part of his/her job. However, the employment trainer's work does not end here. Due to the nature of intellectual disability, situations may arise during the work stage that could jeopardize the worker's adaptive capacity and demand the intervention and support of a person specifically trained to confront and solve them. Consequently, the support is permanent, albeit diverse, as circumstances require.

## EVALUATION OF PROFESSIONAL INCLUSION BASED ON RESULTS

Rehabilitation programmes for disabled people, including those of professional inclusion, currently face, around the world, two challenges: to demonstrate their economic and programme viability, and to use the personal and organizational results for the continuous improvement of the person and of the programme. Both challenges arise from the quality revolution of the 1980s and the reform movement of the 1990s, which have produced a series of changes in the way in which people perceive the desired objectives, characteristics, values, responsibilities and results from human services programmes, including professional inclusion of disabled people. The main characteristics of these changes involve focusing on the results and not on the input, being guided by objectives relating to results of value and referring to people, redefining clients as users and decentralizing authority (Mawhood 1997; Newcomer 1997; Wholey 1997; Gardner and Nudler 1999; Shalock 2001; Hakes 2001).

The broad analysis of alternatives to professional inclusion and of the results obtained from it, leads to the conclusion that there is not only one path, one system, one method, alternative or model that is unique and definitive. The objective is to place each person (with singular cognitive and personal characteristics, and specific aptitudes, limitations and support requirements) based on the best alternative for the individual in question.

Obviously, the final objective is full professional inclusion in ordinary employment.

However, to reach this point, experience teaches that the straight road is not always the best route, and previous steps have to be followed (I refer to the ladder) which will lead to final success. Although supported employment is currently one of the most used and positively considered models based on results, it involves difficulties and processes that are fundamentally based on the following questions: how to approach continuous support, what happens when it is reduced, and who pays the high price implied by the system (Parent *et al.* 1991).

## PROFESSIONAL INCLUSION AS GLOBAL THERAPY

The best we can do today for a person with Down syndrome is 'prepare them for employment and find them a job' (Perera 1998). This is because work is a fact of adult life for all people, disabled or otherwise. The type of employment, salary received and opportunities open to us directly affect the way we perceive ourselves and the way society values us, in addition to the level of freedom we have on the socio-economic level (Wehman *et al.* 1987).

Everyone aspires to a job that is socially recognised and to receive a salary that allows him or her to live comfortably. Salary is a decisive factor for quality of life on both the emotional and material levels. In general, the better paid a person is, the more freedom they have to establish themselves, independently, in society (Brolin 1985).

Starting out from this idea, we can understand the situation of the disabled person who finds himself or herself in a care centre, with no possibility of paid work. Giving this person the opportunity to work not only signifies the salary they will receive, but also recognition of their social value by the family and acceptance in the community. Another important advantage is the opportunity to make friends and establish affective connections with non-disabled people (Verdugo and Jenaro 1993).

'People are what they do' (Montobbio 1992). This is why employment gives the individual with Down syndrome the ability to make decisions; it transforms them into an active person, dignifies their economic situation, allows them to obtain what they want and provides them with security and responsibility (González Yagüe 2000).

Any disabled person whose residual ability can be converted into a useful value should, as such, be considered a worker. The extraordinary social value of this possibility means that people with mental retardation (including those with Down syndrome) can be equal to non-disabled people in the workplace, where it is possible for technology to compensate for human limitations (Casas and Miró 1993).

Society's lack of confidence in the ability of people with disability to carry out paid work is the main obstacle to integration into work and society (Núñez 1983). Integration in the workplace is the key to social integration (Kiernan *et al.* 1989).

All of these ideas, many of which are fundamental principles in the majority of professional inclusion models, reinforce the value of professional inclusion as therapy.

Finally, I would like to refer to a study carried out recently at the Asociación Síndrome de Down de Baleares (ASNIMO – SEMPRE VERD), with the aim of evaluating 26 subjects with Down syndrome, aged between 22 and 36 who were longitudinally followed up over 4 years and who worked as operatives in a greenhouse that cultivates and sells ornamental tropical plants. Every month, professionals in charge recorded data relating to three variables: (a) personal (cognitive and behavioural), (b) social and (c) economic. The results from this study (Perera 2002) demonstrate a significant increase (more than 20% in 82% of cases) in the following variables:

(a) Personal variables:
    1. Self-esteem and confidence in oneself
    2. Feeling of usefulness
    3. Definition of personality traits
    4. Personal autonomy
    5. Ability to adapt to the new
    6. Promotion of abilities
    7. Awareness of the need to make an effort
    8. Belief that effort will translate into new abilities
    9. Awareness of their limitations.
(b) Social variables:
    1. Experience with integration
    2. Learning to coexist, share and relate to others
    3. Learning to compete
    4. Social status (participation in community life)
    5. Security for the future (pension – retirement)
    6. More awareness of the value of money
    7. Increase in level of aspiration.
(c) Economic variables:
    1. Ceasing to be passive subjects (a burden on society)
    2. Becoming productive subjects.

# REFERENCES

Beeghly, M. (1999). Temperament in children with Down syndrome. In J.A. Rondal, J. Perera and L. Nadel (eds), *Down syndrome: a review of current knowledge.* (pp. 111–123). London: Whurr.

Bellver, F., Moll, B., Roselló, R. and y Serra, F. (1993). Un recurso eficaz para la inserción sociolaboral de personas con minusvalía. Una experiencia en la isla de Mallorca. *Siglo Cero.* 24(3):15–24.

Berry, P., Groeneweg, G., Gibson, D. and Brown, R.I. (1984). Mental development in adults with Down syndrome. *American Journal of Mental Deficiency.* 89: 252–256.

Brolin, D.E. (1985). Career education material for exceptional individuals. *Career development for exceptional individuals.* 8:62–64.

Buckley, S. and Sacks, B. (1987). *The adolescent with Down syndrome: life for teenager and for the family.* Portsmouth UK: Portsmouth Down Syndrome Trust.

Caltagirone, C., Nocenti, U. and Vicari, S. (1990). Cognitive functions in adult Down's syndrome. *International Journal of Neuroscience.* 54: 221–230.

Canals, G. and Doménech, M. (1991). *Proyecto Aura. Una experiencia de integración laboral.* Barcelona: Ediciones Milán – Fundación Catalana síndrome de Down.

Carr, J. (1995). The development of intelligence. In D. Lane and B. Stratford (eds), *Current approaches to Down's syndrome.* (pp. 17–86). London: Cassell.

Casas, J.M. and Miró, D. (1993). Centros de Empleo Especial. In *Plan nacional de empleo.* (pp. 143–167). Madrid: Real Patronato de Prevención y Atención a Personas con Minusvalía.

Cicchetti, D. and Beeghly, M. (eds) (1990). *Children with Down syndrome: a developmental perspective.* New York: Cambridge University Press.

Cunningham, C.C. (1995). Desarrollo psicológico en los niños con síndrome de Down. In J. Perera (ed.), *Síndrome de Down. Aspectos específicos.* (pp. 121–151). Barcelona: Masson.

Cuskelly, M. and Gunn, P. (1993). Maternal reports of behavior of siblings of children with Down syndrome. *American Journal of Mental Retardation.* 97:521–529.

Cuskelly, M., Jobling, A. and Buckley, S. (2003). *Down syndrome across the life span.* London: Whurr.

Devenny, D. (2006). The contribution of memory to the behavioral phenotype of Down syndrome. In J.A. Rondal and J. Perera (eds), *Down syndrome neurobehavioral specificity.* (pp. 85–100). Chichester: John Wiley & Sons Ltd.

Fidler, D.J. (2006). The emergence of a syndrome specific personality profile in young children with Down syndrome. In J.A. Rondal and J. Perera (eds), *Down syndrome neurobehavioral specificity.* (pp. 139–152). Chichester: John Wiley & Sons Ltd.

Flórez, J. (2003). La inserción de las personas con síndrome de Down en el trabajo. *Revista Síndrome de Down.* 20:110–115.

Gardner, J.F. and Nudler, S. (eds) (1999). Quality performance in human services: leadership, values and vision. Townson, MD: Brookes.

González Yagüe, A. (2000). Propuesta de trabajo sobre Centros Ocupacionales. *Comunicación a las I Jornadas sobre Deficiencia y Sociedad. Integración laboral del deficiente.* Unpublished manuscript, Universidad de Madrid.

Hakes, J.E. (2001). Can measuring results produce results: One manager's view. *Evaluation and Program Planning.* 24:319–327.

Helios, II (1995–1996). Programa de la Unión Europea a favor de las personas con minusvalía. Reporte anual grupo 17. Transition and Flexible Employment. EU Comission. Brussels.

Hodapp, R.M. (1996). Cross domain relations in Down's syndrome. In J.A. Rondal, J. Perera, L. Nadel and A. Comblain (eds), *Down's syndrome psychological, psychobiological and socioeducational perspectives.* (pp. 65–79). London: Whurr.

Hodapp, R.M. (2006). Total versus partial specificity in the behaviour of persons with Down syndrome. In J.A. Rondal and J. Perera (eds), *Down syndrome neurobehavioral specificity*. (pp. 125–137). Chichester: John Wiley & Sons Ltd.

Hodapp, R.M., Evans, D.W. and Gray, F.L. (1999). Intellectual development in children with Down syndrome. In J.A. Rondal, J., Perera and L., Nadel (eds), *Down syndrome: a review of current knowledge*. (pp. 124–132). London: Whurr.

Jordán de Urríes, F.B., Verdugo, M.A. and Vincent, C. (2005). *Análisis de la evolución del empleo con apoyo en España*. Madrid: Real Patronato sobre Discapacidad.

Kiernan, W.E., Shalock, R.L. and Knutson, K. (1989). Economic and demographic trends influencing employment opportunities for adults with disabilities. In W.E. Kiernan and R.L. Shalock (eds), *Economy, industry and disability. A look ahead*. Baltimore, MD: Brookes.

Luckasson, R., Coulte, D.L., Polloway, E.A., Reiss, S., Schalock, R.L., Snell, M.E., Spitalnik, D.M. and Stark, J.A. (1992). *Mental retardation. Definition, classification and systems of supports*. Washington, DC: American Association of Mental Retardation.

Luckasson, R., Borthwick-Duffy, S., Buntinx, W., Coulter, D.L., Craig, E.M., Reeve, A., Schalock, R.L., Snell, M.E., Spitalnik, D.M., Spreat, S. and Tasse, M.J. (2002). *Mental retardation. Definition, classification and systems of supports*. Washington, DC: American Association of Mental Retardation.

Martínez, S. (2001). Valores de referencia. Los centros y servicios para el empleo como nódulos para la inclusión y la calidad. In M.A. Verdugo and F.B. Jordán de Urríes (eds), *Apoyos, autodeterminación y calidad de vida*. (pp. 219–243). Salamanca: Amarú.

Mawhood, C. (1997). Performance measurement in the United Kingdom (1985–1995). In E. Chelimsky and W.R. Shadish (eds), *Evaluation for the 21st century: A handbook*. (pp. 134–144). Thousand Oaks, CA: Sage Publications.

Montobbio, E. (1992). La integración social de las personas con discapacidad intelectual: instrumentos, métodos y profesionales. In *Síndrome de Down: Para llegar a ser una persona autónoma*. (pp. 451–422). Barcelona: Fundación Catalana para el Síndrome de Down.

Nadel, L. (1999). Learning and memory in Down syndrome. In J. Rondal, J. Perera and L. Nadel (eds), *Down syndrome: a review of current knowledge*. (pp. 133–142). London: Whurr.

Nadel, L. (2006). Neuropsychological aspects of Down syndrome. In J.A. Rondal and J. Perera (eds), *Down syndrome neurobehavioral specificity*. (pp. 67–83). Chichester: John Wiley.

Newcomer, K.E. (ed.) (1997). *Using performance measurement to improve public and non-profit programs*. San Francisco: Jossey-Bass Publications.

Núñez, A. (1983). Elaboración. *Plan Nacional de Empleo*. (pp. 15–50). Madrid: Real Patronato de Prevención y Atención a Personas con Minusvalías.

Parent, W., Kregel, J., Wehman, P. and Metzler, H. (1991). Measuring the social integration of supported employment workers. *Vocational Rehabilitation*. 1:35–49.

Pascual, A. (2003). Empleo con apoyo: una estrategia para el acceso al empleo de las personas con discapacidad. In *Discapacidad y Empleo: nuevas perspectivas*. Madrid: Universidad Internacional Menéndez Pelayo.

Perera, J. (ed.) (1995). *Síndrome de Down: aspectos específicos*. Barcelona: Masson.

Perera, J. (1998). Empleo y síndrome de Down. *Revista Down*. 12:17–21.

Perera, J. (1999a). *Programa de acción educativa*. Madrid: CEPE.

Perera, J. (1999b). People with Down syndrome: quality of life and future. In J.A. Rondal, J. Perera and L. Nadel (eds), *Down syndrome: a review of current knowledge*. (pp. 9–26). London: Whurr.

Perera, J. (2002). Innovació i experimentació en els serveis socio-laborals per joves amb la síndrome de Down. *Revista Enginy*. 12–13:49–57.

Programa ECA Caja Madrid de Empleo con Apoyo (2005). http://inico.usal.es/ecacajamadrid

Pueschel, S., Bernier, J.C. and Pezzullo, J.C. (1991). Behavioural observations in children with Down's syndrome. *Journal of Mental Deficiency Research*. 35:502–511.

Pueschel, S.M., Myers, B. and Sustrova, M. (1996). Psychiatric disorders and behavioural concerns in psychological, psychobiological and socioeducational perspectives. In J.A. Rondal, J. Perera, L. Nadel and A. Comblain (eds), *Down's syndrome psychological, psychobiological and socioeducational perspectives*. (pp. 179–190). London: Whurr.

Pueschel, S. (1998). Visual and auditory processing in children with Down syndrome. In L. Nadel (ed.), *The psychobiology of Down syndrome*. (pp. 199–216). Cambridge, MA: MIT Press.

Puig de la Bellacasa, R. (1995). Rehabilitación profesional. In S. Sánchez, P. Gil and J.L. Castillejo (eds), *Diccionario Enciclopédico de Educación Especial*. IV, p. 1763. Madrid: Santillana.

Rondal, J.A. (1995). Especificidad sistémica del lenguaje en el síndrome de Down. In J. Perera (ed.), *Síndrome de Down: aspectos específicos*. (pp. 93–107). Madrid: Masson.

Rondal, J.A. (2006). Specific language profile. In J.A. Rondal and J. Perera (eds), *Down syndrome and other genetic syndromes of mental retardation*. (pp. 101–123). Chichester: John Wiley.

Schapiro, M., Haxby, J.V. and Grady, C.L. (1992). Nature of mental retardation and dementia in Down syndrome: study with PET, CT and neuropsychology. *Neurobiology of Aging*. 13:723–734.

Seltzer, M., Krauss, M. and Tsunematsu, N. (1993). Adults with Down syndrome and their aging mothers: Diagnostic group differences. *American Journal of Mental Retardation*. 97:496–508.

Shalock, R.L. (2001). *Outcome-based evaluation (2nd edn)*. New York: Kluwer Academic/Plenum Publications.

Switzer, M. (1986). *A model of human rehabilitation*. Baltimore: Williams and Wilkins.

Verdugo, M.A. and Jenaro, C. (1993): El empleo con apoyo. Una nueva posibilidad laboral para personas con discapacidad. *Siglo Cero*. 24:5–12.

Verdugo, M.A. and Jordán de Urríes, F.B. (2001). *Panorámica del empleo con apoyo en España*. Madrid: Real Patronato sobre Discapacidad.

Verdugo, M.A., Jordán de Urríes, F.B. and Bellver, F. (1998a). Situación actual del empleo con apoyo en España. *Siglo Cero*. 29(1):23–31.

Verdugo, M.A., Jordán de Urríes, F.B., Bellver, F. and y Martínez, S. (1998b). Supported employment in Spain. *Journal of Vocational Rehabilitation*. 11:223–232.

Vizcarro, C. (1995). Terapia. In S. Sánchez, P. Gil and J.L. Castillejo (eds), *Diccionario Enciclopédico de Educación Especial*. IV, p. 1921. Madrid: Santillana.

Wehman, P., Moon, S., Everson, J.M., Wood, W. and Barcus, J.M. (1987). *Transition from school to work. New Challenges for youth with severe disabilities.* Baltimore, MD: Brookes.

Wholey, J.S. (1997). Trends in performance measurement. In E. Chelimsky, W.R. Shadish (eds), *Evaluation for the 21st century: A handbook.* (pp. 124–133). Thousand Oaks, CA: Sage Publications.

Wishart, J. (1992). *El desarrollo de las dificultades de aprendizaje en los niños pequeños con síndrome de Down. Para llegar a ser una persona autónoma.* Barcelona: Fundación Catalana Síndrome de Down.

Wisniewski, K., Kida, E. and Brown, T. (1996). Consequences of genetic abnormalities in Down's syndrome on brain structure and function. In J.A. Rondal, J. Perera, L. Nadel and A. Comblain (eds), *Down's syndrome psychological, psychobiological and socioeducational perspectives.* (pp. 3–19). London: Whurr.

Wootton, A.J. (1991). Offer sequences between parents and young children with Down's syndrome. *Journal of Mental Deficiency Research.* 34:324–338.

# 12 Quality of Life

**CARLO BACCICHETTI**

## SUMMARY

Life expectancy for people with Down syndrome has increased dramatically throughout the world over the last fifty years. The purpose of this study is to describe the functional performances at home and in the community of 320 persons living in the community with Down Syndrome.

*Methodology*: a questionnaire asking for information on home living, activities, health, family and friends, leisure time and employment was filled in for each person with Down Syndrome.

*Major result*: only 1 per cent of adults are competitively employed and almost all have few opportunities to interact with unaffected people. In order to prevent regression and Alzheimer-like symptoms we must educate more DS individuals to independent living in the normal community.

## INTRODUCTION

Cohort studies have indicated that the survival of persons with Down Syndrome (DS) has dramatically increased over the past fifty years. Early childhood survival in particular has shown major improvement, due in large part to advances in cardiac surgery and in general health management. The substantial increase in survival across the study period means that the life expectancy of DS people is approaching that of the general population, but the development is accompanied by a range of significant mid-life health problems.

To develop life expectancy data for DS, Baird and Sadovnick (1987) studied 1341 DS people identified by the British Columbia Health Surveillance Registry from more than one million consecutive live births in British Columbia from 1908 to 1981. Survival to 68 years of age, predicted from the available data, is better than in previous estimates, but is still much poorer than for the general population: about 44.4 per cent and 13.6 per cent of live-born DS individuals will survive to 60 and 68 years, respectively, compared with 86.4 per cent and 78.4 per cent of the general population.

*Therapies and Rehabilitation in Down Syndrome.* Edited by Rondal
© 2007 John Wiley & Sons Ltd

In the Western world there are now more DS people who are in their mid-teens or older than there are DS children (Steele 1996). As the relative prevalence of DS at birth lessens and as life expectancy increases this intellectual disability condition will eventually come to be most commonly represented amongst the elderly. This shift in chronological age and its implications have not been clearly recognized by the community of professionals.

## EPIDEMIOLOGICAL DATA

To date, few studies have examined the daily activities of young people and adults with DS who live in the community. This lack of information may be explained, in part, by the different orientation of earlier research on DS. Until recently, research has focused on infant and child development, which is not surprising, given that prior to relatively recent advances in medicine (for example use of antibiotics, nutritional improvements, and the introduction of modern cardiovascular surgery), persons with DS usually had relatively short life-spans, and often died before reaching adulthood.

Most of the existing systematic behavioural research on young and adult DS people has focused on mental development (IQ) (Berry *et al.* 1984) and adaptive behaviour (Silverstein *et al.* 1985). Moreover, these and similar investigations on behaviour have most often used samples of persons who resided in institutions rather than in community residences. Because the type of residence (for example public versus community residential facilities) obviously influences community participation and adaptation (Bruininks *et al.* 1981; Hill and Bruininks 1981), it seems critical to assess the activities of persons living in the community as well as in institutions, because they are likely to differ.

A census of all DS subjects living in the community was initiated in 1988 in the provinces of Belluno and Treviso, in the Veneto Region of north-east Italy. There are 945 000 inhabitants in this area, and we estimated that about 500 would have DS: this figure was obtained by processing the data of a previous survey in part of the same territory. The names of these people were obtained from a list of subjects with mental disability requiring some form of assistance that had been prepared by a medical commission. To these identified subjects a questionnaire was mailed containing items on their medical history, cytogenetic analysis, social integration, and relative life conditions; they were also instructed to ask for help from their attending physician in filling out questions on medical information.

Five hundred and forty questionnaires were sent out, and 320 replies were received.

Changes in the age distribution of the DS syndrome population during the ten years of the period studied can be observed in Fig. 12.1.

In Fig. 12.2 the changing age structure of the population identified in childhood as having a learning disability is observed.

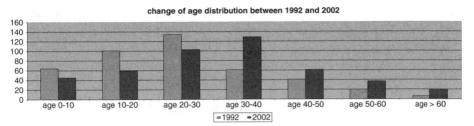

**Figure 12.1.** In 1992 mainly young DS adults aged 20–30 years are observed (blue column), whilst ten years later, in 2002, 30–40-year-old (purple column) subjects are increasing.

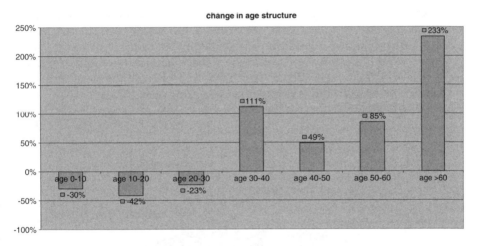

**Figure 12.2.** Over a period of ten years DS children aged 0–10 years are reduced by 30 per cent, whilst subjects aged 40–50 years are increased by 49 per cent and those aged 50–60 by 85 per cent.

In conclusion, we observed in two provinces of the Veneto region an increased survival of DS people, who in 2002 are in large measure adult and aged individuals. But does the prolongation of life coincide with an increase in its quality?

## QUALITY OF LIFE

Quality of life has been portrayed as a developing model or models within the field of developmental and intellectual disability (see Goode 1994; Renwick *et al.* 1996). In this context, it is essentially a sociological and psychological construct. Initially there were considerable disagreements about the nature of quality of life (Wolfensberger 1994), and a number of issues still have to be resolved (Hatton 1998). However, there has been a growing consensus in the last few years, both in terms of definition and constructs involved (Brown 1997). For example, in terms of definition, the notion of well-being in a variety of domains is well accepted.

Felce and Perry (1997) have indicated five areas of well-being:

- Physical well-being
- Material well-being
- Social well-being
- Emotional well-being
- Productive well-being

The twofold purpose of our investigation was to collect information by questionnaire content on home living, activities, health, family and friends, leisure time, employment and relationships with the law, in order to develop a strategy that would prevent, where possible, the complications that make the existence of these subjects demanding, in both social and personal terms.

The main results of the investigation are visible in Fig. 12.3:

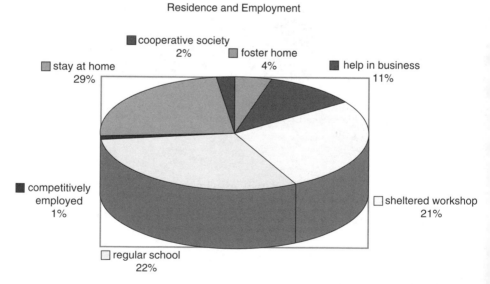

**Figure 12.3.** The findings on type of residence indicate that most DS people lived with their parents (96 per cent) at the time of the survey. The remainder lived in foster homes (4 per cent). None of them lived alone, in large-group homes, or in nursing homes. Locations of residences were evenly distributed among urban (46 per cent), suburban (24 per cent), and rural (30 per cent) settings.

Participation in the community is an important aspect of modern life. Despite the fact that much is known about the short- and long-term benefits of community involvement, general consensus over the goal of integrated participation still does not exist. For example, parents and teachers may be reluctant to support community participation because they fear that individuals with intellectual disabilities will be rejected and even abused by their non-handicapped peers. In our country (Italy) family is the most protective structure, and this is the reason why the majority of DS persons stay at home, as can be seen from Fig. 12.3.

## EDUCATION

Since 1970 in Italy a dramatic increase has occurred in the number of persons with disabilities, and particularly those with DS, integrated into the state school system.

With respect to education, most subjects under the age of 30 attended regular, as opposed to special, schools; and none attended residential schools. The majority of people in their twenties, as well as the older ones who were beyond school age, were receiving training in sheltered workshops.

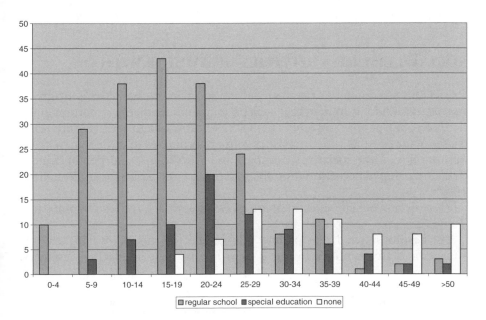

**Figure 12.4.** The results of the questionnaire on education received are reported here.

As young children grow and develop, the state school system takes much of the responsibility for training students in a variety of basic skills for competence in daily living and employment. Teenagers educated in mainstream classrooms showed fewer behavioural difficulties (Buckley *et al.* 2006). As students progress through school, educational goals shift. The notion that secondary special education programmes need to focus on instruction in functional adult skills is currently receiving much attention. This emphasis on planning for transition from school to adult life is a reflection of the realization that persons with disabilities have the right to live and work in 'normal' community settings, and to receive the necessary supports to do so.

## EMPLOYMENT

Regarding employment, of the sample of individuals beyond school age, only 1 per cent of DS people were reported to be competitively employed (for the last 5 years). Some of the major impediments to their employment were described as follows:

1. The appearance, slowness, lack of skills, and non-flexibility of DS people
2. The lack of sympathy of employers and other employees
3. Structural problems of the economy, particularly levels of unemployment
4. Institutional inhibitions
5. Overprotective parents and problems in using the transportation system.

## SOCIAL/LEISURE ACTIVITIES OF ADULTS WITH DS

Participation in community, vocational and social leisure activities is an important aspect of life. It follows that such participation is equally important in the lives of young people and adults with DS. Vocational and social leisure activities provide persons with disabilities with opportunities to develop new skills, earn money, form social relationships and friendships, and demonstrate a degree of competence and autonomy, among other things (Lakin and Bruininks 1985).

The results of the questionnaire about sport activity are reported in Table 12.1.

The results showed that people with intellectual disability had basically similar bodily capabilities to those of people without intellectual disability.

**Table 12.1.** Participation in sports activity of DS adults

| | |
|---|---|
| Yes | 41 |
| No | 132 |

However, the functional performance of elderly adults with intellectual disability was more impaired. We postulate that the slower functioning responses may be explained by a less physically active lifestyle, that may accelerate the onset of disease and result in symptoms associated with ageing that are detrimental to health. It is therefore important that persons with intellectual disability participate in physical activity and exercises in order to promote health and prevent disease.

The answer to the question 'With what groups of friends do you spend your time?' was as shown in Table 12.2.

Participation in social events is reported in Table 12.3.

It appears that many older DS people have few opportunities to interact with persons other than with a limited number of similarly disabled peers (for example in sheltered workshops), their families, paid professionals and other staff members. As important as this limited number of interactions is, they should not preclude participation in other social relationships. Full participation in the life of a community is a long overdue goal for citizens with DS. Moreover, it is a basic human right that has often been denied. Although much progress is occurring in the areas of the education and training of people with DS, it is through community participation that the skills we strive to impart are expressed. It is essential, therefore, to upgrade the scope of research and development on the community participation of people with DS.

From the answers to the questionnaire, it emerges that the main inadequacies for the subjects with this kind of disability are the following:

**Table 12.2.** Groups of friends in contact with DS adults

| | |
|---|---|
| None | 135 |
| Neighbours | 12 |
| Workers in human services | 20 |
| Co-parishioners | 5 |
| Relatives | 14 |

**Table 12.3.** Participation in social events of DS adults

| Event | Several times each year | Seldom | Never |
|---|---|---|---|
| Movies | 27 | | 141 |
| Concerts | 17 | | 151 |
| Circus | 14 | | 154 |
| Restaurants with friends | 21 | 42 | 105 |
| Village festivals | 44 | | 124 |

- unemployment, which represents the most important problem;
- lack of possibilities for a life independent from the family of origin; and
- general lack of a social life.

## CONCLUSIONS

Although it was recognized over a hundred years ago that DS people might get a 'sort of precipitated senility', the understanding of this relationship was for a long time a largely neuropathological one. Numerous studies reported evidence of plaques and neurofibrillary tangles in the brains of DS people who had died in early adult life. Some studies retrospectively looked for evidence of decline and reported evidence of personality changes, functional decline and the presence of neurological dysfunction (Oliver and Holland 1986). This was followed by cross-sectional clinical studies, and later by more robust data about the probable age-related prevalence of clinical dementia (i.e. Alzheimer disease).

The neuropathological studies seemed to indicate that all persons with DS would develop significant Alzheimer-like neuropathology as early as in their thirties, yet as the clinical studies were undertaken it became apparent that there were DS people living into their fifties and sixties who were clearly not developing dementia.

This apparent discrepancy is now well established and remains an important research issue. Clearly, there are environmental factors that both increase and decrease the risk of developing Alzheimer disease with age.

Ageing is, of course, associated with more than just biological changes, cognitive decline and increasing risk of physical and psychiatric disorders. It is also associated with significant social and economic changes. It is perhaps in this aspect of ageing that there are some of the greatest contrasts between people with and without learning disabilities.

First, for most of the population life is structured into infancy, childhood, working adult life and retirement. But for people with learning disabilities, many of the usual expectations of life are not available. The most striking example is work. Although supported employment schemes and more meaningful daytime occupations are becoming available to people with learning disabilities, provision in this area remains seriously deficient.

One of the central themes in our culture is the perceived and real contribution that each person gives to society through employment. Individual identities are closely linked to occupations. Beyond identity, occupations play a key role in determining a person's social activities, associates, and in many ways, his/her future opinions and attitudes. Social status is frequently connected to occupation (Warr 1984).

Society's view of unemployment is often negative, considering it a socially unacceptable status for its members. People frequently express the belief that those who knowingly choose unemployment are not doing their fair share for society and themselves. For the unemployed the level of social acceptance may be significantly limited.

For those who are perceived by society as unemployable, the level of acceptance can be even more severely reduced. Such persons are often regarded as not having the capacity for gainful employment, and thus as being in need of a caring and nurturing support system. Accompanying these views is the tendency to pity such persons and to cast them into a role of permanent dependence.

Emphasis placed upon transition from school to work acknowledges that employment preparation must occur over a period of several years (Chadsey-Rusch *et al.* 1986; Kusserow 1984; Paine *et al.* 1984). Such preparation must include opportunities to develop interests, identify skills and develop abilities.

It is essential that educational curricula provide a chance for students with special needs to plan for the future and to examine opportunities that may be available once schooling is completed (Kiernan and Petzy 1982; Mithaug *et al.* 1985). Expectations on the part of educators, parents and special needs students that employment would be a desirable and achievable goal, functional curricula, and real work experiences are necessary components in a positive transition process from school to work (Hasazi *et al.* 1985; Rusch 1986; Wehman *et al.* 1985).

## THE GOAL OF INDEPENDENT LIVING

'Independent living' is an expression often used to describe a desirable community-based goal for persons with developmental disabilities. It is misleading, however, to think of independent living for everybody as a final condition that can be arrived at as a result of training, and beyond which assistance or instruction is no longer required. Apart from the odd mountain man, or survivalist hermit, few people could live up to such stringent criteria. Most of us depend on advice and assistance from a number of personal and professional sources, ranging from family and friends to car mechanics and tax accountants.

In other words we rely on a variety of informal and formal support systems. This applies equally to all members of society, disabled and not.

The difference lies in what supports are necessary and the extent to which one can procure or be assisted in procuring those services. Many elderly people, for instance, make their own way in the community with minimal daily living assistance. Yet, there are others who, without such programmes as Home Health Care and Meals on Wheels, would be forced to live in more restricted settings. In either case, the informal support of friends and family remains essential.

Similarly, for persons with developmental disabilities, active family support and supported residential and employment programmes offer increased opportunities for genuine participation in the community. Such assistance may take the form of help with the basics of banking and budgeting rather than investment consultancy or advanced medical care, but the difference is only a matter of focus. Programming for independent living implies assessment of an individual's lifelong needs, the designation of appropriate instructional and support services to be delivered in the least restrictive environment possible, and evaluation procedures that address quality of life from a client-centred perspective.

# REFERENCES

Baird, P.A. and Sadovnik, P.D. (1987). Life expectancy in Down syndrome. *Journal of Paediatrics.* 110:849–54.

Berry, P., Groeneweg, O., Gibson, D. and Brown, R.D. (1984). Mental development of adults with Down syndrome. *American Journal of Mental Deficiency.* 89(3):252–6.

Brown, R.I. (1997). *Quality of Life for People with Disabilities: Models, Research and Practice.* Cheltenham: Stanley Thornes.

Brown, R., Taylor, J. and Matthews, B. (2001). Quality of life – ageing and Down syndrome. *Downs Syndr Res Pract.* 6(3):111–16.

Buckley, S., Bird, G., Sacks, B. and Archer, T.A. (2006). Comparison of mainstream and special education for teenagers with Down syndrome: implications for parents and teachers. *Downs Syndr Res Pract.* 9(3):54—67.

Cummins, R.A. (1997). Assessing Quality of Life. In Roy, I., Brown (ed.), *Quality of life for people with disabilities: models, research and practice.* pp. 116–50. Cheltenham: Stanley Thornes.

Felce, D. and Perry, J. (1997). Quality of life: the scope of the term and its breadth of measurement. In Roy, I. Brown (ed.), *Quality of life for people with disabilities: models, research and practice.* pp. 56–71. Cheltenham: Stanley Thornes.

Goode, D.A. (ed.) (1994). *Quality of life for persons with disabilities: international perspectives and issues.* Cambridge, MA: Brookline.

Greenspan, S. and Delaney, K. (1983). Personal competence of institutionalized adult males with or without Down syndrome. *American Journal of Mental Deficiency.* 88:218–20.

Hanley-Maxwell, C., Rusch, F.R., Chadsey-Rusch, J. and Renzaglia, A. (1986). Reported factors contributing to job termination of individuals with severe disabilities. *Journal of the Association for the Severely Handicapped.* 11:45–52.

Hardison, M.G. (1994). Pictorial Paradox – reminiscence therapy for nursing home elderly. *Public Health Reports.* 109(2):178–9.

Hasazi, S., Gordon, L.R. and Roe, C.A. (1985). Factors associated with the employment status of handicapped youth exiting high school from 1979 to 1983. *Exceptional Children.* 51(6):455–69.

Hatton, C. (1998). Whose quality of life is it anyway?: some problems with the emerging quality of life consensus. *Mental Retardation*. 36:104–15.

Hill, B.K. and Bruininks, R.H. (1981). *Family, leisure, and social activities of mentally retarded people in residential facilities*. Minneapolis: University of Minnesota, Department of Psychoeducational Studies.

Kiernan, W.E. and Petzy, V. (1982). A systems approach to career and vocational education programs for special needs students: Grades 7–12. In K.I. Lynch, E. Kiernan and L.A. Stark (eds), *Prevocational and vocational education for special needs youth: a blueprint for the 1980s*. pp. 107–32. Baltimore, MD: Paul H. Brookes Publishing Co.

Kusserow, R. (1984). *A program of inspection on transition of developmentally disabled young adults from school to adult services*. Washington, DC: US Department of Health and Human Services, Office of Inspector General.

Middleton, D. and Buchanan, K. (1993). Is reminiscence working?: Accounting for the thera-peutic benefits of reminiscence work with older people. *Journal of Aging Studies*. 7(3):321–33.

Mithaug, D., Horiuchi, C. and Fanning, P. (1985). A report on the Colorado statewide follow-up survey of special education students. *Exceptional Children*. 51:397–404.

Paine, S.C., Bellamy, G.T. and Wilcox, B. (eds) (1984). *Human services that work: from innovation to standard practice*. Baltimore, MD: Paul H. Brookes Publishing Co.

Renwick, R., Brown, I. and Nagler, M. (1996). *Quality of life in health promotion and rehabilitation: conceptual approaches, issues and applications*. Thousand Oaks, CA: Sage.

Rhodes, L. and Valenta, L. (1985). Industry based supported employment. *Journal of The Association for Persons with Severe Handicaps*. 10(1):12–20.

Rusch, E. (1986). Competitive employment issues and strategies. Baltimore, MD: Paul H. Brookes Publishing Co.

Steele, J. (1996). Epidemiology: incidence, prevalence and size of the Down Syndrome population. In B. Stratford and P. Gunn (eds), *New Approaches to Down Syndrome*. pp. 45–72. London: Cassell.

Taylor, S.J. (1994). In support of research on quality of life, but against QOL. In D. Goode (ed.), *Quality of Life for persons with disabilities: international perspectives and issues*. Cambridge, MA: Brookline.

Warr, P. (1984). Work and unemployment. In P.J.D. Drenth, H. Thierry, P.J. Wiliems and C.J. Dewolff (eds), *Handbook of work and organizational psychology*. Vol. 1, pp. 413–43. New York: John Wiley & Sons.

Wehman, P., Kregel, J. and Barcus, J.M. (1985). From school to work: a vocational transition model for handicapped students. *Exceptional Children*. 52(1):25–37.

Wolfensberger, W. (1994). Let's hang up 'Quality of Life' as a hopeless term. In D. Goode (ed.), *Quality of Life for persons with disabilities: international perspectives and issues*. Cambridge, MA: Brookline.

# Conclusions

## JEAN-ADOLPHE RONDAL AND ALBERTO RASORE QUARTINO

This ambitious treatise has taken us on a long journey, from perspectives on genetic therapies to the qualitative but essential question of the quality of life in people with DS. The latter is the central, and actually the unique, final objective of the remediation efforts. It has become in recent years, and rightly so, the subject of reflections, opinions, positions, and some research. As important as is the question of high levels of quality of life for people with intellectual disabilities, one has also to bear in mind that it also very much depends on the availability of a proper education and effective intervention. Major progress has been achieved in these respects over the last few decades at the research and clinical levels, although it is correct to point out that some parts of this increased knowledge have still to translate into daily intervention activities in many countries, and that the specialized training of many field professionals still needs to be strengthened.

Recent work on Down Syndrome (for example, Rondal and Perera 2006) has attracted attention to the neurobehavioural specificity of DS as a syndrome, showing that children with DS exhibit a specific developmental profile, with strengths in social understanding and visual learning and memory, and more difficulties with motor processes, speech and language, and auditory–vocal short-term memory.

The possibility of implementing a gene-based therapy in people with intellectual disabilities is still remote. But it is no longer science fiction. The problems are very complex indeed, particularly in relation to DS, because it is a chromosomic condition and not a single or multi-gene one such as the Fragile-X or Williams Syndromes, for example. This notwithstanding, the perspectives are real, but it will take years of additional research to implement them. It is already clear, however, that any effective germ-line therapy will involve the use of embryos, because its aim is to alter the targeted genes in every cell of the developing body, something that can best be accomplished at the embryonic stage. Present-day bans or severe restrictions on the public funding of human embryo research in various countries (for example, the United States of America) do nothing to favour of this much-needed type of research. The

*Therapies and Rehabilitation in Down Syndrome.* Edited by Rondal
© 2007 John Wiley & Sons Ltd

field of assisted reproductive medicine has witnessed major developments in recent years. Some will permit gene therapy to go beyond the experimental stage, such as, for example, the cloning procedure, which can be combined with cell replacement therapy in order to overcome rejection by the recipient's immune system. One way to do this might be to combine stem-cell work with the cloning technology developed in private laboratories (Green 2001); but for this trend of research to gain momentum, publicly funded research will be necessary.

Medical research has permitted the alleviation of a large number of physical problems, developmental and otherwise, in people with DS. More such benefits will follow with the advent of refined clinical approaches and more powerful molecules. The difficult ageing problem and the frightening spectre of Alzheimer Disease in DS remain. There is reasonable hope, however, of arresting the devastating course of the disease in people of advancing age through the use of particular drugs, some of them now in the final stages of testing and approval by the official bodies in the United States and elsewhere in the Western world.

Cognitive intervention (language and otherwise) is advancing rapidly along technical lines. We now have at our disposal a deeper knowledge of the major problems involved. Effective steps for treatment have been taken and are currently available. The main persisting problems relate to filling the gap between research and clinical and educational practice.

Inclusive schooling for children with DS has been gaining ground in recent years. In a number of countries much remains to be done legally in this respect. Teachers' training should also be clearly oriented in this direction. The movement is already on its way, under strong impulsion from parents and specialized associations seeking the best opportunities for their children.

Lastly, the involvement of parents in the education of their DS children has been the subject of researchers' attention in recent years. Parents' attitudes and motivation are rightly seen as key variables in successful longer-term interventions.

All in all, although problems of all kinds linked to the task of promoting individual development, mainstream school education, and social and workplace inclusion for DS people do remain, a reasonable confidence is called for. The knowledge base is comprehensive and detailed. The basic interventional and clinical tools are there, and should be employed to the maximum extent for the benefit of any child with DS.

Let us hope that our societies will continue to have the good sense and the goodness of heart to keep funding extensive research, powerful clinical applications, and adequate schooling, and to promote the social and professional integration of these wonderful people craving to become full members of our societies despite their involvement in adverse natural conditions for the presence of which they themselves bear no share of individual responsibility.

# REFERENCES

Green, R. (2001). *The human embryo research debates. Bioethics in the vortex of controversy.* New York: Oxford University Press.

Rondal, J.A., Perera, J. (eds) (2006). *Neurobehavioural specificity in Down syndrome.* Chichester: Wiley.

# Index

Abeta (amyloid beta) peptides 2, 7
acetylcholinesterase (AChE) 21, 22
acetylcholinesterase inhibitors 53
acute lymphoblastic leukaemia (ALL) 48
acute megakaryoblastic leukaemia
      (AMKL) 48–9
acute myeloid leukaemia (AML) 48
adenocorticotropin 21
S-adenosylhomocysteine 30
S-adenosylmethionine 30
aetiological therapies 44–5
ageing 43, 44, 51–3, 202
      language intervention and 66–7
allergies 53
alopecia 19
Alzheimer disease (AD) 11, 207
      antibody technology 13
      dementia in 2, 52, 202
      language deterioration 67
      neurological defects 20, 21–2, 202
      pharmacological treatment 53
amyloid beta (Abeta) peptides 2, 7
amyloid cascade hypothesis 7
amyloid precursor protein (APP) 2, 7
β-amyloid precursor protein (β-APP) 24
amyotrophic lateral sclerosis, murine
      models 7
anal imperforation 49
aneuploidies 1
anthracyclines 48
antibiotics 32
anticholinesterase drugs 53, 57
antiepileptic drugs 21
anti-interferon antibodies 19
antioxidant enzymes 51
antioxidants 53
apoptosis 24, 48
ARA-C 48, 49
arginine 36
atlanto-axial instability 50

atrioventricular canal defect 49
auditory defects 50–1
autoimmune diseases 46–8
autoimmune polyendocrine syndrome type 1
      (APS-1) 46

babbling 70–1
balance 110, 113–14, 116
basal forebrain cholinergic neurons
      (BFCNs) 21
Bayley Mental Development scores 92–3, 97
behavioural traits 182–3
bilingualism 66, 83–5
body schema 110, 111–12
brain abnormalities 2, 21
      murine models 3–4

calcipressins 7
calcium 55
cancer, testicular 48
candidate genes 4–12
      chromosomic location 4–5
      corrective strategies 6–12
      definition criteria 4–6
      expression level 6
      expression territories 5
      functions 5
      protein activities 8–12
      protein targets 7–8
      RNA targets 6–7
carbon metabolism 29–32
L-carnitine 52
catalase (Cat) 51–2
cataract 50
CBS (cystathionine β-synthase) gene 30
central nervous system 110
cerebellum granule cell precursors (GCP)
      8–9
cerebral asymmetry (lateralization) 110, 114
chromosome 22 4, 4–5, 18, 19, 23–4, 33

*Therapies and Rehabilitation in Down Syndrome.* Edited by Rondal
© 2007 John Wiley & Sons Ltd